Daily
Guideposts,
1983

Daily Guideposts, 1983

GUIDEPOSTS
Carmel, New York 10512

Grateful acknowledgment is made to Kathy Mills, Youth Coordinator, and to Tracy Tidwell, Projects Chairman, and the youth of the First Methodist Church of Tuscumbia, Alabama, for permission to use the Halloween Treat Card for the October 31st devotional by Drue Duke. We also thank the Houston Police Department for using excerpts from their leaflet, "Rules for Raising Delinquent Children" in the September 30th devotional by Glenn Kittler. "Seven Days Toward a Better You," by Arthur Gordon, is adapted from a Spiritual Workshop that originally appeared in Guideposts Magazine. The anecdote on Taizé, in the devotional for June 2nd by Arthur Gordon, is reprinted with permission from the Reader's Digest.

Designed and illustrated by Elizabeth Woll.

Introduction

What you now hold in your hands is a guidebook for the journey that lies ahead in 1983. Your traveling companions for the year are the writers who will meet you and walk with you along the way, offering firm handclasps of friendship, quiet communion, and warm embraces of fellowship as they share their own experiences along the path you now travel.

Your compass is the Scripture verse that sets a true course for each day's march. Your benediction is the daily prayer. Each day of the year you are invited to take one step further into an understanding of God's Word, to walk in fellowship with a trusted friend and to discover, through communion with God, a practical guidepost to victorious living — one day at a time.

This is our seventh edition of *Daily Guideposts*. Over one million people have used these volumes over the years. This all-new edition has certain added features to make it a uniquely personal volume for you, the reader.

The Prayer-Poems that introduce each month were specially written for this volume by Alice Joyce Davidson. Inspired by the Psalms, they set a tone of praise and thanksgiving for you to carry with you through the year.

Pattern for a Blessed Life. Marilyn Morgan Helleberg's meditations on The Beatitudes will help you start each month with one of Jesus' great lessons for living and we hope will inspire you to find a blessed pattern for your daily life.

Journeys in Faith. At mid-month, Elizabeth Sherrill examines the life of an Old Testament character, drawing parallels between his walk with God and your own. We suggest that you take this opportunity as a Mini-Bible-Study-Program. Read the suggested Scripture, contemplate the teachings and apply them to your immediate concerns.

The Monthly Praise Diary. Space for you to record praise for a special blessing or prayer for a personal concern is provided at the end of each month. (Find the page numbers by referring to your Daily Guideposts Bookmark.) We suggest that after you have read the devotional for the day you immediately turn to the Diary and jot down a thought, prayer or praise. By recording just a few daily words you can create your own journal of your walk in faith through 1983.

All who have contributed to this volume have done so out of a desire to witness to the presence of God in their own lives and a willingness to share their experience with you. It is our prayer that through the year you will come to know them as trusted friends. May they lead you to a richer understanding of the Word of God and may your year be blessed with a new understanding of His love.

THE EDITORS

January

Every day will I bless thee; and I will praise thy name
for ever and ever.   —PSALM 145:2

Thank You, Father, thank You,
For this year fresh and new,
Another chance to know Your love—
To show my love for You....

Another chance to make amends
For yesteryear's mistakes,
To ask forgiveness and forgive
Those little hurts and aches....

Thank You for this day that brings
New dreams, new plans, new hopes,
Along with all the strength I need
To climb the steepest slopes....

Thank You, Father, thank You,
For this day fresh and new,
A chance to grow, a chance to show
My boundless love for You!

—ALICE JOYCE DAVIDSON

PATTERN FOR A BLESSED LIFE

...And he opened his mouth, and taught them, saying,
Blessed are... —MATTHEW 5:2-3

1

When my friend Carolmae ended our phone conversation with "Have a blessed day," the words made me think. What would a truly blessed day be like? Happy? Of course. Peaceful? Yes. Love-filled? Definitely. But the dictionary reminded me that it would be, above all, a *consecrated* day.

Then I thought of all the "blesseds" in Jesus' Sermon on the Mount. I turned to Matthew 5 and as I read the Beatitudes, it became clear that Jesus had given us a pattern not only for a blessed day but for a truly blessed *life*. Yet how could I, with all my faults, live up to the pattern? The task seemed overwhelming and so I developed this plan: During 1983 I am going to take one part of Jesus' pattern and on the first of each month with God's help, I will try to *really live* that virtue.

Even though my attempts will be imperfect, I know that if I sincerely try to live each one of the Beatitude virtues, my life will become blessed beyond measure. Will you join me in this spiritual adventure? It could change our lives!

I will begin each January day, Lord, by consecrating it to You.
Build in me a commitment to live a blessed life.

—MARILYN MORGAN HELLEBERG

2   *If any man serve Me, let him follow Me...* —JOHN 12:26

I folded back the cover of my new calendar to hang over my desk. There was a page between the cover and the January sheet. On it in bold letters was printed:

8

429 WAYS TO HAVE A GOOD YEAR

12 Months of	52 Weeks of	365 Days of
Prayer	Sunday Services	Bible Study

The twinge of sadness that I always feel as I put away an old year was quickly dispelled. I was about to embark on a brand-new, unblemished year, and I'd been sweetly reminded of how my year could be rewarding and fulfilling.

And there was more:

> 6 weeks of Lent
> 52 Wednesdays of prayer meetings
> 5 weeks of Advent
> 52 weeks of tithing
> 12 months of family devotions
> 365 days of grace....

Lord, may all my days in the new year be filled with ways to draw closer to You.   —DRUE DUKE

---

3 *For all have sinned, and come short of the glory of God...*
                                        —ROMANS 3:23

Sam and I were kids together. We played together, went to school together, and on Sundays we were in the same Sunday-school class. He was my friend, and I looked up to him.

One day he told me he'd decided to be a minister. "I'm going to be a pastor of a big church," he said, "and I'm going to go out and find all sorts of poor, needy people and bring them into my church and mix them up with the rich people so that the rich can help the poor and..."

I was very impressed by his Christian faith.

Then it happened that the dollar and thirty-seven cents I had kept in a red Prince Albert tobacco can, and hidden in a secret place that only Sam and I knew about, was missing.

"I betcha the guys over on Dundee Road took it," Sam said when I reported the loss.

Two days later at Sam's house, looking for a pencil, I opened the drawer of the desk in his room. There was the red Prince Albert tobacco can! I knew it was mine because I'd scratched my initials on it.

It hurt. It hurt something awful. It hurt so much that I cried to Mother about it, "I thought he was a Christian!"

"Don't give up on him," she said tenderly. "He needs you. Most of us are trying to be good Christians." Then she said something that has helped me all my life. "Keep your eye not on the Christian, but on *Christ*."

Father, help me see Your saving Grace behind the imperfections of my Christian brothers and sisters.   —VAN VARNER

---

4   *A soft answer turneth away wrath...*   —PROVERBS 15:1

In one of my favorite Peanuts cartoons, Snoopy gives a crabby Lucy a big kiss. "That's how you break up a 'crab-in'," he tells us.

I remember a time when someone handled me like that. My parents had been called away and Aunt Miriam offered to take me home with her for the day. "I don't want to go to your house," I protested. "You never have anything I like to eat and there's nothing to do." I knew of course that neither was true. Aunt Miriam cooked superbly and lived in a huge old farmhouse with wonderful places to play both indoors and out.

She didn't say a word. Instead we drove home and in the middle of a sticky August day, she cooked fried chicken, corn-on-the-cob and chocolate pudding while Uncle Jim hung a swing from the old black walnut tree.

Aunt Miriam could have reasoned with me — explained all she'd done in the past to love me. She could even have become angry and spanked my bottom! But if she had done those things, would I still remember the scene? Today that memory fills me with a deep awareness of how much I must have been loved.

I think Aunt Miriam and Snoopy are right. The best way to handle a "crab-in" is with love.

Dear Lord, Who loves us even when we are most unlovable, help us to love others like that too.   —PATRICIA HOUCK SPRINKLE

---

5   *. . . Do violence to no man, neither accuse any falsely. . .*
　　　　　　　　　　　　　　　　　　　　　　　　—LUKE 3:14

We had just moved into our new home and were putting things in place when I noticed that a box of silverware was missing. No one in the family seemed to have seen it. Queer. I searched for days — and then I suddenly remembered that a friend's son who had helped us move had a theft record.

Oh, well, there really isn't anything I can do about it now, I thought. I wrote off the loss in my mind — and, yes, I "wrote off" the young man too.

Several years later, while cleaning out the bottom of a cabinet in the basement, I heard a clang. What was that? Using a flashlight, I saw a fork. I also saw little flat wooden feet — parts of the silverware box! Apparently the box had upended and become wedged there in the cabinet when we moved and my cleaning had just jarred it loose.

How ashamed I felt for having blamed the youth! I said a little prayer that day as I polished the new-found silverware — I confessed my sorrow over the unjust accusation that I had made and I asked God to cleanse my tarnished heart. Although I had committed an injustice against the boy, I had committed an even greater one against myself by harboring a groundless accusation.

Father, help me to practice love and understanding toward others, disavowing all judgment and prejudice. —ZONA B. DAVIS

---

6 *...I will never leave thee, nor forsake thee.*
                                                    —HEBREWS 13:5

Not long ago we bought a new pup — a border collie that we named Duffy. Duffy follows a long line of family dogs — Queenie, Mitzie, Heidi, Scampy and Prince, to name a few. Because we live in town, Duffy can't run at will but must get his exercise in the back yard or on a leash. He particularly looks forward to jogging with me in the morning, but like many young dogs, is easily spooked by loud noises, roaring chain saws, passing cars, and barking dogs which throw themselves against fences in an attempt to intercept us.

If he gets nervous, I draw in on his leash and pull him closer to my pants leg. Then I speak to him in a quiet voice: "It's okay, Duffy. Don't be afraid. I'm right here." And when I do this, his ears relax and he settles back into a smooth stride, his fluffy tricolored coat flowing in the breeze.

It's good to have a Master to Whom one can draw close when worries and fears abound. Good to have Someone whisper our names and say, "It's all right, don't be afraid, I'm right here."

Lord, thank You for Your promise never to leave me, nor forsake me. —FRED BAUER

7 *For ye were sometimes darkness, but now are ye light in the Lord: walk as children of light...* —EPHESIANS 5:8

I remember that as a child I was trudging past a church one day when I suddenly felt raindrops splash against my cheeks. Quickly I ducked inside for shelter and perched on the edge of a pew to wait out the storm. Large stained-glass windows that had seemed to be slate-gray from the outside were now penetrated by light and I will never forget my delight at seeing their transformation into radiant colors!

On some mornings I feel like the outside of those windows — drab and nondescript. I awaken full of anxiety and doubt:

I wasn't invited to a friend's party... or considered for that promotion... or included in the office luncheon. It's just not fair.

What a contrast that misery is to joy I feel on the mornings when I take time to pray:

Good morning, Lord. Keep me company through the hours ahead. Let me share Your love with others today. And thank You for giving me this wonderful life!

The light principle is again fulfilled. I am transformed — just like the radiant stained-glass windows — as God's Light pours through me.

I will illuminate the gift of each new day, Lord, by the Light of Your Presence within me. —DORIS HAASE

8 *Now no chastening for the present seemeth to be joyous, but grievous: nevertheless afterward it yieldeth the peaceable fruit of righteousness...* —HEBREWS 12:11

The other day, sitting quietly on our little dock that

overlooks a tidal creek, I saw a mother raccoon lead her three babies out of the tall grass on the far side of the creek and onto a fallen tree that stretched out to deep water. She dove in gracefully and swam around, chirring at the little ones, coaxing them to join her. They just looked dismayed; obviously they had never tried to swim. This was to be their first lesson.

The mother climbed back up on the tree, took one baby in her mouth and swam across the creek with it. She did the same with the second. The third waited expectantly for his free ride, but nothing happened. The mother called to him from the far bank; she didn't go back to him. He grew increasingly agitated, crying piteously and dipping one timid paw into the tide. The mother's answering calls became fainter. She was leaving him — or so she seemed to want him to think.

Finally, with a desperate plunge, the baby threw himself into the creek and floundered frantically to shore, where I was sure that in a minute or two he would brag to his siblings about how brave he was.

An analogy? I think so. That raccoon mother chose the toughest of her babies for her little lesson in loving. She tested him because she knew he could respond. She seemed to abandon him, but she never did.

Need I go on…?

Dear Lord, when I think You have forgotten me, let me remember that baby raccoon. —ARTHUR GORDON

---

9   *Notwithstanding the Lord stood with me, and strengthened me…* —II TIMOTHY 4:17

I have a vivid childhood memory of the day that my little brother Wade and I were playing hide-and-seek. He was hiding, I was seeking. After searching for a long time, I heard frantic, muffled cries coming from the bathroom. Finding the door locked, I hurried to tell my mother. She grabbed a kitchen chair, rushed outside and dragged it behind her across the grass. She placed the chair under the bathroom window and stood on it.

"The window screen is locked," Mother said with a note of desperation in her voice.

Then the strangled sound of Wade's cry filtered through the window. At that moment my mother, an average-sized woman, reached up with her bare hands and tore the sealed screen right off the window and wrenched open a steel lock. She climbed through the window and found my brother wedged inside the clothes hamper.

Mother never again equaled that incredible feat of strength. She did not ordinarily possess such power.

But the memory of my mother standing on the chair beneath the window gives me hope. I remind myself that no matter the problems life brings, God will give me the resources I need in order to cope — when the time comes.

Help me to live with the confidence that what I need to meet life's challenges, You will provide at the right time. —SUE MONK KIDD

---

10   ... *The will of the Lord be done.*   —ACTS 21:14

"Thy kingdom come, thy will be done." Familiar words. But there was a time when I didn't know if I could honestly pray them.

Lynn and I had been discussing marriage but we faced a huge obstacle: I was still in graduate school; she would soon begin an eight-year doctoral program. Our options were few. Financially, we couldn't both be in school at the same time. We could wait to be married — but eight years of separation was a long time. Or one of us could leave school and work, at least temporarily. We prayed for guidance but we saw no satisfactory solution.

As the weeks wore on, the pressure of uncertainty set in. I had written to *Guideposts* for a job — it would be near the school to which Lynn had applied — but I had heard nothing.

One day as we tensely waited for the mailman, Lynn was staring at my mailbox and suddenly she started dictating a letter. "Dear Norman," she said wistfully and then she began to spell out all our hopes and dreams to the publisher of *Guideposts*, Dr. Norman Vincent Peale. It wasn't a letter, really, but *a prayer to God*, a heartfelt rendering of our situation. It was Lynn's way of telling Him, and me, that she was ready to accept His will for our lives.

From that moment on, "Dear Norman" became our secret code for a quick and earnest prayer, meaning, "Father, Thy will be done." And the more frequently we used it, the more peace we found.

After another month we became engaged. I got my job, Lynn was accepted at her school. And we learned afresh the power in those words — "Thy will be done."

Father, however I say it, I will surrender my will to You.

—JEFF JAPINGA

---

11 *For where two or three are gathered together in my name, there am I in the midst of them.* —MATTHEW 18:20

The teacher grimly handed my husband and me the results of what the computer had to say about our son's math ability. We looked at the report long and hard. It said, in effect, that there was no way he could pass eighth-grade math. The teacher offered no words of encouragement and Jeremy was convinced he would fail.

Our family began to pray with him and for him, and my husband began a task of nightly tutoring. Jeremy's sister encouraged him in the things he did do well, such as painting and writing. And I reminded him that Christians have a secret power in Scripture. "I can do all things through Christ which strengtheneth me." (Philippians 4:13) Anxiously, we waited.

Then Jeremy brought home a 97 on a math test. Several more good grades brought his average up, and he passed math. The computer was wrong!

Now when I face seemingly impossible situations — when an unseen computer says, "You can't possibly do that. You will fail" — I remember Jeremy's passing math and I ask my loved ones to pray me through.

Lord, when I am weak, lead me to the fellowship of believers for strength. —MARION BOND WEST

12

That was the true Light, which lighteth every man that cometh into the world. —JOHN 1:9

Each evening at sunset my husband and I walk our dogs down the hill and across the neighboring school grounds. One night as we circled the schoolhouse, he pointed out the power lines looping up to the pole, which was silhouetted against the pink sky in a perfect black cross. Just below its outspread arms there was a rectangular box — a transformer, my husband told me.

"A device for altering the ratio of current to voltage," he explained. "In other words, a transformer gets the electricity from the large line and reduces it to usable current. Electricity can heat houses, run huge machines, light up the world. But without that transformer to reduce and direct it, the electricity would be too powerful for us to use. There would just be a big explosion."

Then he pointed to the visible cross. "Christ is like that transformer. Without Christ, God couldn't really show Himself to us.

The power would be too great, people couldn't comprehend it, there would simply be an enormous explosion. But by sending Christ to live among us and show us the way, God focused and localized His power on the cross."

Now every time I see electric lines, I think of God's great power and of how, by following Jesus, our lives can be brightened and transformed.

Dear Lord: The world is filled with simple but exciting symbols to remind us of Your greatness. Thank You for giving us eyes that we might see them. —MARJORIE HOLMES

---

13 *Let your speech be alway with grace...* —COLOSSIANS 4:6

When I was a new cat owner, I read a newspaper article claiming that household pets, especially those that did not go outdoors, adjusted to the routines of their owners. Any sudden change of routine on the part of the owner could cause the animal to become upset or withdrawn. Working at home as I do, I thought that I spent plenty of time with my pet. But during some weeks my schedule was irregular and my cat would grow unusually quiet and distant. The article stated that when this kind of reaction occurred, the owner should explain the situation to the animal. Although the pet would not understand, at least it would not feel abandoned. I followed the article's advice — and it worked!

Late one afternoon I was preparing to leave my apartment with a visitor. I went over to my cat, who was perched on his favorite chair. "Now, Louie," I said, bending down to his level, "Mr. Davidson and I are going out for something to eat. You have everything you need, so you take care of the apartment and I'll be back around ten o'clock and I'll tell you all about it."

"What in the world are you doing?" my friend gasped. I told him about the newspaper article. He asked, "And that works?"

I nodded.

Halfway through dinner my friend said, "I've been thinking about you and your cat. Wouldn't it be nice if people communicated with one another like that? There would be less hurt, less argument, less pouting, less misunderstanding." I thoroughly agreed with him.

When I arrived home that night, Louie was waiting for me just inside the door. He arched his back and rubbed against my legs, purring all the while. I began to tell him about my evening. Yes indeed, my friend was right. Would that we humans could learn the art of communicating with one another. Love and understanding would surely follow.

Father, let me always speak with love and understanding to others. —GLENN KITTLER

---

14 *Even so faith, if it hath not works, is dead, being alone.*
—JAMES 2:17

I used to wonder why James stressed the value of works. I always thought that faith was enough — that works were okay but not really necessary.

Then I tried to learn to fly a plane. My husband, a pilot, described the controls to me and gave me some reading materials. But only when I actually sat in the pilot's seat and got the plane into the air did I finally *understand* the principles of flying. Only then could I truly trust — have faith in — the plane.

I thought about it later. Maybe that's what James meant when he said that faith without works was dead — just as a grounded plane is 'dead.'

Now I might *hear* about God, I might *read* about God and I might believe all that I hear and read. But only when I actually put into practice what I hear and read, can I understand. Then I can 'turn on' to His spiritual power.

I'm trying to actively apply God's Word to my daily life. And sure enough — my faith takes wings and flies.

But I still need You, Lord, as the copilot. —MADGE HARRAH

JOURNEY OF FAITH

15 Your traveling companion is ABRAHAM
...who stepped into the unknown. —GENESIS 11 - 25

God's marching orders to Abraham are the very ones He gives to you and me at the start of each new year: "Leave the past behind. Venture with Me into territory you have never glimpsed!"

Leave behind old hurts and hates, old limitations. And leave the good as well: last year's insight...the truth that yesterday was so stretching. Dare for the better! Abraham's country and kindred were not evil — they were simply not all that God had in mind for him.

Where will God lead you in 1983? You will know only by setting out. The *direction* was all God would show Abraham in the beginning, not the *destination.* The journey itself, the putting one foot after another in faith, is the great training-ground in trust.

What can we learn from Abraham?

OASES. The journey to which God called Abraham was across arid plateaus and steep hill country.

How would Abraham water his sheep and goats and feed the men, women and children who depended on him? By consulting caravaneers who traveled the route before, learning the location of wells and planning each day's trek to end at an oasis.

The Bible is *your* caravaneers' handbook, as you venture into challenging terrain in 1983. And this book, *Daily Guideposts,* can provide you with refreshment during your journey; a daily, weekly, monthly oasis for your spirit.

BUILDING AN ALTAR. God's guidance was progressive, revealed

little by little as Abraham passed through the land. And each place where God's will, God's nature, God's purpose became clearer, Abraham *built there an altar* — a place of worship, marking the ground as Holy — an acknowledgment of the truth he had encountered. Your Monthly Praise Diary in this book can be your way of building altars along your personal route: a place to record insights, praise, thanksgiving.

THE UNSEEN CITY. Abraham died without ever reaching his destination — the city whose builder and maker is God. But he died *in faith* — not in disillusionment — not having received what he was promised, but having seen it and greeted it from afar. This is the essence of faith: The confident affirmation of what is still — in our time frame — future tense.

The walk of faith is not for those who need quick results; it is for those for whom, for now, the journey in God's company is enough.

Measure my steps, Lord. . . One step at a time is fine with me.

—ELIZABETH SHERRILL

---

16 *. . . If any man hear my voice, and open the door, I will come in to him, and will sup with him, and he with me.*
—REVELATION 3:20

Whenever I'm in Denmark, I make an effort to go to Copenhagen's great Protestant cathedral, *Vor Frue Kirken.* Around its walls there is a series of colossal statues of the twelve apostles. They face the central statue on the high altar, that of Jesus Christ.

There's an interesting story about the creation of that particular work. Its sculptor, Bertel Thorvaldsen, in preparing his clay model, had created a Jesus figure with arms raised high in a gesture of imperious leadership. Pleased with his accomplishment, he left his studio to let the soft clay harden overnight. When he returned in the

21

morning, however, he was startled to find that Jesus' arms, the arms that Thorvaldsen had so carefully fashioned into a stance of authority, had drooped. They no longer commanded; no, they seemed to have fallen into a gesture of pleading.

At first Thorvaldsen was bitterly disappointed. But they say something amazing happened to him as he stood gazing at the transformed statue. He now saw before him the image of the *true* Jesus, the Man of compassion. At that moment Bertel Thorvaldsen became a Christian. And eventually he was led to chisel on the base of the finished statue: "Come unto Me."

No, Jesus does not *command* us to follow Him. He *invites* us. It is the most important, most beautiful, most rewarding invitation you and I will ever receive.

Jesus, I accept. —NORMAN VINCENT PEALE

---

17 *... Stand ye still, and see the salvation of the Lord with you... fear not, nor be dismayed... for the Lord will be with you.* —II CHRONICLES 20:17

Every night during World War II my mother went to her Bible in search of guidance for her sons in the service. She would read and then pray specifically for one of them. Around midnight on Thanksgiving Eve in 1944 she was reading the above scripture and praying for my brother Mac, who was marching with General Patton's army across France.

The sergeant of a reconnaisance platoon, Mac was standing in the middle of a road, ready to lead his men through some woods to a crossroad beyond which an enemy strong point was suspected to be. A seasoned soldier, Mac knew it was against all rules to move down that road in plain sight; normal procedure called for fanning his men out so they could move through the cover of the woods in a shallow wedge. Yet for no apparent reason, after standing in thought for a moment, he walked them right down the middle of the road in a column.

They found that the crossroad was unoccupied and turned to walk back. There, on the reverse sides of the trees, they saw the signs, *Minen!* — posted to warn German soldiers approaching from that direction that the woods were mined. "Had we gone through them," Mac wrote in an exchange of letters, "we would have been blown apart. Keep praying for me, Mother. He is with us — and with you."

It is good to know that You hear those who are praying for me, Father. Sometimes all I can do is stand still for that moment and follow Your guidance. —ELAINE ST. JOHNS

---

18 *... Though I speak with the tongues of men and of angels, and have not charity, I am become as sounding brass, or a tinkling cymbal.* —I CORINTHIANS 13:1

I'll admit that my habits of torturing toothpaste tubes into yielding the last milligram, turning out the lights the second a room is vacated, and urging the members of my household to don another sweater instead of turning up the thermostat can become, well...a little tiresome. I know I'm right about these matters but I also recognize that I'm a little quick to scold when others don't follow my example.

The other morning I was surprised to see my wife Judy leave the upstairs room that I use for a retreat when I want to read late, which I had done the previous night.

"Looking for a magazine?" I asked, since I sometimes spirit them away upstairs.

"No," she answered.

"Is the radiator acting up again?"

"No, no, everything's okay," she replied.

"Well, then, what's the attraction on the third floor at seven in the morning?"

"I noticed some lights on," she said, "and I just went up to turn them off."

An instant pang of remorse — and an enormous tug of affection — squeezed my heart. Of course it was *I* who had left the lights on; but had it been Judy who had done it, I would have made certain that she *knew* about it.

Later, at breakfast, I said, "You know, you would have been perfectly justified in jumping all over me for having left the lights on last night."

Judy looked at me thoughtfully and then smiled. "You know the folks I always think of when it comes to being justified?" she asked.

"Who?" I inquired.

"The Pharisees."

Lord, teach me to value kindness above "rightness."

—JAMES McDERMOTT

---

19 *I beseech you therefore, brethern, by the mercies of God, that ye present your bodies a living sacrifice, holy, acceptable unto God, which is your reasonable service.*
—ROMANS 12:1

Do you like words? Have you ever studied a common word that you use every day — a word whose meaning is entirely clear to you — and suddenly, under close examination, found that its ordinary meaning has changed into a fresh and exciting, even inspiring usage?

Here's a word, once obvious, that has new meaning for me:

DEVOTIONAL. The editors of *Daily Guideposts* call the book you now hold in your hands a collection of "devotionals."

When I discovered not long ago that "devotional" comes from the same Latin root as "vow," my feeling for the word deepened. A vow, of course, is a promise, especially a promise made to God. And so it is that whenever I write or read a "devotional," I find that I'm not just seeking inspiration — I'm pledging myself *again* to God.

And that, I hope, is what you too are doing, this very second!

Lord, I pledge myself to You all 365 days of the year.

—VAN VARNER

---

20 *Verily I say unto you, Whatsoever ye shall bind on earth shall be bound in heaven...* —MATTHEW 18:18

Yesterday I shared with you my fascination with words. Today I would like to share another word that holds deep meaning for all those who love and worship our Creator.

RELIGION. The nouns "religion" and "ligament" share the same Latin root. *How odd,* I thought at first. There are two meanings for "ligament" in my dictionary: 1) a bond or tie serving to connect one thing with another; 2) in anatomy, a band of tough tissue connecting bones or holding organs in place.

Suddenly the word "religion" took flight in my imagination and ever since it has meant more to me than just a noun that stands for a system of belief. Now it is a vivid and intensely personal word. When I see it or say it, I am aware of a tough and strong connection that holds me fast, a beautiful tie that forever binds me close to God!

I want to be connected to You every day, dear God. —VAN VARNER

21 *If the Son therefore shall make you free, ye shall be free indeed.* —JOHN 8:36

Early one morning I noticed a bird lying just outside our patio door. I brought him into the house and took him to the bathroom to wrap him up in a towel. His eyes were closed. He was limp but seemed to be breathing. No blood. Suddenly he flew out of the towel. Frightened, he flew around in circles, screamed at me and finally landed on the shower rod. He was worn out, and so was I.

Standing on the rim of the tub, I dropped some water into his open panting mouth and said softly: "Look, bird, I'm your only hope. If you don't let me save you, you don't have a chance. Let me hold you and then I'll set you free. Please trust me...."

The situation seemed familiar, but I couldn't figure out why. Just then the weary bird relaxed and allowed me to cup my hands gently around him. He remained perfectly still as I walked through the house to the edge of our yard and set him high in a pine tree. Immediately he flew off. A part of my heart soared with him as I realized why the situation had seemed familiar. When I feel like that poor bird, trapped and frightened, God reaches down to help me. But only when I *surrender* can He set me free.

Jesus, I give in. Please show me The Way. —MARION BOND WEST

---

22 *.... And having done all, to stand.* —EPHESIANS 6:13

I remember that as a young man I once went to my father with a set of problems that troubled me. Father listened with interest but also with increasing exasperation for nothing seemed to ease my worries. Finally he said, "Son, go read Ephesians!"

"Ephesians?" I was astonished. "What for?"

"Because there," he said, "you'll find the greatest antidote in the world for worry. It's where St. Paul advises the Ephesians, once they've done everything they can, to just stand.

"You're in danger of becoming a chronic worrier," my father went on. "There's nothing wrong with *some* worry if it impels you to take action against your difficulties. But when you've taken that action, when you've done all you can do, it's just plain senseless to go on worrying. How much better to stand quietly, as St. Paul says. Or sit quietly. Or even lie down. In other words, *relax*.

"If you have a problem, do the best you can with it. Then leave it in God's hands. Angels," my father concluded, "can do no more."

I think he was right.

When trouble comes, Lord, I'll stand with You at my side.
—ARTHUR GORDON

---

23 *...Thy face, Lord, will I seek.* —PSALM 27:8

I have fond memories of my grandmother's visits to our house when I was a child. During her stay there was no talking or conversation allowed on Sunday mornings until we returned from church. Emergency remarks were permissible, but no chitchat. I accepted this rule without question: It was just Grandma's way. And I dearly loved her. But when I became a little older, I asked her why she imposed this curious restriction on herself and others.

She replied, "Going to church means going to the House of God. It is no casual visit, Glenn. Now when you plan to visit friends, you think of them ahead of time, deciding what kind of gift to take — flowers, candy, a book. Something. When you plan to visit God's house, you should think of Him ahead of time too and prepare the only gift He asks for: yourself. *You must prepare yourself, Glenn.*"

So may I suggest that this morning you take a tip from my

grandmother: *Prepare yourself.* You are a housewarming gift for God Himself!

Father, today I bring myself to You, ALL that I am.
—GLENN KITTLER

---

24   *I will give thee... hidden riches of secret places.*
—ISAIAH 45:3

When my husband and I went through customs on our return from abroad, the man inspecting my luggage pulled out my worn and marked-up Bible and flipped through its pages. Then he held it by the covers, pages dangling, and shook it.

"Sorry, lady," he said. "It's just that people often hide large amounts of currency or other valuables between the pages of a Bible. Once I even found a diamond in one! You just wouldn't believe the treasures people try to smuggle in that way!"

What that inspector didn't know was that my old Bible was just loaded with hidden riches that his inspection missed completely. My special treasures hiding there were gifts, most of them easy to find because they're marked. There's a star in the margin by Isaiah 54:13 because the Lord gave me that present when my son was suffering emotional turmoil. Psalm 139, verse 9, stands out in shining yellow because I marked it with a highlighter while traveling alone on an airplane to New York to be met by strangers. "For Sue at Bill's death" is written in the margin after the words of Luke 4:18, "...He hath sent me to heal the broken-hearted...." Why would I want to hide diamonds or money in the pages of a book that is studded with riches as priceless as these?

Don't hesitate to write in your Bible. Those names, dates and other markings will become your treasure maps!

Guide me, Lord, as I mark the hidden riches in Your Word.
                                    —MARILYN MORGAN HELLEBERG

---

25 *Set your affections on things above, not on things on the earth.*   —COLOSSIANS 3:2

The telephone hadn't rung all day. No one had stopped by to say hello. Nothing had come in the mail. My husband was away on a business trip...and I was lonely.

I tried not to think about it for I had plenty of work to do. But every time I stopped typing, I was acutely aware of the silence. Had the whole world forgotten that I existed?

I have friends and loved ones, I thought. *So why do I feel this lonely? Maybe I ought to call them.* So I telephoned a few friends — but no one was home. Finally, in desperation, I closed my eyes and bowed my head. "God," I said, "I'm a little lonely right now..." and for the next few minutes I poured out my feelings to Him. Then — after a few tears, a few sighs — a warm, peaceful feeling enveloped me. Yes, Someone *does* care—all the time. I had only to reach out to Him to know that He was right there...constantly there.

I hadn't remembered to keep in touch with Him, that's all.

The next time that I feel lonely, I'm going to call a Friend. In fact I'm going to reach out and touch Someone.   —PHYLLIS HOBE

26 *...What doth the Lord require of thee, but to do justly, and to love mercy, and to walk humbly with thy God?*
—MICAH 6:8

Once while driving in an area famous for its timber industry, I came upon a bridge that had collapsed, victim of a heavy, log-carrying truck whose driver had failed to observe the load-limit sign. The sign was still standing at the entrance to the bridge, its big, bold letters forewarning motorists that the weight limit was ten tons.

"Too bad," said a stranger standing nearby. "She served the community for nearly fifty years. Carried millions of tons of logs in her time."

I found the man's observation interesting. The bridge had no doubt carried millions upon millions of tons in its lifetime but then somebody made the mistake of asking it to carry more than ten tons *at one time.*

What we can learn from this little story is that while our potential is great, we can make only so many commitments for a given time. Like the bridge, we can carry millions of "ten-ton loads" in a lifetime — *one load at a time.*

Lord, help me to know myself — and show me how I can best serve You.
—FRED BAUER

27 *Ye cannot serve God and mammon.*　　—LUKE 16:13

The great composer Verdi once dashed off an opera that lacked his usual excellence. Just the same, the opening-night audience liked it, and Verdi was delighted when the theater thundered with applause and there was a standing ovation at the final curtain.

But his joy was short-lived. In the balcony he saw his former teacher, Rossini, still seated. His face was grim, his hands clasped in his lap. He was not applauding. Disappointment was etched in his face.

So many times I find myself satisfied with the adulation of my peers. But the question comes before me: Is my Teacher pleased with what I am doing? Is it something He would approve of? Or will He be looking down, disappointed in me?

Somehow the noise of the crowd becomes very unimportant when measured against pleasing my Lord.

Are You satisfied with me, Jesus?   —DRUE DUKE

---

28 *Rejoice with them that do rejoice, and weep with them that weep.*   —ROMANS 12:15

I helped my bride into our sub-compact car, carefully smoothing her dress as she settled into the bucket seat. We were on our way to our wedding and had to be careful of her beautiful white gown.

"You're sure you want to stop now?" I asked Lynn as we backed out of the driveway. Weeks before we had decided that on the way to the church we would stop at a local nursing home where Lynn had regularly been visiting a few patients. Lynn would be wearing her gown, I my tux. "I just hope you don't get that dress all mussed up," I warned, "and what if somebody talks too long? It's bad luck to be late to your own wedding."

"Honey, we're stopping," Lynn said, laughing.

So down the hall of the nursing home we strolled, receiving double-takes all the way. Finally Lynn tugged me into one of the patient's rooms. And there on the face of a lovely, white-haired woman I saw the biggest grin I had ever seen, as joyful as that of any of the guests we would see at the wedding ceremony that evening.

I guess Lynn had anticipated the joy we would bring to her friend at the nursing home but she probably did not expect my change of heart. The lovely senior citizen caused it, really. "Most people try to be my friend by showing interest in *my* life," she told us, "but you have let me have interest in *yours*."

I haven't forgotten that. I'll be a good listener, sure. But I can go one step further — I can be a good sharer too.

For blessings, O Father, we thank You. And for people with whom to share them. —JEFF JAPINGA

---

29 ...Perfect love casteth out fear... —I JOHN 4:18

My friend Rhoda was teased relentlessly by her classmates about her deep fear and hatred of cats. Later, in college, an understanding teacher helped her overcome her fear.

"You don't have to contend with such a thing alone," the teacher told her. "We fear what we fail to understand, then we hate."

She gave Rhoda an exercise to follow. Walk briskly, breathe deeply — and list one thing, to start, about an imaginary cat.

"I thought my heart would burst," Rhoda told me later. "But I finally was able to think of a cat's feet making little tracks."

Rhoda added to her list daily. There came a time when she was able to appreciate the cat of her imagination. And still later a time when she could love the cuddly warmth of her own real, live pet cat.

Today when I encounter a situation I fear, I remember my friend Rhoda. I don't have to contend with such a thing alone. I go for a brisk walk, breathe deeply, and with a prayer, search for a positive quality to build on.

Lord, here's another positive thing I've overlooked....
—JUNE MASTERS BACHER

30

Behold, I am the Lord, the God of all flesh: is there any thing too hard for me? —JEREMIAH 32:27

When I was a child, my daddy carried me to the ruins of a Civil War prison in the little town of Andersonville, Georgia. As we walked about the ghostly old walls, we came upon a stream of water bubbling from the ground through a wall. And there my daddy read me the true story of the stream as it was engraved on the historical marker above it.

During the war the inmates of Andersonville Prison ran out of water. Their only source had been a nearby stream, which became contaminated. With hope nearly gone, fourteen prisoners bowed their heads in prayer and asked God to send them water. And so it happened that a fresh, clean spring broke suddenly out of the ground and flowed through the prison. It still flows today. And the name of the spring is Providence.

I remember the awe I felt that day as I stood beside the mysterious silver spring. It reminds me that similar miracles can still happen. God comes like a spring of hope when things seem bleakest. And that is why you and I should never give in to despair. God *does* provide. Always.

Father, I am thirsty. Teach me to pray. —SUE MONK KIDD

31

I will shew thee my faith by my works. —JAMES 2:18

I was only nine years old at the time but I've never forgotten what happened. I was skating on a pond with five or six of the neighborhood youngsters. Watching us was Mrs. DeBrett, a widow who gave many of us our piano lessons.

Suddenly a child who had strayed from the group fell through the ice and, to our horror, did not come up. While we children stood transfixed, Mrs. DeBrett raced across the ice, shedding her heavy coat, scarf, gloves and hat as she went. She plunged into the hole and disappeared under the ice. It seemed an eternity before she surfaced with the child in tow. She threw him onto the ice and pushed him toward us.

"Get him home!" she shouted at one of the boys. "The rest of you get a ladder."

We raced to a nearby barn where we grabbed a ladder and ran back with it. We slid it out to her and watched, still astonished, as she spanned it over the hole and finally extricated herself. Surprisingly composed, she made her way back across the ice, picking up her discarded clothes as she went. She managed a weak smile when she reached us at the pond's edge.

"Mrs. DeBrett," someone said, "you could have drowned under that ice."

"Yes," she replied calmly, "but there would be a nice, warm place waiting for me if I had." And she was gone.

In all the years since that incident I have thought about the fire of Mrs. DeBrett's faith that propelled her into the freezing waters, about her firm belief in Jesus' promise of preparing a place for her that made her capable of the most courageous act I have ever witnessed. Mrs. DeBrett gave me my first glimmer of faith in action, and the gallant application of her belief set a standard that I have wanted to live up to ever since.

Dear Jesus, lead me to make my acts as bright and shining as my beliefs. —JAMES McDERMOTT

Praise Diary for January

1

2

3

4

5

6

7

8

9

10

11

12

13

14

15

16

17

18

19

20

21

22

23

24

25

26

27

28

29

30

31

February

Dear Lord,
I get a sunny kind of feeling
When Your loveshine warms my heart—
My troubles turn to bubbles
And my fears and doubts depart....

Thank You for that feeling,
That warm and special glow—
I pray that I can pass it on
To everyone I know....

Please use me as a ray, Dear Lord,
To make each day much brighter,
By word or deed to fill a need
And make a burden lighter....

And let me use Your loveshine
In everything I do,
That in a humble way I'll be
A mirror, Lord, of You!

—ALICE JOYCE DAVIDSON

PATTERN FOR A BLESSED LIFE

...Blessed are the poor in the spirit: for theirs is the kingdom of heaven.   —MATTHEW 5:3

1

"I don't know what's the matter with me," Kim said. "I've been reading books on prayer, listening to inspirational tapes and praying to be touched by the Holy Spirit and yet nothing changes. I'm about ready to give up!"

Larry, the leader of the prayer workshop, startled us all with his resounding reply: "Good! Giving up is the best thing you could possibly do right now!" Kim flashed a puzzled look at him as he continued, "Sometimes we strain so hard for spiritual experiences that we miss the real thing. Be poor in spirit, Kim. Just be empty before God, leaning on His love. Go ahead — give up!"

By the end of the workshop, Kim was quietly radiant as she said good-bye to Larry. "You know, after you told me to give up, I just let go. I felt as though I were falling and I guess I was...because I fell right into the soaring wings of the Holy Spirit!"

Lord, empty my spirit to make room for Your Spirit.

—MARILYN MORGAN HELLEBERG

2

Ye are all the children of light, and the children of the day: we are not of the night, nor of darkness.

—I THESSALONIANS 5:5

As I walked down the driveway to the mailbox, Stevie from next door came shuffling by. He's usually a cheerful little guy, but today he frowned and his head was down.

"Something wrong?" I asked.

"Yeah," he replied as he kicked a chunk of icy snow into the street. "The groundhog saw his shadow and we're gonna have six more weeks of winter!"

So that's why he was so gloomy! And I realized there is a grain of truth in that superstition — a truth that has nothing to do with the weather. How often we let predictions of gloom spoil an otherwise sunny day. How many times I've looked in the direction of the shadow instead of in the direction of the sun.

If the world seems gray today, let's remember that a shadow is evidence that the sun *is* shining!

I'll turn my back on darkness, Father, by facing your Son.
—MARILYN MORGAN HELLEBERG

---

3   *He that findeth his life shall lose it: and he that loseth his life for my sake shall find it.*   —MATTHEW 10:39

Call her Mary. That's not her real name but her story is true. In her teens Mary led an irregular and dissolute life. In her twenties she married, bore her husband three children and calmed down somewhat. Still, she was short of being an exemplary wife and mother. In her thirties, just when it seemed as though her marriage might end and she would lose her children, Mary came to know Jesus. She invited Him into her life and accepted His guidance.

After that Mary became a virtuous and hard-working wife and mother, giving an inordinate amount of time to her church and to helping others. She spent little on herself — in fact, she gave away money, even her jewelry and her clothes. So radical was her change of character that her family feared for her sanity and maneuvered her into a hospital for a psychiatric testing.

The results of the tests? The doctors reported that Mary was in fine mental health. Anyone, they said, who freely ministered to others as she did, whose thoughts were centered beyond herself, was in no danger of losing her sanity. Illness, they added, occurs when a person's sense of self becomes the center of his or her universe.

Gradually Mary learned to temper her good deeds and give priority to her family's needs. Today Mary's family is truly happy — and Mary's is a happy story. It reveals not a mere secret of sanity but *the* secret of happiness: not self, but others.

Loving You first, Lord, sets me on the road to loving others.
—VAN VARNER

---

4   *Yea, the sparrow hath found an house, and the swallow a nest for herself.* —PSALM 84:3

Construction of the house in the block down the street seemed to be progressing nicely. Then — all of a sudden — the work came to an abrupt halt. When I saw the contractor's car in the driveway, I strolled over to inquire.

"Come with me," he said, a twinkle in his eye.

He led me around the house and through the back entrance. There he pointed to the space where the electric fuse box was to be installed. He motioned me to be quiet but to peek into the opening. Inside I saw a small brown-twig nest that held a little bird, its bright, inquisitive eyes fixed on me.

The contractor led me away and spoke in a low voice lest the tiny tenant be disturbed. "We're letting the birds finish their job," he said, "before we go on with ours."

A warm glow enveloped me as I walked home. The contractor's consideration of the little bird was a reminder to me of my God-assigned responsibility to protect all of God's creatures — great and small. An important task — one that I relish sweet reminders of from time to time.

Father, for all the marvelous creatures You have given us to enjoy — and to protect — I thank You. —DRUE DUKE

5   *Sufficient unto the day is the evil thereof.* —MATTHEW 6:34

Whenever I find myself overreacting to things, I try to recall a little episode from one of our trips to Florida. Our motel faced a quiet, salt-water lagoon. The day was hot and still. From our window I could see an old fellow fishing from a dock not far away. Rather, he was more or less fishing. He was tilted back in a chair, hat over eyes, apparently asleep. His tall bamboo pole was propped against the railing, line trailing in the water.

Even as I watched, a large creature of the deep — a big redfish, probably — seized the line and yanked the pole completely off the dock. Into the water it slid, where it began streaking out toward the center of the bay. I was thrilled. A small rowboat was moored to the dock. Hot pursuit would enable that lucky angler to overtake this splendid fish!

Determined not to miss a detail, I flung the window wide. As I did so, the old boy turned his head about an inch and spoke to his life companion in the house behind him.

"Mamie," he said, "they got another pole!"

Well, that was years ago. But to this day, when I feel my blood pressure soaring because the car battery is dead, or we're overdrawn again at the bank, or the frozen pipes have burst, or some other disaster looms, I try to remember to murmur to myself, "Mamie, they got another pole!" Then I can smile — and my blood pressure returns to normal.

Lord, keep me from overreacting — with a smile.
                                                        —ARTHUR GORDON

---

6   *Ask, and it shall be given you...*   —MATTHEW 7:7

The summer I was eighteen a handsome young man joined our church. How I wanted a date with him! So I prayed fervently, "Please, God, let Charles ask me out." Sure enough, one hot August evening Charles came by the house and asked me out. The only hitch was, it was the wrong Charles.

And there was the time when I prayed, "Please, God, let this car just get to the repair shop." So then, directly in front of the repair shop — but across the street — the motor died in Atlanta's four o'clock traffic. As I paid the towing charge, I had to smile ruefully. I got precisely what I asked for.

Last week we had anticipated our first weekend away since our youngest son was born. "Oh, Lord, give me just one morning when no child's voice wakes me up," I sighed. The request was granted all right — but the conference schedule was such that I was up and dressed before the children would have awakened anyway!

God takes prayer seriously. He honors sincere requests of the heart but He expects us to ask for specific things. He is not interested in generalities and half-considered requests.

Prayer is one of the most exciting adventures I know. But be careful of what you pray for — you may get exactly that!

Dear Lord, teach us to pray with careful thought and humble hearts.   —PATRICIA HOUCK SPRINKLE

---

7   *I will therefore that men pray every where, lifting up holy hands...*   —I TIMOTHY 2:8

For the most part I work at home and I don't often have a chance to share in the Prayer Fellowship meetings in the *Guideposts'* offices on Monday mornings. And I used to feel left out. One morning, though, I was there and I want to tell you about it.

The staff members took their places at the long table in the conference room; a stack of letters from readers was passed around; each person silently read a few of them and then chose one to read aloud. After each reading we discussed the steps that *Guideposts* could take — as a magazine and as a family — to help the writer of the letter. Someone said a prayer as we all joined hands, our heads bowed.

Suddenly a warmth filled the room. And I realized that people all across the country, even all across the globe — countless thousands of people — were in that room with us at that moment, joining us in prayer. *Like a tidal wave of faith*, I thought, *certainly reaching God.*

Since then I have found that wherever I am, whatever I am doing, on Monday morning at 9:45 I can pray in fellowship with others, my voice joined with thousands of voices in one great psalm to God.

This day, God, I will add my voice to the chorus. —GLENN KITTLER

---

8 *... And, lo, it was all grown over with thorns, and nettles had covered the face thereof, and the stone wall thereof was broken down.* —PROVERBS 24:31

As a child I loved to visit Uncle Mart Sutton's "mansion." A large, many-gabled house, it sat high atop a hill, surrounded by flowering trees and singing birds. Inside, there were lush hanging ferns, billowing white curtains, colorful embroidered cushions on plump, overstuffed couches, and fine china. Looking down from the top of the hill, we could see acres of fields basted together with a winding little creek; often we saw deer.

Recently we returned to the house after an absence of many

years. The longer I looked around, the more I ached. No gate welcomed us. Pushing through tangles of undergrowth, we finally found the house — rundown but still beautiful. The front lawn was pink with wild sweet peas that almost frothed with bees. Looking up to the second floor, through a broken window, we could see juts of honeycomb. The lovely room with its once tight-stretched carpet and quilt-covered bed was now a great beehive. Beyond the house, the formerly sturdy barn leaned into the slope of the hill as though on its knees.

A chill ran down my back. I wondered: *Can spiritual decay occur as gradually and insidiously as the decay that had felled the house and barn? Can neglect and unconcern bring about the downfall of one's spiritual house?* I pray — and *I will pray* — not.

Lord, help me to be constant in spirit; steady in discipline; faithful in prayer...always. —ZONA B. DAVIS

---

9   ...*Follow me, and I will make you fishers of men.*
—MATTHEW 4:19

There is a story I love about Thomas Merton, the Trappist monk. A man of joy and laughter, he was quite good with a camera and often photographed the simple beauty of the Kentucky hills around his monastery.

One day he sent a photograph to a friend with this announcement: "The only known photograph of God." The color snapshot showed gentle green hills under a vast blue sky. And at the top of the picture, dominating the scene, there was an immense sky hook, the kind used in construction to lift heavy objects. It looked like a gigantic fishing hook suspended from heaven.

That story always makes me smile. For the truth in it goes very deep. God can indeed be found in an image of a hook dangling over the world. Ever-seeking, ever-loving, God desires fellowship with men. God fishes...and waits. And most amazing, He invites me to go fishing with Him...to be a "fisher of men." Today, why not cast your hook along with God's? Tell someone about His love.

God, I know that my only lasting joy in life is to be caught by You.   —SUE MONK KIDD

---

10 *For where your treasure is, there will your heart be also.*
                                    —LUKE 6:21

The first time my then future wife Judy took me to visit her family I discovered that her mother and I shared an affection for paperweights. Over the years I had gathered a modest accumulation, but Mrs. Vanderveer's collection was exceptional. She'd been collecting them over a lifetime, and when I saw the twenty objects in a lighted display case, they took my breath away.

"Come see my best ones by my chair on the table," Mrs. Vanderveer said, leading me to her living room. And there were two stunning Baccarat weights whose pellucid crystal contained dazzling bursts of color.

"Wow!" I said.

"But this, of course, is my favorite," she said, picking up a flat, four inch circle of clay on which a chubby little hand had left an imprint. She touched it lovingly and said, "Judy gave this to me for Christmas twenty-five years ago. It's been my most precious one ever since."

At first I thougt *how corny!* But then I thought: *Now here's a woman who* really *knows* what to *collect.*

Help me to know, Lord, what to truly value in life.
                                    —JAMES McDERMOTT

11 *. . . I will forgive their iniquity, and I will remember their sin no more.* —JEREMIAH 31:34

My grandmother insisted on everything being in its proper place. I have learned a lot over the years from her embroidered sampler that hung above the mantle:

DON'T PUT IT DOWN,
PUT IT AWAY!

Then, last week it occurred to me that I'd been violating her rule for years. The realization came when I spoke unkindly to a loved one.

"Forgive me," I begged. And he did. And God heard.

But still I went around in a state of remorse. Unable to forgive *myself*. I carried the burden of guilt and put it down beside me everywhere I went — walking on eggs lest I commit the same wrong. Until I realized that there was yet another prayer I must offer:

Lord, when I commit a sin, don't let me put it down beside me. Let me put it away — as You have done when I asked forgiveness.

—JUNE MASTERS BACHER

12 *O that there were such an heart in them, that they would fear me, and keep all my commandments always, that it might be well with them, and with their children for ever!* —DEUTERONOMY 5:29

Here are ten guidelines that have particular meaning for us today:

You cannot keep out of trouble by spending more than your income.

You cannot help the poor man by destroying the rich.

You cannot establish security on borrowed money.

You cannot bring about prosperity by discouraging thrift.

You cannot lift the wage-earner by pulling down the wage-payer.

You cannot strengthen the weak by weakening the strong.

You cannot help small men by tearing down big men.

You cannot build character and courage by taking away man's initiative and independence.

You cannot help men permanently by doing for them what they could and should do for themselves.

You cannot further the brotherhood of man by inciting class hatred.

We owe much to Abraham Lincoln, whose birthday we celebrate today and the ten guidelines set forth above — written by him — surely seem worthy enough to follow the Ten Commandments set forth by God. Each leads us toward a clear conscience and true Christian brotherhood.

Help us, Father, to obey all words of wisdom that show us how to be staunch friends to our fellow man. —ISABEL CHAMP

---

13 *For unto every one that hath shall be given, and he shall have abundance...* —MATTHEW 25:29

"My folks couldn't afford to buy me a bicycle," John Havilcek, Boston Celtic basketball great, once told me, "and I felt cheated. I ran everywhere — to school, to deliver groceries, to basketball practice. I suppose all that running helped me to develop my legs and my stamina."

Interesting. Those who enjoy the finer points of basketball know that movement *without* the ball is one of the keys to success in the game. The player who keeps running can eventually elude his guard, receive the ball and score. John Havilcek was perpetual motion personified. The lack of a bike when he was a youngster may have aided the development of those sturdy legs that ran other teams ragged.

If you feel that you have been shortchanged in some way, take inventory of your situation. Assay your strengths. Chances are that God has some compensatory gifts in mind that more than offset the negatives. Ask Him to show you how to make the most of what you have.

Keep me from self-pity, Lord, and raise my sights. —FRED BAUER

---

14 *As the Father hath loved me, so have I loved you.*
—JOHN 15:9

Some days I don't like myself very well. Like yesterday. In the morning I had an argument with my husband. The afternoon mail brought a rejected manuscript. Then at 10:00 p.m., I realized I hadn't visited my mother-in-law in over a week. Feeling a failure on all fronts, I phoned my daughter Karen, and we prayed together.

And today I got a valentine in the mail! It was just a folded piece of white paper with some heart-shaped stickers on it. On the front it read: *A Valentine for Marilyn.* Inside was this message:

> As the Father hath loved me,
> so have I loved you.
> > All my love,
> > Jesus

I couldn't hold back the tears. How blessed to be so loved even when I feel unlovable!

I'm pretty sure I know whose human hand fashioned that valentine, but I also know that the One Who spoke those words speaks them to me now and that (imagine!) He really does love me!

Do you know anyone who would like to receive a valentine from Jesus?

Thank You, Lord, for Your precious love.

—MARILYN MORGAN HELLEBERG

JOURNEY OF FAITH

15 Your traveling companion is *ABRAHAM'S SERVANT* ... *who journeyed for another.* —GENESIS 24

Throughout the Old Testment great value is placed on faithful servants. It isn't until the New Testament, however — when God Himself comes to earth in the form of a servant — that servanthood is seen not just as acceptable, but as *the* God-given calling of all believers.

What are the standards by which a servant is judged? There is only one standard: his master's evaluation. Anyone else's opinion is simply not important. And so it is when we become servants of God, we need not care about satisfying anybody else.

For our model servant, let's choose Abraham's. How do we know he was a good one? Because Abraham thought so and gave him charge of all that he had. Now watch the way this good servant carried out his assignment.

He understood his orders. So often we catch a glimpse of a divine mission and dash off without knowing the limits of our assignment. But the experienced servant of Abraham, before setting out on *his* journey, made sure he understood what he was *not* to do.

Limited tasks can be the hardest of all. To speak a word, to offer a

FEBRUARY 1983

helping hand, to invite someone to church — and *then to take our hands off,* this is the heart of servanthood.

He knew how to wait. Having placed in God's hands the choice of a wife for his master's son, he "...held his peace, to wit whether the Lord had made his journey prosperous or not." Only after the sign from God was given, did he draw from his saddlebags an enormous ring and two golden bracelets.

He put his master's interest first. After the long trek from Canaan to Mesopotamia, Abraham's servant was surely tired and hungry.

Rebekah and her family agreed to the betrothal, but wanted her to remain at home at least ten days. Now, Abraham's servant was not a young man; ten days to rest and enjoy fabled Near Eastern hospitality would not be self-indulgent before setting out on the rigorous journey homeward.

But he is steadfast. "Hinder me not, seeing the Lord hath prospered my way; send me away that I may go to my master..." Abraham's servant's errand was not just a job; it was a trust that came ahead of everything.

That I may go to my Master...

Lord, show me that all servanthood leads to You.
— ELIZABETH SHERRILL

---

16 *...I am not come to call the righteous, but sinners to repentance.* —MATTHEW 9:13

I recently overheard a man tell a woman that he never goes to church.

"It's full of hypocrites," he said.

"Well, thank God!" she replied. "If only saints were allowed in, I'd be in big trouble."

Me too.

What a comfort it is to know that I'm welcome in God's house despite my shortcomings. And it's even greater comfort to know that when I truly repent and ask God's mercy, my sins are forgiven.

On this day of penitence, Lord, open my heart to Your cleansing love. —MADGE HARRAH

---

17 *But every man hath his proper gift of God, one after this manner, and another after that.* —I CORINTHIANS 7:7

When I moved into the dormitory at college, I could see plainly that my roommate and I were not at all alike. Bruce was from the nearby state capital; I was from a small, upstate town. He had been the sports editor of a suburban newspaper; I had written only two sports stories for our local paper when it was short-staffed. He had a car; my parents delivered me to school.

The pattern didn't seem to change. When he got plums, I got pits. He would get an "A" on a final exam with only a few hours of study; I would work all day for a "B." He was named general manager of the campus radio station; I was news anchor. It seemed that I was always a step and a half behind. What I wanted to be, he *was*.

One day during the broadcast of a football game (Bruce was doing play-by-play; I was keeping statistics), our school (prestigious in losing) was being sorely beaten on the field. I leaned out the window of the radio booth to gauge the reaction of our fans and saw an old gentleman holding up a sign. "We are not Undefeated," the sign read, "but We are Proud."

I looked over at my roommate, chattering away, and back at the sign. And right in the middle of that football game — where one team was very good and the other was very bad; where one coach liked running plays and the other preferred passing; where Bruce announced and I kept stats — I realized that God had created diversity and called it *good*. I did not have to do play-by-play or ease through Advanced Reporting class to be proud of who I was.

No, I am not Bruce, who is still my best friend and today a television sports producer for a large independent station, but *I am Jeff. And I am proud!*

Thanks, Father, for letting me know that by being myself, I'm being all that You want me to be.   —JEFF JAPINGA

---

18   *Better is it that thou shouldest not vow, than that thou shouldest vow and not pay.*   —ECCLESIASTES 5:5

Last year all my friends were talking about their New Year's resolutions...and I felt guilty because I hadn't made any. So when I opened the freezer to poke in a little carton of leftovers and saw dozens of similar cartons frozen into solid blocks of frost, I determined to make a resolution: *This year I will faithfully defrost the freezer.*

Well, I kept putting it off until one day I discovered that apparently someone had kicked loose the cord sometime earlier and I hadn't noticed it. With soapsuds and soda in midsummer, I finally fulfilled my New Year's resolution!

I think that maybe a lot of us live our lives as we do our New Year's resolutions. In January we say, "This year I'll take more time for volunteer work."

Days, weeks, months pass and we don't follow through. We don't call on our neighbor — until our car won't start one morning. We don't begin to tighten our budgets — until we lose a job. We don't take more time for volunteer work — until we feel downright ashamed.

And sometimes we even put off talking with God — until we're confronted by a problem or a disappointment. I think I'll take a further step this year and resolve: *I will keep my resolution.* That way, God will be hearing from me all year 'round!

Father, I know that a resolution is a commitment. Help me to be constant, as You are constant with me. —ISABEL CHAMP

---

19 *But the fruit of the Spirit is love...* —GALATIANS 5:22

My dog Trooper is thirteen years old. Among animals, he's a real senior citizen.

Trooper can't do a lot of the things that he used to do. He's almost totally deaf now and he doesn't hear people when they come to the door. It embarrasses him when they suddenly appear and he barks — even at friends whom he knows. It's his way of insisting that he's still looking out for me, and I appreciate that.

But now that Trooper is old, I find that I look out for him too. I don't like to leave him at home alone for more than a few hours at a time. And when I'm away, if he's outdoors and it begins to rain, I dash home to give him shelter. For years he has followed me from room to room. Now when I'm going to another part of the house, I tap him on the shoulder to let him know that I'm on the move. He wants to be with me and I enjoy his company. We're old friends and time isn't going to change that.

Some people say that having a pet is too much trouble. "You get so attached to them," they tell me.

Maybe so. But maybe love means that you allow yourself to get attached. I would like to think that when I'm on in years, the people I love will feel attached to me.

Lord, let me know the grace of love that increases with time.
—PHYLLIS HOBE

20

The heavens declare the glory of God; and the firmament sheweth his handywork. —PSALM 19:1

Last night I was reading a slender book, *God and the Astronomers*, by Robert Jastrow, an eminent astronomer. In it are facts that made my mind reel. According to Dr. Jastrow, most of his colleagues now believe that the universe began about twenty billion years ago in a stupendous fiery explosion that hurled the galaxies into infinite space where they are still receding from one another at ever-increasing speeds over ever-increasing distances.

Scientists think they even have detected lingering radiation from that inconceivable blast.

The main point that Dr. Jastrow makes is that the evidence indicates that the universe had a specific beginning at a definite point in time, just as the first verse of Genesis says: *In the beginning God created....* Jastrow writes: "The scientist has scaled the mountains of ignorance; he is about to conquer the highest peaks; as he pulls himself over the final rock, he is greeted by a band of theologians who have been sitting there for centuries."

How marvelous that the only answer to the unanswerable still must be expressed in a simple, three-letter word: *God.*

Heavenly Father, when scientific facts awe and frighten me, let me remember that the same Power that created such vastness also has the tenderness to care about me. —ARTHUR GORDON

21

For whatsoever things were written aforetime were written for our learning, that we through patience and comfort of the scriptures might have hope. —ROMANS 15:4

I didn't seem to have enough time in the mornings to read

my Bible, I'd get up at five and write until six. Then I'd shower, dress, eat breakfast, make my lunch and leave for work by seven. Each moment was filled, I thought — until a friend told me that she times her three-minute egg every morning by twice repeating the Lord's Prayer and the Twenty-third Psalm.

What a good idea! Then I wondered: *If she can pray and recall an entire Psalm twice in three minutes, what can I accomplish in five minutes?* I began boiling my morning eggs at six-forty and setting the timer for six forty-five. After that I opened my Bible and read until the bell rang. The eggs done, I closed the Book.

Now I never complain about lack of time in the morning. My new routine puts me in God's Presence for five minutes at the start of each day... and that adds up to nearly thirty hours each year!

If you are as busy as I am, perhaps this idea can be helpful to you too.

Lord, I will spend time every morning in Your Word.

—DORIS HAASE

22 *...Ye should earnestly contend for the faith which was once delivered unto the saints.* —JUDE 1:3

Last February on George Washington's two hundred and fiftieth birthday, I attended a meeting of the Daughters of the American Revolution. It was a meeting to honor him, the one who led us to nationhood. As I sat there, I thought that so much of our nation's history had depended upon his leadership. What would our country be like today had Washington failed?

Then the program began with a woman telling a story about the fateful night when Washington knelt in the snow at Valley Forge. It was during one of the darkest chapters in the Revolutionary War. The American troops were tattered and cold and many thought that the army could not hold out much longer. Washington knelt there that winter night and prayed. As he did, he was overheard by a colonist who happened to be walking home through the woods. When the man reached his house, he confidently told his wife, "Do not worry any longer, dear. Washington will win."

"But how do you know?" she asked.

"Because he first seeks God's guidance," he replied.

General Washington did win, against all odds. And the destiny of our nation was shaped forever.

After hearing that story, I became more determined than ever to pause and seek the guidance of God before I face the tasks and battles of my life. For if God can shape the destiny of a nation, surely He can shape the destiny of one small life.

Thank You, God, for Your guiding hand upon the birth of our nation and upon all who call upon You. —SUE MONK KIDD

---

23 *This is the day which the Lord hath made; we will rejoice and be glad in it.* —PSALM 118:24

A group of old friends. An informal dinner. A question: "What was the best day of your life?"

"The beautiful April day when we were married," Roberta and Hal said.

"The day little Vicky was born," Victor mused.

"The day I was fired from my first job — it was my 'best' and 'worst' day." Tony laughed. "That day made me take stock of myself and it set me on a new path that has since led to contentment in every area of my life."

And so we talked. Then Elizabeth, who had been silent, spoke up. "I think," she said in a soft voice, "that the best day of my life is *today*."

"Why is that?" I asked.

"Because it's the day I value the most. After all, I can't retrieve yesterday, I'm not sure of tomorrow, but this day *is* — it's mine, to make it into whatever I want it to be. And because it's now, and I'm alive in it, it's the *best* and I thank God for it."

What was the best day of your life? Or, perhaps, as Elizabeth would say, "What *is* the best day of your life?"

Today, Lord, this new day to be lived for You. —VAN VARNER

---

24 *Bear ye one another's burdens, and so fulfill the law of Christ.* —GALATIANS 6:2

February ought to be called Feb-*blah*-ary. Brief gray after-noons, no sign that spring will ever come, two days without mail, Christmas joy receding and Easter still too far away to be celebrated — in my calendar, February is the *longest* month of the year! So one snowy February evening at a church meeting when I was asked to tell what God was doing in my life, I blurted out, "Keeping my annual February depression from becoming suicidal."

Silence. Shocked silence from the group, embarrassed silence from me. I hadn't intended to be quite that open.

But the next morning I received a telephone call from a woman who said, "Thank you for your honesty last night. I'm depressed in February too but I've never said so since I became a Christian. It seemed…well, weak, not really walking with the Lord, I guess. Could we call each other when we're feeling low?"

I was so relieved. Why is it that we Christians don't like to acknowledge that in the closets of our lives we sometimes harbor doubts and fears, feel depressed, get terribly hurt? Often it is only through admitting our troubles that we are able to share the troubles of others and bring about a healing — for them and for us.

59

Let us share with others the joys and sorrows of life. How else can we rejoice and weep together?

Dear Jesus, help us to share all *our joys and* all *our sorrows with one another.* —PATRICIA HOUCK SPRINKLE

---

25 *...We will give ourselves continually to prayer...*
—ACTS 6:4

Ironing was the one household chore I disliked most until a neighbor shared her secret.

"When I iron, I pray for the people whose clothes I am ironing — especially for the time when they will be wearing them. That way they have prayers stored up for them."

The next time I faced the ironing pile, I decided to try her secret.

Over one of my husband's shirts I prayed: "Lord, bless Jerry when he wears this shirt. Help him at work with each decision he has to make. Keep him safe and remind him of my love for him." The shirt looked great.

Ironing our twin boys' jeans, I continued: "Father, please enable the boys not to fight when they wear these pants. Help them to really enjoy each other and to share their things. Help them in school to be good learners." Done.

My nineteen-year-old daughter's blouse had been on the ironing board for months! "Father," I prayed as I ironed, "please bless Jennifer when she wears this blouse. Protect her. Let her want to please You and help her reach out to others." The blouse looked lovely.

Soon there was only a skirt left. Mine. I began to iron. "Lord, I just wear this skirt around the house. It's harder to be a wife and mother than I thought it would be. Help me show Your love to the people with whom I live. Remind me to smile when I wear this skirt. Thank You." I was finished. And *I was* smiling.

My friend was right. Ironing, or any chore, doesn't have to be a drag. I had found that my special "ironing" prayers bring added blessings to my family — and to myself.

Father, if there be a dreaded task for me to perform today, help me find its blessing through prayer. —MARION BOND WEST

---

26 *But I know, that even now, whatsoever thou wilt ask of God, God will give it thee.* —JOHN 11:22

While I was driving south on a major highway near my home, I came upon a towering outcropping of rock that must have been part of a big hill or a small mountain before the highway was put through. I don't know how it was done but at some time someone had obviously lowered himself down the face of the rock and in bold black letters painted the words, "GOD FORGIVES!"

Then most likely at a later date, someone else had lowered himself down the rock and in bold red letters added: "WHEN YOU ASK!"

I'll get no answers, if I don't ask. Father, please forgive me for.... —GLENN KITTLER

27 *If ye then, being evil, know how to give good gifts unto your children, how much more shall your Father which is in heaven give good things to them that ask him?*

— MATTHEW 7:11

Sometimes when God gives me a "No!" answer and I find myself questioning His wisdom, I have only to think of Ann and the red wings.

Although Ann was being raised in a devout Christian family, she arrived at a doubting stage early in life. Was God real? Were prayers heard? To discover the answers, she prayed fervently to God for red wings as proof of His good intentions — and nothing happened! No red wings — ergo, no God.

"Yet as I grew older," Ann told me, "that was the very fact that brought me to my knees with a hosanna of thanksgiving as I realized how *good* God is. Imagine having to go through life with red wings!"

How we could enrich our faith by looking all the way back through the years and remembering — with gratitude — the times that He said "No!"

Father, let me accept equably Your "No" along with Your "Yes" as facets of Your infinite wisdom and loving care.

— ELAINE ST. JOHNS

28 *I do set my bow in the cloud, and it shall be for a token of a covenant between me and the earth.* — GENESIS 9:13

One day last winter when Norman and I were sailing to Rio de Janeiro on the great ocean liner, *Queen Elizabeth II*, we made a stop at Salvador, the oldest city in Brazil. The ship anchored in the waters off the city, which is located at the southern end of a beautiful, bluff-formed peninsula. Boats were lowered to take passengers ashore. Although the day was very hot and uncomfortable, a brief shower helped to cool things off. As the rain ended, Norman and I went out on deck to watch the last of the shore boats return. The QE2 prepared to set sail again. Grinding noisily, the winches hoisted the boats from the water and crewman were laboriously maneuvering them back into their stanchions when someone cried out, "Look!" Everyone turned, passengers and crew alike, and for an unforgettable moment the world seemed to hush.

There, spanning the sky high above the blue water and the steep green hills of the Brazilian coast, was a magnificent rainbow. But more — above that another perfect arc had formed: We were looking at a *double* rainbow! On our entire trip we had not seen a more spectacular sight.

"It's a miracle," someone said quietly.

And then I heard the deep voice of one of the crewman as he said something so unexpected and yet so simple that I find myself repeating the sentence over and over again, like a watchword:

"*Every day* is a miracle."

Father, show me today's miracle and know that I thank You for it.

—RUTH STAFFORD PEALE

Praise Diary for February

1

2

3

4

5

6

7

8

9

10

11

12

13

14

15

16

17

18

19

20

21

22

23

24

25

26

27

28

March

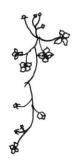

God is our refuge and strength, a very present
help in trouble.   —PSALM 46:1

For howling winds
That make me bend,
And make me stronger
In the end,
I thank You, Lord!

For hurricanes
That tear at roots,
Forcing me
To grow new shoots,
I thank You, Lord!

For winds of love,
I thank You, Lord,
The soothing breeze
Of faith's reward,
I thank You, Lord!

—ALICE JOYCE
DAVIDSON

PATTERN FOR A BLESSED LIFE

Blessed are they that mourn: for they shall be comforted.
—MATTHEW 5:4

1

When my father died suddenly, we tried to console ourselves by saying, "Well, at least he didn't have to suffer through a long illness." I managed to get through the funeral without a tear by telling myself that Daddy wouldn't want me to grieve.

Then on the day after the funeral, one of my father's patients came to the door and said, "Fifteen years ago your dad tried to save my only son's life but Jimmy died anyway. While everyone else was trying to cheer me up, your father did the only thing that really helped. He cried with me."

She put her arms around me and tears started to roll down her face. With that something stiff and cold within me broke loose and all of my pent-up grief came pouring out in great, body-wracking sobs.

What a blessed release! What a healing grace. In that moment I was enfolded in the arms of my loving Heavenly Father.

Praise You, God, for the gift of tears...and for Your Fatherly arms that hold me when I cry. —MARILYN MORGAN HELLEBERG

2

...And he which soweth bountifully shall reap also bountifully.
—II CORINTHIANS 9:6

The owner of a large estate gave his gardener some red roses to take home to the employee's wife. But she never received them. On the bus that afternoon the gardener sat next to a widow who spoke of her loneliness. Knowing his wife would understand, he gave the roses to the widow.

But the widow didn't get home with them either. At the grocery store she came upon a young girl in tears. The girl's mother was very ill. "Here," she said, handing the flowers to her, "give them to your mother and tell her I'll be praying for her."

Gratefully the girl accepted them and took them to her mother. The bedridden woman was cheered by the roses, but she didn't keep them. "They're too beautiful not to share," she told her minister when he came to visit her the next day. "I'd like the church to have them." So the pastor took them and placed them in the sanctuary, where they were appreciated by his congregation. After the service, the minister gave single roses to some of the church members as they left. The enjoyment of the flowers was extended once more before they wilted.

My friend Helen Steiner Rice once wrote a beautiful poem entitled, "Flowers Leave Their Fragrance on the Hand of the Giver," and the words are true. Every good deed, every kindness, every thoughtful action, has a way of blessing the giver and multiplying the gift. Like the ripple effect of a stone tossed into water, the circles that emanate can reach many unseen shores. So it is with love shared.

Thank You, Father, for Your love. Today I'll pass it on.
—FRED BAUER

---

3 *To every thing there is a season, and a time to every purpose under the heaven...* —ECCLESIASTES 3:1

I wanted to give the morning to God in prayer and meditation. But the boys dawdled over breakfast. Then my husband had a problem he wanted to discuss. Our tenant missed her ride to work and when I offered to take her, I remembered that I needed to make a bank deposit. By the time I returned home, the morning was half gone.

"Oh, God, I wanted to give You the *whole* morning," I lamented. Fetching a cup of tea and a Bible to my favorite chair, I sat down and...sure enough, the phone rang.

"Just wanted to let you know your order has come in," said a cheery voice from a nearby department store. "Will you be in today to pick it up?"

"Not likely," I said curtly.

"Fine." She ignored my tone. "We're open all day every day to serve you."

As I hung up, her words rang in my ears: *Open all day every day to serve you.* I had wanted to give my morning to God. Instead, God had sent me dawdling children, a puzzled husband, a needy tenant and a stranger, and I had dealt perfunctorily with all of them so I could "give time" to God.

In shame and penitence I bowed my head to once again offer God *all* my time.

Lord of all time, take my day and let it be consecrated wholly to Your service. In Jesus' name, Amen. —PATRICIA HOUCK SPRINKLE

---

4   *Yet man is born unto trouble, as the sparks fly upward.*
                                            —JOB 5:7

My friend Robbie Thompson and I were talking about the Great Depression of the 1930s, which both of us remember vividly.

"I couldn't get a job anywhere," he said. "No welfare, no unemployment insurance back in those days. I didn't know how I was going to live. I was scared!

"At that time the postal rate for letters went from two cents to three — a big jump! We all complained. After all, times were hard enough. But complaining got us nowhere. Then I had an idea. I took my last four dollars and bought a very secondhand bicycle. I went to all the merchants on Main Street and told them I would deliver their bills to customers by hand — for a cent and a half apiece.

"I must have looked fairly trustworthy because several of them took me on. By pedaling fast I was able to earn about two dollars a day. Back then with that you could buy a week's supply of groceries. I couldn't complain now. My resourcefulness helped me make it through the darkest of times!"

His words made me think: Yes, trouble can be painful. It's never really welcome. But if it makes you wake up, get going and take action, you're bound to find your way through it. And maybe discover a new strength you didn't know you had.

Lord, show me a creative way through my problem today.
—ARTHUR GORDON

---

5 *I waited patiently for the Lord; and he inclined unto me, and heard my cry.* —PSALM 40:1

At the beginning of Lent we were looking forward to spending time together at a woodsy retreat grounds beside a lake. However, I didn't expect the type of solitude that our leader proposed immediately upon our arrival. He announced that, "While we spend these two days together, we will not speak to one another except at mealtime. This is an opportunity to look into God's Word undisturbed by others and to let Him speak to our hearts."

At first I was averse to the idea. *So this is what I'm giving up for Lent — a time of fellowship with friends whom I never see enough of anyway!*

But then I recalled that Jesus Himself needed to be alone. He often retreated too — from His disciples, His best friends — to go into the wilderness or a garden to pray.

If Jesus needed time apart, why shouldn't we?

Whether you live alone or with a boisterous, busy family, try turning off the television, the radio, the stereo — even if only for a day. Give your spirit a chance to privately and lovingly listen to God as He speaks directly to you...and you alone.

Lord, quiet my soul that I might hear Your special message for me. —ISABEL CHAMP

---

6 *Six days may work be done; but in the seventh is the sabbath of rest, holy to the Lord...* —EXODUS 31:15

A clergyman was once asked what he thought about people who had to work on Sundays. He replied, "It should not detract from a man's reverence to do what is required. Even Jesus spoke about the ox in the ditch on the Sabbath. But if your ox falls in the ditch *every* Sabbath, you should either get rid of the ox or fill up the ditch!"

There is a beautiful truth in these words. There are times when emergencies, illness or conflicting work schedules prevent us from attending church. But those exceptions should not become habitual or be allowed to serve as an excuse.

One day of the week was especially set aside for us — and for Him.

Father, wherever I am this day, I will spend it with You.
—GLENN KITTLER

7

...God hath commanded you, that ye may live, and that it may be well with you... —DEUTERONOMY 5:33

It began shortly after his wife died. He was sixty-five then and he decided to retire. At first Mr. Breckinridge, an old friend of the family, was busy enough and cheerful enough, but when his hearing started to fail, his whole attitude changed. You could see old age in his eyes and in the sag of his shoulders. He stopped going out and began to complain of loneliness. He even refused to see a doctor. He seemed to be ready for death.

His hearing worsened until one day at a friend's urging he agreed to see an ear doctor. Sitting before the specialist, a what's-the-use expression on his face, he closed his eyes. The doctor began to explore first his right ear and then his left, using a number of instruments and fluids.

Suddenly there was a loud noise in the room.

"What's that terrible racket?" Mr. Breckinridge shouted.

"*That*, Mr. Breckinridge," the specialist said sternly as he pointed to an object on the filing cabinet nearby, "is the whirring sound of the blades of my electric fan. I have just removed a large amount of wax from your right ear. I shall now remove a similar amount from your left ear. After that you may go home. I will not need to see you again." Then he asked in a whisper: "Do you hear me, Mr. Breckinridge?"

Close to tears, Mr. Breckinridge nodded. And from that moment hence, our old family friend decided that he was young again. Before the year was out, he had even remarried. I remember that it was a lovely Christmas wedding.

Funny, isn't it, how many people trick themselves into old age, squandering the life that God gave them by not living it to the fullest?

Father, no matter how old I may be, keep me growing younger!
—VAN VARNER

8   *...I will go before thee, and make the crooked places straight...*
                                                —ISAIAH 45:2

We were cross-country skiing when we rounded a curve and found ourselves before a frozen lake.

"Let's cut straight across," my husband suggested.

I studied the scene. The ice gleamed like a mirror. *Breakable?* I wondered. "Ski across a lake?" I asked. "What if the ice should give way?"

"I'll check it out," my husband replied. Gingerly he slid his skis out onto the ice, where they cut two silver ribbons behind him. "Solid," he announced. "Now stay right behind me. It will be safe *if you follow in my trail.*"

So we wound our way in a serpentine course out over the ice. Halfway across I had a sharp stab of doubt: *What am I doing out here?* My skis seemed to move slower and slower. I was not unlike Peter walking after Jesus on the Sea of Galilee, filled with doubt — and sinking.

"Come on," Sandy called, glancing back at me. I looked up at him and began to inch forward, following his trail in the ice. Gradually my doubts eased and my skis pushed ahead with renewed confidence.

We made it of course. But the little adventure taught me a lesson — a lesson for those uncertain moments when life seems about to crack and give way beneath my feet. When my eyes focus only on the problem, I am apt to sink into doubt and become immobilized. But when I concentrate on Jesus and *follow His trail,* my faith burns bright and I move steadfastly ahead. The lesson is as old as the Sea of Galilee but still true for us today. Jesus is always there, up ahead...ever leading the way.

When I am on thin ice, Lord, sustain me.

                                           —SUE MONK KIDD

9   *Charity (love) . . . beareth all things, believeth all things,
    hopeth all things, endureth all things.*
                                            —I CORINTHIANS 13:4,7

The odor wafting from the kitchen was unmistakable —
oatmeal-raisin cookies, my favorite. It made me feel both hungry
and perplexed.

"Honey, what are you doing?" I asked Lynn, peering around the
door into the kitchen.

"Obviously I'm baking cookies," she replied.

"Yes, but shouldn't you be studying? You have a test and two
papers due next week. If you leave things until the last minute,
you'll regret it. I learned that the hard way."

Lynn stared at me, visibly angry. "This is the third time this week
you've told me that I should be studying. Did it ever occur to you
that I'm capable of deciding for myself how much study I need? If
baking cookies is going to make me fail, isn't that *my* problem?"
And with that she slammed the kitchen door.

I had my hand on the knob of the door to open it and voice a loud
protest — when something made me stop. Had I listened when I
had been told to study instead of going to the basketball game? Or
when I nearly wrecked the car because I had ignored the warnings
about icy roads? Some lessons have to be learned the hard way, I
guess — by experience.

Yes, I would stop being a nag. Hereafter I would trust Lynn to
God, pray for her as she studied, believe in her ability to handle her
own affairs, and whatever happened, always let her know I loved
her. I'd even sample a few of her oatmeal-raisin cookies tonight.

*Thank You, Father, for the freedom to do it our way, with Your
love.*   —JEFF JAPINGA

10   *... Let not thy left hand know what thy right hand doeth.*
                                          —MATTHEW 6:3

When our son, Paul, was critically injured in a car accident, I received a post card that read: "You don't know me, but I just want to tell you that someone who cares is praying for Paul every day." It was signed, "A friend in Jesus." After Paul was home from the hospital, another card came: "I was reading in Romans 8 today, and verses 18, 28 and 31 seemed to be meant just for you." When our son was fully recovered, a third card came, with only five words on it: "Praise God for answered prayer!"

I'll probably never know who sent those cards, but of this I'm sure: It was a person of humility who wanted to give comfort and didn't care about receiving credit for it. Since then, I've kept a packet of post cards handy, and when I'm moved to pray for someone, I follow the example of my anonymous "friend in Jesus." I know that those prayers are specially blessed, because part of the blessing spills on me.

How about letting an anonymous post card carry your message of loving concern? Send it on the wings of prayer, and it will bless two — the one prayed for and you.

Lord, let this little card be a reminder of Your great love.
                             —MARILYN MORGAN HELLEBERG

11   *But other fell into good ground, and brought forth fruit, some an hundredfold, some sixtyfold, some thirtyfold.*
                                      —MATTHEW 13:8

When my friend Peggy returned from a trip to her home town, she told the following story:

"I dropped in to visit my former church. Seeing a new directory of members, I thumbed through it and happened to see David's name. I smiled, remembering the Sunday morning that he walked to church with my girlfriend and me. Although he was a declared atheist, we coaxed him to come inside. Reluctantly he followed us through the wide doors. I remember how quiet he was after the service. I've often wondered what happened to him. Now, just think — he's a member!"

And Peggy's story did make me think.

I know people who turn away at the mention of God. I have often thought, *There's no use in talking to them.* But how do I know that for sure? In Jesus' parable many of the sower's seeds never had a chance to grow. And the sower couldn't tell "good ground" from bad. But unlike me, he kept right on sowing. Some seeds — we know not how or when — take root in their own time.

Keep sowing — that is Jesus' message to us.

Let me be the sower, Lord, and leave the growing to You.

—DORIS HAASE

---

12   *...When thou doest thine alms, do not sound a trumpet before thee...*   —MATTHEW 6:2

My grandmother used to say that one of the greatest satisfactions in life is doing good on the sly.

Years ago in England there was a young boy who worked twelve hours a day in a factory at a job that paid next to nothing. The boy loved to read, but he owned no books and was too poor to buy any. Every day on his way to work he passed a shabby, secondhand bookstore and if a book lay open in the window, he would stop and read the two pages that were visible.

One day he noticed that such a book was open to the *next* two pages. The day after that, the following pages. The boy read on, day after day, until he came to the last page. At that point the man who owned the bookstore appeared and told him that he could come in, browse around and read anything he wanted to at any time. Thus Benjamin Faregon was helped on the way to becoming a successful writer.

He had been given a passport to the world of books by a man who knew the joy of doing good on the sly.

Why don't we all reach out more often to others in secret ways? It may take imagination, a little effort, a little time. But the dividends are enormous.

Father, give me the vision to see the needs of others, and the imagination to act selflessly.   —ARTHUR GORDON

---

13 *Let us therefore come boldly unto the throne of grace...*
                                                    —HEBREWS 4:16

When I first started scheduling time for my daily prayer, I was a little self-conscious about it. I wondered what my family would think about my going off into the bedroom and closing the door for a half-hour twice a day. But then I read about the mother of John Wesley, the founder of Methodism. She had a large family and couldn't find a private corner in the house, so she would sit on a kitchen chair and cover her head with her wide apron. There, in her makeshift "prayer room," she would meet her God. What an eloquent statement that must have made to her family about the importance of the Lord in her daily life!

That story about Mrs. Wesley erased my hesitation. Now my prayer time is very precious to me and my family recognizes it.

Do you spend time alone with the Lord each day? Do those you live with know it? It could be the most powerful example you could give them.

Today, Lord, let my actions speak of You.
—MARILYN MORGAN HELLEBERG

---

14 *Every good gift and every perfect gift is from above...*
—JAMES 1:17

I have always lamented my rather dim eyesight and I became convinced that it held me back. In high school I lost a government surveying job in Idaho because of it and later I was turned down by the Navy for having faulty vision. When I finally joined the Army, I was relegated to the job of clerk-typist because, as a sergeant said, "You'd be more dangerous in the field than the enemy." But the other day I saw a newspaper headline — "Inventor Lost Sight as Youth" — that changed my attitude.

It seems that a man named Ralph R. Teetor lost his eyesight in a boyhood accident. Nonetheless he became president of the Perfect Circle Company, a leading manufacturer of automotive piston rings, and invented numerous automobile gadgets as well as a fishing-rod holder, a locking device and a power lawn mower. He was a trustee of Earlham College in Indiana and at one time he served as president of the Society of Automobile Engineers. He died in February, 1981 at the age of ninety-one.

Obviously Mr. Teetor was not a man who spent much time in lamenting his lack of sight. He learned early that circumstances don't deny achievement — *people* do. What he did was to make the best of those gifts that God *had* given him. And that's what I need to do too.

Lord, let me live up to the special qualities the You have given me.
—JAMES McDERMOTT

JOURNEY OF FAITH

15 Your traveling companion is *NOAH*
...who walked with God. —GENESIS 6 - 9

If your efforts this month to know more of God seem at odds with the values around you, Noah knew the feeling. He too stood alone in the world.

What was his secret? How does one go against the crowd? The answer rests in four words: *Noah walked with God.*

He didn't run to Him only when rain clouds darkened the sky. Nor look for Him in some earlier, more godly age...or ahead to a promised millennium. Daily, hourly, Noah kept step with God, so that when the floods came, he was prepared.

Would God warn only *one* man of the impending catastrophe? Would he save only *one* family when there was wood enough for a whole flotilla of arks? From what the Bible teaches us about God, we can be quite sure that He told not only *some* others, but *all* others. What Genesis records is that *only one man heard.*

Noah heard because of that faithful daily walk. When the sun was shining and the birds were singing Noah kept close to God. And when the saving Word was spoken, Noah heard.

Noah not only heard God's instructions, he acted on them. Because of his long patience in obedience, he understood the guidance he received: what, when, how to build — in exact dimensions and specific figures. So he built the ark and waited.

Now the waters increased, and bore up the ark. And the same flood waters that swept away everything and everyone else only served to float the ark higher. The torrents which destroyed others lifted Noah closer to God.

There must have been times in his unlit and confining quarters when Noah was sure that God had forgotten him. The days when they had walked together on solid earth, belonged to another world from this endless dripping on the roof, the ceaseless rocking on the floods of change.

Change cuts us loose from our moorings, sets us adrift in a world from which every familiar landmark has vanished, where we question not only God's goodness but His very existence. Noah learned that God does not forget. A dove arrives with a wisp of greenery in her beak — one tiny leaf that proclaimed life was emerging when all appeared to be dying.

The covenant God makes with Noah as the flood subsides is unconditional. God *will* perform it. What security this gives us! For hope that depends only on ourselves is not hope at all.

> *Lord, I will welcome the rain as well as the sunshine this month. And as my boat crosses the waters, I will watch for Your signs of hope.*

— ELIZABETH SHERRILL

---

16 *And the peace of God, which passeth all understanding, shall keep your hearts and minds through Christ Jesus.*
—PHILIPPIANS 4:7

Late again. I was on the Hollywood Freeway headed for my office in downtown Los Angeles. Red brake lights flashed in front of me and traffic came to a complete stop. I groaned in exasperation. As the minutes passed, I became increasingly agitated and soon I was a tense bundle of anger and frustration.

The apostle Paul had a different approach to roadblocks. When his plans were thwarted and he was immobilized in prison, he wrote of peace: "Rejoice in the Lord alway...."

Caught in that traffic tie-up, could I have experienced God's peace with Paul's serenity? In the future I will try. I will: Rejoice...relax...pray...give thanks...enjoy God's Presence.

God, help me to use roadblock experiences for discovering unexpected moments of peace with You. —DORIS HAASE

17

Be of good courage, and let us behave ourselves valiantly for our people, and for the cities of our God...

—I CHRONICLES 19:13

It's the bottom of the third inning in one of our team's most important softball games of the season. Bases loaded...two outs...our opponent's leading hitter at bat. I'm shortstop.

Here's the first pitch. The batter hits a hot smash to my right. I field the ball cleanly and throw it to first. The ball sails high over the head of the first baseman, into the bleachers — two runs score.

I fling my glove to the ground, then kick it. In the next play, still steaming mad, I boot another ground ball. Finally out of the inning, I head for the farthest corner of the bench. Not far enough from my coach though — I see him coming.

"Japinga!" He sits down next to me, puts his arm around my shoulders. "Success is never final. Failure is never fatal. It's courage that counts. You're going to go out there next inning and hold your head high? I hope so."

I have never forgotten that moment although it took place quite a few years ago. I repeat those words whenever I make an error or face failure — and not just on the softball field. It's my prayer for strength and courage to go on my way again, head held high, confident in God's forgiveness and support.

How do you react to adversity *or* success? It's courage that counts.

Whatever the obstacles today, Father, give me the courage to walk tall.

—JEFF JAPINGA

18

By this shall all men know that ye are my disciples...
—JOHN 13:35

One day recently my former grade school held an open house and I went back for a visit. Warm memories flooded over me...the smell of chalk dust, recess bells, Mrs. Anderson, my fourth-grade teacher. *Whatever happened to her?* I wondered.

I found her in one of the classrooms. She hadn't changed very much — her hair a little grayer perhaps. She was sitting at her desk, an open book before her, a circle of children around her. Each child read from the book in turn. They were slow and read haltingly, but when they finished, Mrs. Anderson clapped her hands and gave each one of them a hug.

The school principal, standing behind me in the doorway, said "None of those children could read when she began to work with them. Everyone else had given up on them — but not Mrs. Anderson. She won't stop now until they can read as well as she can."

I noticed that her classroom wasn't as well equipped as some of the others. "How does she do it?" I asked. "She doesn't have very up-to-date materials."

"Oh, she has tools that never go out of style — love and patience," the principal smiled.

I realized then that Mrs. Anderson hadn't given us just the ability to read and write...she had given us lessons in love as well.

Today, Lord, may I do my work with tools that are never out of date: the tools of my heart. —PHYLLIS HOBE

19 *Where no counsel is, the people fall...* —PROVERBS 11:14

A group of children at our church was practicing for an Easter special. When the youngsters first came out on the platform, they maintained a semblance of order but soon this was lost and all became mass confusion. No one knew where to go or what to do. They were milling around and tripping over one another.

"Stop!" called the director. "Let's begin all over. And this time be sure that you're following the right *leader*."

And I thought to myself: With so many leaders in the world today, I too need to be sure that I am following the right One.

Jesus, You are the Leader who shows me The Way.
—ZONA B. DAVIS

20 *...God is love. We love him, because He first loved us.* —I JOHN 4:8, 19

Easter will be here two weeks from tomorrow. That gives you just enough time to "grow" some Easter baskets for those special people in your life. Here's how.

First line a basket with heavy plastic, trimming the top to fit around the edge (use pinking shears if you have them). Then fill the basket with vermiculite or planting soil. Gently pour in just enough water to cover the soil. On top of this generously sprinkle wheat seed, found in feed or health-food stores. Cover the basket with light-weight plastic (ordinary food wrap) to help the wheat sprout and prevent mold.

Set the planted basket near a sunny window — but not in direct sunlight — and in several days the tiny green wheat spears will poke thorough the soil, making a nice grassy nest.

For the pièce de résistance add colored Easter eggs or fresh-cut flowers. Or a chocolate bunny. Or jelly beans. Tie calico or silk ribbons to the handle of the basket or plait them around the sides.

Between now and Easter you can hand-make gift cards by lightly sketching spring flowers on folded rectangles of parchment. Then letter in God's love message — or one of your own choosing. You could even use the Scripture verse at the top of today's devotion.

And then — the most important part of all — add an "I love you!" of your own.

Father, I just want to tell You that I'm thinking of You today and that I love You.   —ISABEL CHAMP

---

21   *Let us offer the sacrifice of praise to God continually, that is, the fruit of our lips giving thanks to his name.*
                    —HEBREWS 13:15

Spring at last! I could hardly wait to get the new fruit trees in. Their roots wrapped in brown burlap, their branches bare, they looked as though they might be dead. But a red tag wired to the top of the first potential tree assured me that it was a "Gravenstein Apple."

The second tree's tag identified it as a "Petite Plum" and the third tree was called a "Hale Peach." There was even a small picture of the mature tree in full flower on the reverse side of the tag.

I tucked each tree into its respective hole, spreading its cramped toes, watering and then covering all with lush, loamy soil. And, of course, all the while I was envisioning myself picking fruit from them each autumn in the years ahead.

The trees reminded me of the fruit spoken of in Scripture and I thought, *Our minds are much like an orchard. We can deliberately choose the fruit we want to plant in them.*

Paul tells us that "the fruit of the Spirit is love, joy, peace, longsuffering, gentleness, faith, meekness and temperance."

Not only in the lovely springtime, but in all seasons, I would like to cultivate only the choicest of fruits.

Lord, help me to enrich the garden of my soul with the fruits of Your blessings. —ISABEL CHAMP

---

22 *And God said... Be fruitful, and multiply, and replenish the earth, and subdue it: and have dominion over the fish of the sea, and over the fowl of the air, and over every living thing that moveth upon the earth.* — GENESIS 1:28

The other morning while I was writing at the dining-room table, I heard a loud thud against the picture window. A bird-feeder hangs just outside the window and occasionally a confused chickadee or titmouse crashes into the glass.

Sensing that a bird had just met such a fate, I jumped to my feet and raced outside. The little creature lay there on the ground. Cupping the bird in my hands, I identified it as a young Carolina wren. No doubt it was from a nest in the porch rafters.

After waiting for a couple of minutes without seeing any signs of life in the tiny body, I unbuttoned my shirt and held the wren against my chest, hoping that the extra warmth might revive it. Time passed while I stood there, feeling at first helpless and then slightly ridiculous. Here I was, all emotionally involved with a dead bird when I should be inside, hard at work.

Just as I was about to give up my resuscitation efforts, the tawny-feathered creature, all of three inches in length, moved. Withdrawing her from my shirt (by now I was inexplicably calling her Jenny), I opened my hands and peeked inside. Sleepily she opened one eye and then closed it, as though winking at me. Then she winked the other eye before closing both eyes and listing to portside. This routine went on for another five minutes before I coaxed Jenny into standing on one of my fingers without falling over. At last she extended her wings — but nothing happened. Even when I waved my hand in an upward motion, trying to supply some momentum, she held on.

To make a long story short, however, Jenny finally lifted off, making an abbreviated Orville Wright-type of swoop to the nearest branch, where she perched, tottering, for several more minutes until she was fully recovered.

When I returned to my work a full thirty minutes after the beginning of my mission of mercy, I scolded myself for having wasted so much time. But later that night, when I related the little tale to my wife, Shirley reminded me that my Good Samaritan deed was probably the most important thing I had done all day. And she was right.

Whatever it was that I had been writing at the time has long been forgotten by me, but I still remember Jenny. As a matter of fact, I think she visited the bird-feeder today. No other bird winks like Jenny.

Father, lest I forget, You have assigned to me a most important task — that of caretaker over all Your Creation. —FRED BAUER

---

23 *. . . And when we cried unto the Lord, he heard our voice, and sent an angel. . .* —NUMBERS 20:16

When I was very young, I was enchanted by angels: Michael with his great wings and flaming sword. . . pastel-winged Gabriel standing in the presence of the Lord. . . my guardian angel . . . heavenly hosts. Everywhere I went I listened expectantly, and sometimes I even heard the rustle of wings.

Then I grew up. I forgot all about angels — until one day recently. I was expecting a beloved friend to visit. My yard was not fit to receive anyone. Somehow, in the press of other work, I hadn't noticed that the hedge had become a forest, the weeds were in full bloom, the lawn was a full-fledged meadow. Ruefully I sighed, "Well, I can cook, Lord, but I'll have to leave the gardening to you."

That afternoon a courteous youth and his father appeared at my door. They were looking for a yard to "do." And they "did" mine — to perfection. I took their phone number and later called it, hoping to thank them. There was no answer.

"Well," I surprised myself by thinking, "maybe angels don't answer phones!" And I never saw nor heard from the pair again.

Now I try to be more expectant, watching for the "angels" who pass through my daily life. And I'm content to accept them as such — without wings, without questions, but with a heart full of thanksgiving.

Lord, let me recognize Your messengers as I meet them here, there, everywhere. —ELAINE ST. JOHNS

---

24 *One man esteemeth one day above another: another esteemeth every day alike. Let every man be fully persuaded in his own mind.* —ROMANS 14:5

When I exhibited my abstract painting at an art fair recently, I was surprised that about half the viewers saw what I had intended to be a sphere as a hole. Why, I wondered, did the sphere, a positive shape, register as a negative image with some of the viewers? Later I discovered that, depending upon where I was standing when I viewed the picture, the picture did seem to shift from a sphere to a hole for my eyes, too.

The following Sunday I found myself in disagreement with a

fellow church member over the meaning of a Bible verse. We seemed to see that verse in completely different ways.

I wanted to say, "You're wrong!" but suddenly I thought of my painting. Mentally, I shifted places with him and looked at that verse through his eyes. Ah ha! At once I saw what he was talking about.

Lord, when I insist on being right, help me "shift" to see the light.
—MADGE HARRAH

---

25 *Now unto him that is able to keep you from falling, and to present you faultless before the presence of his glory with exceeding joy...* —JUDE 1:24

Even after all these years I still remember the day in the third grade when I got back that terrible arithmetic paper. I had missed every single problem. Every one. I was so ashamed and angry with myself that I wadded up my paper and slumped down in my seat.

The teacher must have noticed my discouragement because she came over and put her arm around me and whispered, "It's not the mistakes you make that are most important, but how much you learn because of them." Then she smoothed out my crumpled paper. "Now try again."

I did. And that time my teacher wrote across the bottom of my paper, "IMPROVED."

That experience of my childhood is one that I hope I shall never forget. For I still make mistakes. Some of them cause me to feel ashamed and angry with myself. And sometimes when I am slumped down in guilt — berating myself — I can hear God whisper the same words in my ear: "It's not the mistakes that are most important, but how much you grow because of them."

I will never be perfect. But surely the next best thing is to be "IMPROVED."

Lord, may my failures and mistakes be ground from which I grow.   —SUE MONK KIDD

HOLY WEEK
with Norman Vincent Peale

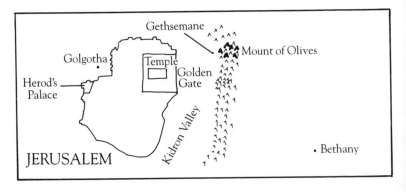

26 THE SATURDAY BEFORE PALM SUNDAY

✝ One never-to-be-forgotten day many years ago, my wife Ruth, our three children and I took a car from the American Colony Hotel in Jerusalem to the little village of Bethany. There we got out of the car and set forth to make the return journey on foot. It is not a long way back to Jerusalem, perhaps only three miles; it is, however, a long way back to the Jerusalem of Christ's day, more than two thousand years. But as you walk that steep and stony and winding path, the years between seem to close like the folds of an accordion.

As you leave Bethany, you pass the tomb of Lazarus, the house of Simon the Leper, the site of the house of Mary and Martha. Moving up over the steep shoulder of the Mount of Olives, you approach the place were Jesus is said to have taught the disciples the Lord's Prayer. You linger for a while at the overhanging height from which Jesus gazed down at the city and wept for it, prophesying its destruction, a prophecy fulfilled seventy years later. Eventually you wind your way down through the Garden of Gethsemane, cross over the Brook Kidron and pick your way through the rugged ravine known as the Kidron Valley until at last you come to Jerusalem's ancient walls.

Today on the eve of Palm Sunday, 1983, I would like to extend an invitation. I would like you to join me on another walk to Jerusalem. In fact, I would like you to come along on an eight-day journey through Holy Week. You will find a map above that I hope you will refer to from time to time.

But for now, look for the village of Bethany. Jesus is having supper there tonight with a number of his closest friends and followers. The mood is restrained. There is a sense of hushed expectancy for in the morning Jesus plans to go to Jerusalem.

---

27 PALM SUNDAY

✝ On that first Palm Sunday, Jesus entered the Holy City of Jerusalem through the Golden Gate. Today that entrance, whose outline I myself have discerned in the stonework, is walled up, not to be reopened until He comes again. But on that Sunday morning He rode a little donkey through that gate, and the city, already packed with visitors preparing for Passover, went wild.

Word had spread of His approach. This was the Man Who, for three years up and down and across the land, had been proclaimed as the long-awaited Messiah. Crowds swarmed to welcome Him. Thrilled, electrified, heady with the thought that they were about to see the King Who would bring them deliverance at last, the throngs rushed to strip the branches of palm trees, to wave the fronds — the symbol of victory — and strew them in His path.

It was a day of victory. And yet few men and women, shouting hosannas as He passed by, really understood that what Jesus was bringing them was personal deliverance, not political. Jesus had a way of confounding people, including His own disciples, because the things He talked about were new to man's thinking, and different. Even so, I like to think that there were people in the crowd that morning who *did* comprehend His true meaning, and I picture them in my mind as waving palm branches in the air and crying our their gratitude. You know them too.

There was the woman taken in adultery. Through Him she had found victory over sin.

There was Simon the Leper. Through Him he had triumphed over disease.

There was Lazarus. Through Him he had gained victory over death.

And there were numerous others, now infecting those in the crowd around them with their enthusiasm and love, passing along their own stories of His healings and other miracles.

Yes, it was a day of victory, for as He rode through the Golden Gate, Jesus Christ was bringing God's children, all of us, then and now, the power to turn defeated lives into lives of triumph.

But it would be a long, full, drama-packed week before the greatest victory in the history of the world would be achieved.

---

28 MONDAY

✝ On Monday Jesus returned to Jerusalem from Bethany and went immediately to the Temple. On the previous day He had observed the merchants and money-changers doing business there, and He had seethed with indignation at the blatant corruption of God's house. On this morning Jesus was a determined and righteously moved Man as He strode into the middle of the busy bazaar and quickly turned it into bedlam. In a flurry of flying coins and fluttering pigeons He drove the money-changers and their customers out of the Temple area. It was the most violent act of His ministry.

On this day, I ask you to keep the picture of the active, angry Jesus in your mind. It is not our customary view of Him, is it? We are all inclined to think of Him as a passive Man, but of course He was not passive. I recall the time that one of the members of my church pointed out this fact to me by asking: "Did you ever notice that nearly everything Jesus said has a verb of action in it: *Come* unto me...*Go* thou and *do* likewise...*Follow* me and I'll *make* you.... "

Jesus expects us to be active too. He expects us to deplore religious pretense as much as He did. He expects us to burn with indignation when we see wrong and injustice. He expects us to be gentle in heart, tough in will, but always ready to do battle for the right. Perhaps is was not easy for Him to be Christ, as it is not easy for us to be Christians.

---

29 TUESDAY

✝ What an exhausting day this must have been for Jesus! Once again He returned to the Temple and sat in its precincts while, over and over, His enemies tried to snare Him into making a misstatement that could be used against Him. Jesus, however, was totally versed in Scripture and His intellect was deeper, His mind more agile, than any of His attackers. He avoided one trap after another and in a rush of illuminating parables and answers, He explained, He prophesied, He denounced His hypocritical opponents. Hours later He took His leave of the Temple for the last time. His public ministry was at an end.

But His private teaching was far from over. On the way back to Bethany, Jesus and His disciples sat for a while on a slope of the Mount of Olives and, tired as He was, He went on expounding great truths. He talked about the destruction of the Temple and about the end of the world, and He tried once more to prepare the perplexed men, who loved Him deeply, for His death and resurrection.

On this particular day each year I like to reread this Great Discourse in the Gospels, especially the 24th and 25th chapters of Matthew. I place myself there in the little group on the rocky hillside. I hear Jesus softly telling me about how He will "come in His glory, and all the lowly angels with Him." I picture in my mind the Last Judgment as the sheep are separated from the goats. And when dusk falls on each Tuesday of Holy Week, I see a weary Jesus wending His way back to His friends' houses for supper, and as I put down my Bible and prepare for the evening ahead, I seem to hear His voice trailing in the distance. I hear Him saying the very words that I try so hard to live by: "Verily I say unto you, inasmuch as ye have done it unto one of the least of these my brethren, ye have done it unto me."

30 WEDNESDAY

In the middle of a frenzied week, this day, Wednesday, was as calm and as soothing as a lullaby. For Jesus this was a time for resting, for gaining strength for the ordeal ahead.

I have the feeling Jesus spent most of the day alone, that somehow His disciples sensed that they should not disturb Him. And yet, as they poked around the little village, how they must have mused and questioned among themselves. They were not brilliant or sophisticated men, and the things Jesus had been telling them were much too momentous for easy weighing or sorting. In spite of His predictions, they did not expect Him to die. After all, He was the Son of God. And what was this all about, this resurrection?

With the gift of hindsight, we today of course know what Jesus meant. On the day that my family and I were there in Bethany, I recall that as a hot sun burned down upon us, we stood by the tomb where Lazarus is said to have lain dead. I would have liked to stand, if possible, on the very spot where Jesus stood when He summoned Lazarus back to life. I walked all around, figuring that at some point my feet must touch the exact spot where He stood.

Then I took out my Bible and asked Ruth to read to us in her lovely voice the words that Jesus spoke on that day: "I am the resurrection, and the life: he that believeth in me, though he were dead, yet shall he live: and whosoever liveth and believeth in me shall never die."

All of a sudden I felt my eyes blinded by tears. I felt a warmth in my heart and I knew for a certainty that what Jesus said was true. "This is the greatest statement ever uttered in the history of time," I told my family. And they too knew that this was true.

But the men around Jesus — the very men who first heard those words — they had to wait, to suffer, before they fully understood their meaning.

You and I do not have to wait. We do not have to suffer. The meaning of His resurrection is a gift freely bestowed on us and as with the life of Jesus Christ, we can freely rejoice in it.

31 THURSDAY

✝ Peter. Poor Peter.

Why is it that on the turbulent night of the Last Supper, on the night that Judas betrayed our Lord, on the night that blood poured from His brow like sweat as He prayed in Gethsemane, on the night He was arrested and confined in the High Priest's house until daylight — why is it that whenever I review the drama of that long night, I always seem to see Jesus through Peter's eyes.

Why? Because Peter is so human, so like many of us, and when dealing with this very human fisherman, Jesus shows both His great humanity and His divinity. When Jesus said at the Last Supper that He was going away, I am sure Peter thought that Jesus was referring to a risky mission, not death, and he offered to go with Him. He even offered boastfully but with all his devotion to lay down his life for Him. And when Jesus said that Peter would that night deny Him three times, this big, strapping fellow was utterly bewildered. He had meant what he had said to our Lord.

Later, after they had taken Jesus from the Garden and most of the disciples had fled in fear, Peter skulked behind, trying to keep Jesus in view but lacking the courage to walk alongside. After Jesus had been taken upstairs in the house of the High Priest Caiaphas, Peter hung around outside the gate until he could gain admittance into the courtyard. Once there, as he warmed his hands by a fire, three women, on three separate occasions, accused him of being one of Jesus' followers, and each time he denied it. The third time, when the cock crowed, Peter remembered, and he went away weeping bitterly.

Poor Peter. No wonder I so closely identify myself with him. He wanted to do good, but he did bad. I try to do good too, and I am sure you do, but we are as human as Peter; we will always fail somewhere, somehow. In time, however, Peter knew that Jesus had forgiven him, and that, for me, is the great message shining out of the black night: For those of us who try, but err, there is always forgiveness.

Praise Diary for March

1

2

3

4

5

6

7

8

9

10

11

12

13

14

15

16

17

18

19

20

21

22

23

24

25

26

27

28

29

30

31

April

Thou wilt shew me the path of life: in thy presence is fulness of joy; at thy right hand there are pleasures for evermore. —PSALM 16:11

I'm singing, Lord, I'm singing
A soul song filled with praise
As with a soft and gentle touch,
You bring on springtime days!

I'm singing, Lord, I'm singing
A song of thanks to You
Renewing life around me,
The spirit in me too!

Glory hallelujah
To He Who dwells on high
Who made the changing seasons,
The sea, the sod, the sky!

Thank You for the miracles
That springtime brings to earth,
For life that's everlasting,
And for my soul's rebirth!

—ALICE JOYCE DAVIDSON

1 ✝ FRIDAY

At midnight, when this terrible day began, most of Jerusalem lay asleep. But Jesus and His captors were awake. His first trial, in the house of the High Priest, was held in the secrecy of darkness, and at daybreak His enemies moved Him as swiftly as they could, first to Pilate, who sent Him to Herod, who sent Him back to Pilate, who sent Him to be scourged, and then on to Golgotha. By noon He had been crucified, and three hours later He was dead.

Dead?

On Good Friday, the most somber of all days on the Christian calendar, I focus my thoughts on Jesus and on His suffering, but I do not linger on the thought of His death. Jesus Christ means LIFE; that thought never leaves my mind; and I spend a part of every Good Friday in prayer for those who are alive today — and especially for those who are living, but dying.

In my ministry I have good reason to see people everywhere who are moving about in the darkness of their own Good Fridays; they are dying spiritually. The Bible says that "there is only one death, the soul that sinneth." I pray for these troubled people. I pray that they will find new strength to fight, that they will come alive again under the mystic touch of Jesus Christ, that they will know that "if any man be in Christ, he is a new creature."

I hope you will pray for these suffering people too, keeping in mind the fact that the meaning of Good Friday, the meaning of Christ's death, is life for all of us — full, rich, wonderful LIFE!

2 ✝ THE SATURDAY BEFORE EASTER

The celebration of the Passover had begun, but for those who loved and believed in Jesus, this was a hollow day of numbness.

The disciples were scattered and in hiding, their emotions a confusing mixture of shock and mourning and fear. And surely, I think, more than one of the men who followed Jesus must have suffered the first painful shudder of doubt. Perhaps Jesus was not the Son of God after all. Could it be that they had been duped?

Doubt. Feeding on hesitation, suspicion and distrust, doubt can destroy.

But doubt can be a healthy thing too. The Spanish novelist Unamuno once wrote that "faith which does not doubt is dead faith." I believe that for I know that open and honest questioning is necessary for anyone who takes his faith seriously. Show me someone who never had a doubt about anything and I will show you someone who is not using the mind that God gave him.

I remember that when I was a theological student I had a professor who said, "I'm going to knock your faith to pieces, boys, and then put it together for you again. If I don't, when you get out into the world, the *world* will knock it to pieces."

That professor helped me to learn that when you struggle through doubt, you toughen your faith.

The day after Christ's crucifixion was a time for doubting. All of us have empty, gnawing days like that. But the next day — ah, that was a day for believing, and believing strongly!

---

3 EASTER SUNDAY

One dew-drenched Sabbath morning I sat in a peaceful Jerusalem garden and listened to a preacher give a sermon. Rising directly above us was the solemn hill of Calvary — so called from before the time of Christ because of the two caves in the side of it that resembled deep-set eyes; they gave the hill the look of a skull. Before us there was an open tomb, and a great round stone, like a millstone or grinding stone, lay in a roughhewn stone trough. It had been laboriously rolled away from the tomb's entrance.

The preacher, a hard-bitten, vigorous man, an Army chaplain, was preaching a sermon much like those I used to hear when I was a boy: It was unequivocating, unrestrained, powerful Christianity, drawn straight from the Bible. "Look," he said, pointing to the tomb, "not even death could hold Him!"

Suddenly I felt a tingling within myself and a flash of insight, a renewed feeling of absolute conviction, as I remembered Jesus saying: "Because I live, ye shall live also." (John 14:19)

If the idea of Jesus Christ's resurrection is astonishing to us today, what must it have been to the people of His time — to those who had seen Him walking and talking and moving in their midst? Sometimes when I try to picture the effect His resurrection had on the populace living then, I see in my mind a very rare and very old Spanish coin. The coin, minted in the fifteenth century, was imprinted with a drawing of the narrow strait between Europe and Africa near Gibraltar, called the Pillars of Hercules. Inscribed at the bottom were the Latin words, *Ne Plus Ultra*, meaning "No More Beyond." To the Spanish of that time, that was it, there was not anything else out there. Then along came Columbus, and when he proved that a new world lay beyond, they had to remove the *Ne* from all the coins. From that time forward they read *Plus Ultra* — "More Beyond."

It is no wonder that you and I are thrilled to celebrate this Easter Sunday, to praise and thank God for the marvelous privilege of saying, "Why, this mortal life is only the beginning. This is only a little bit of the whole; there is More Beyond!"

PATTERN FOR A BLESSED LIFE
Blessed are the meek: for they shall inherit the earth.
—MATTHEW 5:5

4

I visited a small mission church recently, pastored by a former English teacher who had obeyed God's call to the ministry. The lovely little chapel in the basement of the pastor's home is a holy place. The congregation consists of his wife, his two daughters and two gentlemen from the mental retardation center.

The sermon had been carefully prepared and was delivered as though to a congregation of thousands. There was something quietly heroic in the devotion with which Reverend Vreeland conducted the worship and I was moved to tears.

I'm sure that our Lord is pleased with those who win many souls for Him. But I believe He delights just as much in those who, like Reverend Vreeland, quietly and lovingly perform whatever mission He has appointed for them. For those who practice meekness, all the earth becomes a Holy place. What a blessed inheritance!

During April, Lord, help me to do my work quietly and humbly, without concern for personal gain or public recognition.
—MARILYN MORGAN HELLEBERG

5

To every thing there is a season, and a time to every purpose under the heaven...   —ECCLESIASTES 3:1

In my usual morning dash to the office, I drive past a young woman feeding the pigeons on the sidewalk in front of her house.

"How do you find time for that when you have to get to work?" I called to her one day.

"I *make* the time," she answered with a smile. "It always gets my day off to a good start."

And I'll bet she's never late to work. Unlike me. I race time all day long, scarcely stopping to even look at God's world, much less to feed his creatures. Why, I can hardly find time for my morning Bible-reading. While I was brooding about it one day recently, the above words from Ecclesiastes suddenly appeared in my mind.

No time? Oh, yes, there *is*! And it's up to me to define my purposes...to set my priorities...to manage and enjoy the hours that God has so graciously given me.

Today, Lord, I'll make time for....   —DORIS HAASE

---

6 *Even so faith, if it hath not works, is dead, being alone.*
                                                —JAMES 2:17

Last spring two helpless, bawling, orphaned raccoons — a brother and a sister — wandered into our lives and for nearly four months my wife Shirley, the kids and I nurtured them with one goal in mind: to make them self-sufficient, able to fend for themselves when we returned them to the wild.

After several weeks of bottle-feeding, we introduced them (by now our masked bandits bore the names of Bonnie and Clyde) to cereal and fruit. Later we led them to wild blackberries, mulberries, and crayfish at a stream. When they climbed their first trees, we stood underneath the dancing boughs holding our breath for fear they would fall. But their marvelous, handlike paws enabled them to recover from every slip and our worries were for naught.

By early August they were making forays into our woods. Soon their stays lasted overnight, but they returned each morning for breakfast. Then their visits stretched out to every other day; every

106

third day, fourth day. Finally they were gone. Bittersweetly we knew we had completed our job.

The experience reminds me that I have a similar role as a parent — to help my children become self-sufficient. And if that is true, then God must do the same for His creation, all His children. When I pray for His intervention in the work He sets before me, shouldn't I take care that I don't over-petition and under-perform?

Teach me to pray knowing all depends on You, Lord, and to work as though all depended on me. —FRED BAUER

7

And unto one he gave five talents, to another two, and to another one; to every man according to his several ability. —MATTHEW 25:15

Years ago when Martha Berry was struggling to get the Berry School started in Rome, Georgia, she appealed to Henry Ford for a contribution. He reached into his pocket and gave her a dime.

Instead of being discouraged at the size of the gift, Miss Berry determined to use it for the school's good. She bought a package of seed peanuts with it. The seeds were planted and tended, and they yielded a large crop of peanuts which Miss Berry sold.

She again called on Mr. Ford.

"Here's the dime you gave me last year," she said, handing him a coin. Then she told him of the return she had realized from his meager investment.

Mr. Ford was so impressed with her perseverance that, in the years that followed, he gave millions of dollars to the school.

I have wasted many hours fretting over things I don't possess — talents, money, material goods. And then I hear about someone like Miss Berry, and I realize that it is not important what or how much I have. What really counts is how I use that which I *do* have.

Jesus, I'll stop complaining about what I don't have. Today I will find ways to multiply the talents I do have. —DRUE DUKE

---

8 *But a certain Samaritan, as he journeyed, came where he was: and when he saw him, he had compassion on him, And went to him...* —LUKE 10:33,34

When I was in college, some students in the Psychology Department made a week-long experiment that they called the "Good Samaritan Test." They placed various people in strategic spots around the campus, people who were in need of help in one way or another. By week's end they found that if the bell was ringing and students were hurrying to get to class on time, the students were not inclined to stop to render assistance; if they had the time, however, they would go out of their way to be helpful. It didn't matter if the people in need were white or black or yellow, young or old or infirm, or in whatever condition passed then as the current version of the despised Samaritan.

The modern key to being a Good Samaritan, the experiment revealed, was *time*.

I wonder what would have happened to that poor fellow who fell among thieves if the traveling man from Samaria was running late for a business appointment in Jericho. Nowadays, he might still be lying beside the road, for time in the twentieth century is a valuable commodity that we don't seem to give away lightly. Maybe it's easier to give away food, or money, or sympathy.

Anyway, it's something to think about.

Will I be tested today, Lord? —VAN VARNER

9   *But if ye forgive not men their trespasses, neither will*
    your Father forgive your trespasses.   —MATTHEW 6:15

My teenage daughter Julie and I were going through a period when we just couldn't seem to communicate with each other. Over and over again I felt she misinterpreted what I said; then she would resent me and I in turn would feel hurt by her rejection. None of my prayers for Julie seemed to help.

One day a friend said: "You can spend the rest of your life praying for someone to change, Marion, but if unforgiveness is in your heart, no matter how well hidden, God cannot answer your prayers."

Hot tears rolled down my face. Our problem was me! In desperation I confessed my unforgiveness not only to God, but to Julie too.

An indefinable gloom that I hadn't been able to shake lifted like a feather. Most amazing was the immediate change in Julie. We laughed together, prayed together, even went shopping together. Sometimes we held hands for a few moments without speaking.

Soon I saw that she was making mature decisions on her own, without one word from me. Then she began to ask for my opinions instead of struggling against me. One memorable evening I heard her tell a friend on the phone, "My mother and I have a really good relationship." I smiled.

What a powerful gift — this thing called forgiveness.

Father, is there someone who needs my gift of forgiveness today?
                                              —MARION BOND WEST

10 *... Verily I say unto you, Inasmuch as ye have done it unto one of the least of these my brethren, ye have done it unto me.* —MATTHEW 25:40

"Are you hurrying?" Lynn called. "You know I want to be a few minutes early today."

"Be right there," I called back, still trying to calm the nervousness I felt. Ever since Lynn had asked me to accompany her to the Sunday worship service she conducts at the state psychiatric hospital, where she serves as an intern chaplain, I had been uneasy.

How would I handle myself? What if one of the patients began to talk to me? I wasn't trained in psychiatry. How would I respond? What would I say? What would I do?

When we arrived at the hospital, I stayed close to Lynn. Then, as she went to the front, I slipped unobtrusively into an empty pew.

Immediately a young man followed and slid over next to me. "Hi, I'm Joe," he said cheerfully, extending his hand. "And these are my friends, Keith and Jim and Bob. You must be Chaplain Lynn's husband."

I nodded my head, still unsure of myself. But as we sang hymns loudly and off key to a twangy piano, as we shared in prayer and listened to Lynn's sermon, I began to relax. Not because *I* had accepted them but because *they* had so lovingly embraced me.

The lesson I learned that day? God is everywhere — when you look for Him. He was in the hospital, in the hearts of the people there and — when I dared to look — in my heart too.

I'm glad, Father, that Your Presence is not limited to being only where I expect You to be. —JEFF JAPINGA

11 *And if I go and prepare a place for you, I will come again, and receive you unto myself...* —JOHN 14:3

When Virginia Griffin came on night duty at the small hospital near my home, there had been one new admission, a girl in her early twenties who was terminally ill. When Virginia checked on the girl after reading the night report and learning that she was already in a coma, she noticed the young soldier husband, sitting in despair at the bedside. He had made no response to the suggestion that the chaplain visit, and he seemed to be terribly quiet and alone.

When his wife died at two o'clock, Virginia was surprised to note that a red carnation had been carefully tucked in her hair. Otherwise the room was bare, without flowers or even toilet articles. She let the young husband out the front door and watched him walk into the fog. Then she alerted his commanding officer at the nearby Army post....

On her morning rounds Virginia noticed a bit of white paper protruding from a floral arrangement on a table near the room where the girl had died. On the slip of paper were the words: "Pardon my taking the flower, but my wife always wears a flower when she is going somewhere special!"

Father, we thank You for the special somewhere You have prepared for all who trust in You. —ELAINE ST. JOHNS

12 *They shall still bring forth fruit in old age; they shall be fat and flourishing...* —PSALM 92:14

Over the years I have known many elderly people who seemed to be just as busy at their work, their hobbies and their personal interests as they ever were. I have asked several of them how they managed it. Time and again I have been told, "There is so much that I can do for others now that I have the time for it. I may be old but I am not decrepit!"

Ralph Waldo Emerson once said, "We do not count a man's years until he has nothing else to count."

Now that I am approaching the homestretch of my threescore and ten, I find *myself* busier than ever. Not that I am afraid of running out of time, but I feel an urge to do as much as I can for others in the time I have left. I suspect that the decrepitude of old age is not a matter of years but a matter of simply quitting. When we give up as individuals, we also give up as children of God, dismissing the gifts He has given us.

Father, let me give all my years and live all my days — fully — for You.
                                                    —GLENN KITTLER

---

13   *He that is slow to anger is better than the mighty; and he that ruleth his spirit than he that taketh a city.*
                                                    —PROVERBS 16:32

My son is in the fourth grade. Sometimes he writes short themes and brings them home for me to read. I like his writing better than my own. For he tells simple stories that I usually need to hear. Last week he brought this one home to me.

WHAT TO DO WHEN A BOY
POPS YOUR BALLOON
by Bob Kidd

One day I was walking down the street holding a big red balloon in my hand. The pest of the school came up and popped it! It was gone and he ran away. I wanted to chase him and yell a lot and pop his balloon too. But instead I sat down on the curb and took a real deep breath and counted all the way to a hundred. And then I didn't feel like popping his balloon any more.

The End.

Of course he was sending me a message. When he did something "bad," I would sometimes explode in instant anger. Now he was teaching me that when he "pops my balloon," I should take a real deep breath and count all the way to a hundred. Not bad advice for anyone who needs help in being patient.

A truly good story always has some truth that can be distilled from it — a truth that can change a life, even in a small way. And Bob's balloon story made me a more patient mother. For that, I give his story an "A." For Amen.

Lord, when I feel wronged, help me to pause and think before I react too quickly—1...2...3.... —SUE MONK KIDD

---

14 *He that hath my commandments and keepeth them, he it is that loveth me...* —JOHN 14:21

You know how it is — you see a winsome little puppy and it's love at first sight, usually mutual. Then the puppy begins to grow up and get into trouble...and you don't kow what to do.

"Take him to Obedience School," a friend suggested. I really didn't want to do that. It sounded like a harsh solution and, after all, he *was* only a puppy. But eventually, when I was about to run out of shoes because Trooper had chewed them all to shreds, I gave in. I enrolled both of us in an obedience class.

The group met twice a week. All of us were beginners. And at first we thought we would never get through to our dogs. It took a lot of repetition, endless patience and heaps of praise. But eventually owners and pups began to understand what each expected of the other. We owners were learning to speak with loving authority and our dogs began to take pride in their accomplishments. The whole experience brought owners and pets closer together than ever before.

There is a word for this kind of process and I had never understood it until now. It's *discipline*. Discipline is truly an art. Actually, it's an act of love because it says to the other, "I care about you." Never harsh but always firm, it takes time, wisdom...and devotion.

Now I know why God is so patient with me.

Thank You, Lord, for Your love. I want to be obedient that I may be closer to You. —PHYLLIS HOBE

JOURNEY OF FAITH

15 Your traveling companion is *JOSEPH*
... *who traveled light.* —GENESIS 37:45

There is a journey each of us must take — sometimes over and over: The trip to the place we never wanted to go. Maybe it's an early and unexpected widowhood...a crushing financial reverse...the process of aging....

Joseph is good company for such a trek. What must his thoughts have been on that bitter march through the Negeb, the hottest part of the Syria-Egypt caravan route, hands bound behind him, throat thick with the dust raised by hundreds of camels and donkeys? Every step was taking him farther from the home where everything had been going his way.

It would be understandable in such circumstances if Joseph —

and if we — gave in to self-pity. Especially as it all came about while he was doing what his father told him to! When we're heedless and headstrong and disaster overtakes us, it's no more than we can expect. But when we're doing our Father's will and trouble comes ...why, we revolt at the injustice.

Nor is that the end of the unfairness for Joseph. Making the best of a negative situation, he manages, through hard work, to carve out a new life for himself. But a second undeserved blow falls. He is falsely accused of a shameful crime, and powerless to prove his innocence, thrown into prison — now not only a slave, but a slave in disgrace.

Repeated blows often lead to a sense of hopelessness. But they didn't for Joseph. He threw himself with immense energy into every situation in which (however unwillingly) he found himself.

What was his secret? The answer is stated twice: "The Lord was with Joseph."

Cut off from every friend, he was not cut off from God. Locked behind bars, he was not locked out of God's presence. Though no one else, perhaps, in this strange land, knew the God he worshiped, he persisted in solitary faithfulness. He kept his eyes on the Lord's goodness and omnipotence, not on his own disastrous circumstances.

> Lord, when things go wrong this month, I want to affirm along with Joseph: "The Lord is in this situation."

Joseph might easily have responded with resentment, self-pity or even despair, for his problems were the result of human ill will: envy, lies, ingratitude. He saw human nature at its worst.

But human nature was not where his attention was. His eyes were fixed on God. Not: "What have people done?" But: "What is God doing?"

Forgiveness is the name for what we do when we put down our suitcase full of wrongs and injustices.

But how can we forgive the monstrous and terrible? Joseph shows us. The way is not to deny the awfulness of what has happened. Glossing over the truth only separates us from Truth Himself. "You meant evil against me," Joseph tells his brothers. To call it anything but evil would be a lie. But that's not the whole story — or even the most important part. "You meant evil, but God meant good," Joseph says. God is Joseph's focus — first, last and always: "It was not you who sent me here, but God."

The secret of a happy life then is simply this: *God in everything.*

> *Lord, when my route leads into Egypt, I will remember with Joseph: You are my focus — first, last and always.*
> — ELIZABETH SHERRILL

---

16 *Behold, now is the accepted time; behold, now is the day of salvation.* —II CORINTHIANS 6:2

The other night at a dinner party our hostess gave each of us paper and pencil and asked us to write down our favorite word in the language. After dinner, she said, we'd compare our choices and give reasons for our selections.

I was pretty sure the most popular word would be "love," and it was. Rightly so, for it's a tremendous word. But my choice was the word "now." It's a great word, I think. The past behind; the future not happening yet. The moment we are really in touch with — NOW.

Besides, it's a cheerful, dynamic, optimistic word. "*Now* I see what you mean!" "*Now* let's get started." "*Now* thank we all our God...." "*Now* is the time for all good men...." And so on.

Today is going to be a whole string of unique, onrushing, never-returning *nows*. If you can make even a third of them really count, what a day you're going to have. Think about it! *Now!*

> *Thank You for this moment, Lord. Help me to realize its possibilities* — now! —ARTHUR GORDON

17

Wisdom is before him that hath understanding...
—PROVERBS 17:24

One Sunday I worshiped with a small congregation I did not know. In front of me a woman whispered continually to an older woman beside her and I became quite annoyed and distracted. *If she wants to talk,* I thought, *why doesn't she stay home?*

As I left church, I found myself directly behind the women. The preacher greeted the younger one with a big smile. "How nice to have your mother with us. When did she get in from Lebanon?"

The young woman beamed. "Yesterday." Turning, she said something in a foreign language and the older woman extended her hand to the pastor with a shy smile.

"I saw you translating for her during the service," the pastor continued. "Thank you for helping her share our worship."

They moved on and the pastor put out a hand to greet me. "Welcome," he said warmly. "I hope you found something in today's message and that you'll join us again."

As I reached my car, I remembered his text for the day: *I once was blind, but now I see.*

Dear Lord, help me wait until I have all *the facts before I make judgment.*
—PATRICIA HOUCK SPRINKLE

18

...A word spoken in due season, how good is it!
—PROVERBS 15:23

When I worked as a television-station secretary, a certain show was dropped from the programming schedule. Oh, how the mail and phone calls poured in! The viewers were irate. I was on phone duty one day when an angry listener called.

"Why did you cancel *that* program? It was the only good one you had!"

"Did you ever let us know you liked it?" I asked.

"No," he acknowledged with a sigh, "but I can see now that I should have."

The incident made me think. We should never wait until it's too late to show our appreciation. I am grateful to the man who faithfully sets up the folding chairs, adjusts the thermometer and locks and unlocks our church door every week. And to the woman who braves all kinds of inclement weather to guide the school children over the crosswalks. And to the delivery boy who *usually* gets my paper within reach instead of on the roof....

Can you think of a "good deed" any better than phoning or dropping a note to someone today to express gratitude for a job well done?

Father, first I'll thank You for....   —ISABEL CHAMP

---

19   *Behold, we count them happy which endure.* —JAMES 5:11

She was a young housewife, the mother of several small children, and she had spent days in fear and trembling as she underwent a series of tests in the medical clinic. But no examination had yet uncovered the cause of the pain she was experiencing. The last doctor to see her was the throat specialist, a no-nonsense man who examined her briefly, then sat back to review her case history and the test results. After that he studied her for a long moment and then, to her surprise, he opened his arms wide and indicated his shoulder. "Cry," he ordered. And to her utter amazement, she did just that.

"It all gets a little much for you mothers, doesn't it?" he asked when the sobs had subsided. "I admire every one of you. Now I'm going to show you my diagnosis and the prescription." On her chart he wrote: "Diagnosis: Acute motherhood. Prescription: Steadfast prayer."

It was the correct diagnosis. And the right prescription. I know, for I was that young woman. And through the years I have found that as a remedy for problems and disorders, it's the one prescription that always works, one that can help in curing the patient.

Lord, when I steadfastly turn to You in prayer before all else, my life unfolds in harmony. —ELAINE ST. JOHNS

---

20 *And thine ears shall hear a word behind thee, saying, This is the way, walk ye in it, when ye turn to the right hand, and when ye turn to the left.* —ISAIAH 30:21

Gert Pond was a middle-aged woman who loved life. So you can imagine her desolation when she was hit with a crippling form of arthritis that confined her to a wheel chair. A virtual shut-in now, her once-active life came to a standstill. But the spunk inside Gert wouldn't subside. Gert discovered "ham" radio. She got herself a set and soon was her lively, chatty old self again, staying in touch with the world via air waves.

Once Gert set up a rescue effort for two engineers stranded in the desert. And ever since, she has been a kind of unofficial emergency "command post" in Arizona. On many occasions she has gone for days and nights with little sleep, listening for distress calls, relaying messages and directing disaster volunteers. And last year she was named her state's "Amateur Ham Radio Operator of the Year."

Gert Pond's secret? Don't despair at life's roadblocks; turn the corner and find a way around them. If you have failed or feel stymied, perhaps this is just a nudge from God, urging you in a new — and exciting — direction.

Father God, lead me to the other side. —JAMES McDERMOTT

---

21 *Sing unto the Lord a new song, and his praise from the end of the earth...* —ISAIAH 42:10

One day I told my dentist, "I like to hear you sing while you work." He laughed and resumed the tune he had been humming.

The Bible is full of accounts of people singing with joy and happiness — but it also tells of another kind of singing. Singing when there is no reason to sing. Paul sang while he was in prison. After the Last Supper, Jesus sang with His disciples. Knowing of the ordeal He faced, He still sang!

Surely the sound of song in all its manifestations is dear to God.

Recently I heard a minister give voice to song in a most difficult situation. At the graveside of his son, as the young body was being lowered into the ground, the father started to softly sing his favorite hymns — songs of praise!

Is there a joyful occasion in your life today that you can celebrate with song? Is there a pain that you must work through? Why not offer Your Father a sacrifice of singing praises in His name?

Alleluia! Alleluia! Alleluia! Alleluia! —MARION BOND WEST

22 *Continue in prayer, and watch in the same with thanksgiving.*
—COLOSSIANS 4:2

Our prayer group has been meeting for over a year now. Every week we start by bringing our prayer list up to date. We add new names and needs, cross off those for which our prayers have been answered, and give thanks for those blessings received.

Recently, in going over our old lists, we were stunned and thrilled at the number of answered prayers. With brimming hearts, we thanked God for the incredible way He had quietly moved through our lists, healing, comforting, blessing, providing, meeting all kinds of diverse needs!

I guess it's human nature to focus on those stubborn problems for which we can't see immediate results from our prayers and to fail to notice all those that *have* been answered. Why not keep a prayer list yourself? You'll find that your list of requests and answered prayers is a wonderful record of God's love and faithfulness.

Lord, I'll begin my list today. —MARILYN MORGAN HELLEBERG

23 *Let the words of my mouth, and the meditation of my heart, be acceptable in thy sight, O Lord, my strength, and my redeemer.*
—PSALM 19:14

When I visited a friend of mine who is a music director in Minneapolis, he played a tape-recording of a Puccini mass, choir and orchestra, that he had conducted recently. Now I knew that Puccini had written some wonderful operas — *Madame Butterfly, La Bohème, Tosca, Turandot* and others — but I didn't know that he had written a mass.

"Yes," my friend said. "He was just seventeen when he announced to his family that he wanted to write operas. His mother said, 'All right, we will support you. But first you must write a mass.' And he did, the one we just heard."

I was so taken by the beauty of the music that tears came to my eyes. It was then that I gained a new understanding of the development of great talent. The emergence of talent doesn't just happen: It must be encouraged in others by parents and teachers (even by me) when we have the wisdom to encourage reverence as well as skill.

Father, let me remember that great art comes to us only through You. —GLENN KITTLER

---

24 *...Now abideth faith, hope, charity (love), these three, but the greatest of these is charity (love).*
—I CORINTHIANS 13:13

Margot Pickett, the feminine half of the husband-and-wife team that ministers to our church, recently had a novel suggestion in one of her sermons. "Take the verses in I Corinthians 13:4-8," she advised, "and for the word *love*, substitute your name."

Then she followed with an example: "*Margot* suffers long and is kind," she read (albeit somewhat self-consciously). "*Margot* doesn't envy, *Margot* is not puffed up, *Margot* thinks no evil, *Margot* is not easily provoked, *Margot* bears all things, believes all things, *Margot* never fails."

She concluded the sermon with the suggestion that such an exercise might show us where we fall short of St. Paul's standard.

Those majestic verses certainly give us a goal to aim at and they inspire us to strive ever harder for Christ-like motives. I think you'll agree that those in our midst who try to put love first are well on the road toward sainthood — especially if you subscribe to the theory that saints are only sinners who *keep on trying.*

Perfect my ability to love, Jesus. —FRED BAUER

---

25 *...Bless them that curse you...and pray for them...*
—MATTHEW 5:44

She works in an office down the hall from mine. She ignores my "Good mornings" and stares coldly at my smiles.

"I have spoken to her for the last time," I declared to my friend Ethel. "I will ignore her the same way she does me."

"You're foolish if you do that," Ethel said. "The woman may have all sorts of things on her mind, troubles you never dreamed of."

"No," I was adamant. "I think she's just hateful."

"Then she has a real problem. Why develop one of your own over it? Don't you think it would be better for you to pray about it rather than pout?"

Ethel was right, of course, and I started including the woman in my prayers.

Things seem a little better; I think she *almost* smiled today. The big improvement, though, has been in me. I don't resent her any more. Perhaps someday she will return my greeting, and who knows? We might even become friends. I'll keep praying for her, and for that day to come.

Is there someone you could be blessing instead of cursing today?

Lord, bless _____, and help me to change my frown to a smile. —DRUE DUKE

26 *Greater love hath no man than this, that a man lay down his life for his friends.* — JOHN 15:13

Twelve of us in my church youth group had already put two hundred and fifty miles behind us in what had been billed as a four-day, three-hundred-mile bicycle spectacular. Our carefree attitude of the first day was gone, replaced by a deep camaraderie forged in the pain of aching muscles and our common struggle against vicious head winds. Before beginning the trip we had only hoped to be able to finish. Now our plan was to ride triumphantly, all together, down the main street of our town.

We had reached the bottom of a forbidding hill just twenty miles from home when one of the girls pulled up. "My bike is stuck in tenth gear," she announced, fighting back tears. "I've ruined our chances of all finishing together."

Dave stepped in. "We'll switch bikes," he offered. "I might be able to make it on yours." I shook my head in doubt, convinced that the upcoming hills would defeat him.

Dave was valiant in his persistence, even when it meant walking the bike part of the way. Finally, I asked him: "Dave, why did you trade bikes? There's no way we'll make it together."

"Do you remember last night, Jeff, around the campfire? When we talked about laying down one's life for a friend? Well, I doubt that I'll ever be asked to give my life for a friend. But maybe if I can give a little every day — a bike here, a hand there — pretty soon I might have given my whole life, you might say."

A short while later I waited for Dave as he struggled up yet another hill. "How about trading bikes with me?" I asked. "You need a break."

Dave smiled. "You know, we're going to lick these hills yet." And we did, too!

Help me, Lord, to let my love for You show through in my giving to others. —JEFF JAPINGA

27 *A word fitly spoken is like apples of gold in pictures of silver.* —PROVERBS 25:11

When I read the above verse one day, I stopped to wonder: What words, fitly spoken, might be like golden apples?

"I love you." Those are surely golden-apple words.

So are: "I'm sorry, please forgive me," or, "It's all right, I understand."

How about: "Let me help"?

Or: "I couldn't have done it without you"?

How about the simple words, "Thank you" and "You're welcome"?

I find, when I think about it, that language is full of golden-apple words.

Why not share some today with a friend?

I love You, Father. Thank You. —MADGE HARRAH

28 *...In all these things we are more than conquerors through him...* —ROMANS 8:37

"I'll never get that heap on the road," I lamented to my mother. "Almost everything's wrong with it!"

I was sixteen years old and had just bought my first car — a 1930 Ford Model A roadster in sorry condition. I was ready to give up on it. But my mother wouldn't let me.

"Did you know that Socrates had a terrible stutter?" she asked with a hint of merriment in her eyes. "And that Lincoln was overly shy and awkward?

"Socrates and Lincoln had 'almost everything wrong' with them," she went on, "but by the time they had put what was *wrong* with themselves *right*, they had built up so much momentum that it carried them on to greatness."

Well, you guessed it. With Mom's continuing encouragement, I gradually put everything into order with the model A and it ran beautifully. I was the proud driver of a classic auto!

I think that what my mother was trying to teach me was that in every obstacle there lies an opportunity. When things seem unusually difficult, perhaps you are being singled out for greatness.

Lord, help me to be worthy of my difficulties. —JAMES McDERMOTT

---

29 *...For by him were all things created, that are in heaven, and that are in earth, visible and invisible...*
—COLOSSIANS 1:16

Years ago I read a magazine article by Harold L. Irving that made a deep impression on me. It was about a basic law in God's universe: the law of rhythm. We observe rhythm in the ebb and flow of the tides, the seasonal cycles of growing things, the interplay of positive and negative forces of electricity, and so on.

Each of us, Irving said, has been divinely fashioned so as to function in harmony with the law of rhythm. He offered three words as guidance toward this harmony.

The first word is *easy*, meaning moderate or unhurried. Repeat the word frequently during the day, especially when pressure or tensions begin to build up. God's rhythms are unhurried. That's how ours should be.

The second word is *steady*. The concept of "measured motion" governs the movements of the stars and planets with majestic regularity. Speak this word as you go about your appointed tasks and a great sense of purpose will come over you.

The third word is *balance*. All motion, mental or physical, when unhurried and steady, results in a perfect balance of energy. God's universe is always in balance and our lives can be too. Operate your life daily on His divine pattern.

Just three words. But when applied to your life, each one becomes a prayer.

Easy...Steady...Balance...   —ARTHUR GORDON

---

30   *That thine alms may be in secret: and thy Father which seeth in secret himself shall reward thee openly.*
—MATTHEW 6:4

Last year I received a May basket. I don't know who left it on my doorstep. It was a small wicker basket lined with a delicate lace doily and in it were six freshly baked cinnamon rolls, some lovely sprigs of forsythia and this message:

> This little basket comes to say,
> You're a special friend in every way.
> May baskets last for only a day;
> *This* one's meant for *all* of May,
> So...
> Enjoy the rolls, savor the love,
> Then refill the basket with your love.
> Home-baked goodies or something sewn,
> Flowers from your garden, a note, a poem.
> Then pass it on, but don't get caught!
> Do it in secret as Jesus taught.

What a beautiful way to say, "I appreciate you." I felt so special all that day — and so deliciously sneaky when I passed the basket on to someone else this year. You know, I wouldn't be a bit surprised if that basket eventually found its way back to the person who first started it on its travels. That's the way love works!

Help me to find creative ways to pass on Your love, Lord.
—MARILYN MORGAN HELLEBERG

Praise Diary for April

1

2

3

4

5

6

7

8

9

10

11

12

13

14

15

16

17

18

19

20

21

22

23

24

25

26

27

28

29

30

May

*Be pleased, O Lord, to deliver me: O Lord, make
haste to help me.* —PSALM 40:13

The rose is nature's gift of love,
And as I watch it bloom,
I marvel at the sweetness
Of its delicate perfume.

My heart is filled with praise, Lord,
For this very special gift,
And the lesson that it teaches
When my spirit needs a lift....

It's a lesson that in spite of thorns,
The painful barbs of strife,
My faith can bloom as sweetly
Above the trials of life.

—ALICE JOYCE DAVIDSON

PATTERN FOR A BLESSED LIFE
Blessed are they which they do hunger and thirst after righteousness: for they shall be filled. —MATTHEW 5:6

1   Rory was a student in my freshman English class eight years ago. By the age of nineteen he had tried smoking, drinking, sex and drugs and had finally decided that life was nothing but emptiness. Now here he was, standing in my doorway with joy written all over his face. When I asked him why, Rory replied, "Well, I discovered an amazing thing. God had put that emptiness inside of me! He did it in order to draw me to Him. But I kept on trying to fill it with temporary external things — until I realized that the only high that *lasts* is Jesus."

Sometimes I get an empty feeling too, don't you? The next time I do, I'm going to remind myself that God put it there to draw me closer to Him. It will signal me to spend more time in prayer so that Jesus can replenish my spirit with the only lasting nourishment.

I will come to You each day in May, Lord, hungering and thirsting for Your presence. —MARILYN MORGAN HELLEBERG

MEMORABLE MOTHERS OF THE BIBLE
Mother's Day is just one week away and in anticipation of that very special Sunday, Fred Bauer brings us the stories of seven memorable mothers in the Bible.

2   SARAH   *Genesis 17:15-19*

Sarah, which means princess, was a beautiful and loving woman but she was unable to provide her husband with the gift he most wanted — a son. Although she suffered the disgrace and idignity that her culture bestowed on childless women, she remained loyal to her husband, and he to her.

When she was ninety and Abraham was ninety-nine, God made a covenant with Abraham, promising him "descendants through all generations." Abraham thought it absurd to have a child at such an advanced age and he laughed at the idea. But the Lord kept his word and the couple was blessed with a son, Isaac, who was a cornerstone in God's plan for Israel.

Sarah is best remembered for the miracle of her pregnancy and childbirth. But what makes her most special to me is her faithfulness. Despite the anguish that accompanied a lifetime of barrenness, she never lost faith in God or abandoned her husband, whom she loved deeply.

When we are tempted to give up our dreams, when we feel that God has forgotten us or doesn't care about us, when the odds against our achieving seem insurmountable, we need to remember that we serve a God Who deals in the impossible.

Put us in tune with Your plan for our lives, Lord, and in step with Your timetable. —FRED BAUER

---

3 NAOMI   *Ruth 1:5-22*

Naomi is famous not because she was an outstanding mother, which she undoubtedly was, but because she was a very special mother-in-law.

First her husband died; then her two married sons. Facing life alone, did she cling to her daughters-in-law? No. Without thought for herself, she advised them to go home, to return to their parents. One of the women did as Naomi suggested, but the other one, Ruth, would not hear of it and said, "...whither thou goest, I will go; and where thou lodgest, I will lodge: thy people shall be my people, and thy God my God...." Ruth's loyalty is a testament to Naomi's extraordinarily beautiful character.

Yet for me the significant life lesson of the Book of Ruth is in Naomi's example of selflessness. It would have been understandable had she sought support from her daughters-in-law. Instead, she freed them and made no claims on her own behalf.

Someone once said, "That which I struggle to keep, I lose and that which I freely give away, I keep." Naomi well knew the truth of those words.

Lord, teach us to think of You first, others second and ourselves third.
—FRED BAUER

---

4 MOSES' MOTHER *Exodus 2:1-10*

Moses' mother hid her baby for three months in an attempt to save him from Pharoah's evil designs.

Finally, when hope of keeping the infant's existence a secret dwindled, she set in motion an ingenious plan. She would obey Pharoah after all and cast the child into the river! Well, almost. She would make a floating ark of bulrushes and place her baby in it. But she wouldn't exactly set him adrift in midstream; rather, she would place the ark among the shallow reeds growing at the shore. And she wouldn't leave the baby just anywhere; rather, she would leave him at the very spot where she knew that Pharoah's daughter came to bathe every day and hence would surely discover the child. And she would station the infant's sister nearby so that she might appear when he was discovered and volunteer Moses' mother to nurse him.

What a delicious story! The maternal scheming worked out to perfection and a child's life was saved.

How resourceful mothers are when it comes to their babies; how creative and inventive they can be when their children's needs arise; how loving, how giving, how sacrificial when it comes to the flesh of their flesh. God in His infinite wisdom created mothers and imbued them with qualities both tough and tender — tough enough to defy Pharoah's laws and tender enough to protect and nurture a destiny-bound child.

For loving mothers who taught us to love, Lord, we thank You.
—FRED BAUER

---

5 AN UNNAMED MOTHER   *I Kings 3:16-28*

One of the Bible's most heart-warming stories is about the unnamed mother who went to King Solomon to plead for her baby, who had been claimed by another woman.

"This woman and I share the same house," she told the King. "I delivered a son. Three days later she did likewise. But one night she found her baby dead. She took my son from my bosom and replaced him with her dead child. When I awoke in the morning and tried to feed my baby, I found him dead. Then I realized that the infant was not my son but the son of this woman. She has refused to return my child to me."

The other woman claimed that the first woman was wrong, that the child in question was hers. It seemed an insoluble dilemma but Solomon, renowned for his wisdom, determined to find the solution.

"Bring me a sword," he said to his servants. When they did, he ordered, "Now, divide the child in two. Give half to one woman and half to the other." At this the first mother screamed, "No! Don't slay my child. Give him to her!" Thus it was that the King discovered the identity of the baby's real mother.

Solomon knew that no true mother would ever allow her child to be harmed. He reasoned rightly that she would sacrifice her own self-interest, even her life, for her baby's safety. What an eternal blessing belongs to those of us who have had such a mother to care for us, to sacrifice for us, to believe in us. It is from the well of this deep love that we draw faith unto ourselves, faith in others and faith in God.

Father, we thank You for teaching us about sacrifical love. Help us to live it. —FRED BAUER

6 REBEKAH *Genesis 27:1-46*

Rebekah was a very good mother but there was a flaw in her maternal character: She loved one son more than she did the other. Worse, she revealed her feelings when she helped Jacob dishonestly secure the blessing of his blind father, Isaac.

Although the Biblical narrative departs from Rebekah and follows the story of her sons, I am reluctant to leave her without an over-the-shoulder chastisement. Not only was she an instigator of deception but she was responsible for having led Jacob astray.

Parents who play favorites with their children plant seeds of sorrow and resentment that can live for generations. The story of Jacob's and Esau's rivalry, for instance, is like the story of Cain and Abel. And Joseph, the apple of his father's eye, provoked his brothers into jealousy, leading to strife for many years thereafter.

Of course God always brings good out of evil but in our day-to-day dealings with our children — and with each other — isn't even-handedness a worthy goal?

Father, give us the wisdom as parents to disavow all favoritism and to treat equally those whom we love. —FRED BAUER

7   A MOTHER OF NAIN   *Luke 7:11-15*

Nain is a village not far from Jesus' Nazareth home. One day He and His disciples visited the little hamlet.

As they approached the town's gate, a group of mourners appeared, carrying the bier of a young boy. The boy's mother, a widow, had known grief before. Now with the loss of her son, she was truly alone.

Jesus stopped to observe. He told the mother, "Don't weep." Then He walked over to the coffin and touched it, at the same time commanding the young man to arise — and lo, the boy returned to the living.

Those who witnessed the miracle couldn't believe their eyes. The reaction of the mother is not recorded but we can be sure that her heart was filled with joy.

Jesus told the desolate woman, "Don't weep," meaning: "Trust Me, Mother. I love you and I love your son — He is My child. Nothing can remove him from My Kingdom."

Here then is the spiritual key to the healing of grief: "Don't weep." Jesus promises life everlasting — and He demonstrated its truth.

Lord, we thank You for Your healing touch, for Your promise of life eternal.   —FRED BAUER

8   MARY, MOTHER OF JESUS   *Luke 1:42*

Mary, the mother of Jesus, is deservedly the most honored woman in the Bible. Today — Mother's Day — we salute her anew for the role she played in God's greatest drama — the sending of His only Son to us.

137

What an enormous responsibility God placed on Mary's thin young shoulders! But He also supplied her with the grace necessary to carry out His holy assignment.

Motherhood is an awe-inspiring achievement — from child-bearing to childbirth to childrearing. And throughout the ages the sorrows and the joys of motherhood have not varied. Even today — as yesterday — tears and potential heartbreak weigh one side of the scale, happiness and unimaginable contentment the other side.

No tribute to mothers can surpass the loving homage of Mary's cousin, Elizabeth. Although she was speaking of Mary's holy mission and the God-child she was carrying, her words are for all mothers: "Blessed art thou among women, and blessed is the fruit of thy womb."

Today we ask Your blessing on all mothers, Lord, that their children may reflect Your love in joy and praise. —FRED BAUER

---

9 *I exhort therefore, that, first of all, supplications, prayers, intercessions, and giving of thanks, be made for all men...* —I TIMOTHY 2:1

"My son Kevin is going into the hospital two weeks from Monday," a friend said to me in the drugstore. "Please pray for him on that day."

"Of course," I replied. And as I walked away, I thought, *How many times have I said "Of course" and then forgotten about it? Well, not this time!* I took my date calendar from my purse and penciled in Kevin's name across the top of the page for that Monday.

When the day rolled around and I consulted my calendar, as I do each morning, I was surprised to see Kevin's name. Aha! Once again I had forgotten. Without my diary reminder, the day would have come and gone without a single prayer for Kevin from me.

Kevin became the focus of my prayers on that day. I prayed for him when I waited at stop lights, while I was at the dishwasher, when I was in the shower and as I waited in the schoolyard to pick up my children. Later, after I learned that Kevin was at home and successfully recuperating from his surgery, I realized how powerful that encounter with intercessory prayer had been. And so I began to pencil in other names on my calendar — my husband's name on the day he planned to travel, my son's name on the day he had a math test, a widow's name on the anniversary of her husband's death and my minister's name on a special Sunday.

Now I have learned that a date calendar can serve as much more than a mere reminder of daily activities. It can become a *prayer* calendar, bringing my loved ones and God into all the activities of my life.

Remind me, God, to pray for others throughout the hours of my day.
—SUE MONK KIDD

---

10 *Apply thine heart unto instruction, and thine ears to the words of knowledge.* —PROVERBS 23:12

It was a warm, sunny spring morning and the first thing I did was to go out and buy some flats of flowers for the beds around the house. After the long winter I was hungry for the colors and the scents of growing things. I hurried home to begin planting.

But — I soon despaired at the amount of work I had undertaken to do. I had to take out the spade and turn the earth; then I had to mix in peat compost and fertilizer; then rake everything smooth. After a while the project wasn't as much fun as I had anticipated it would be.

But I no longer had a choice in the matter. If I put the plants aside, they would die. *Why,* I mused, *do we have to work so hard before we see any results?*

And then it occurred to me that God must face a similar chore — with every single one of us! First He has to lay the ground work. In fact, it's that early nurture and care that make our very lives possible. We take root according to where and how we are planted. Then it's up to us to ripen and blossom.

Father, help me to grow today...and every day. —PHYLLIS HOBE

---

11 *...Be not highminded, nor trust in uncertain riches, but in the living God, who giveth us richly all things to enjoy...* —I TIMOTHY 6:17

When I visited the Homestake Mine in the Black Hills of South Dakota, our guide told us at the outset that the Homestake is the largest producer of gold in the Western Hemisphere. He added that on the way out we would receive "free samples." This latter remark, I noticed, was of particular interest to a young boy in our group.

The tour was fascinating. We were told of the many painstaking procedures necessary to the drilling and blasting out of tons of granite-like ore from the earth. We watched the laborious processes of separating the gold from the ore — a far cry from my pictures of bright yellow nuggets popping out in some lucky old prospector's pan. "Do you know how much gold is recovered from each ton of ore?" our guide asked. "About one-third of one ounce."

This impressed all of us except the young boy. He was impatient and hurried his parents along, eager to get on with it. Finally as the tour ended, the youngster asked frantically, "The sample...what about the sample?"

"Oh, yes," said our guide, pointing to a huge container piled high with massive chunks of ore. "Take as much as you like."

He hadn't lied — there *was* gold in the ore, an infinitesimal fraction. And I could not help but feel sorry for the boy, principally because in his one-sided obsession he had missed out on all the fascinating things that the rest of us had just seen.

So there's really not much new under the sun. The Midas-minded people continue to miss the real riches of living, don't they?

Don't let me miss today's golden opportunities, God.

—VAN VARNER

---

12 *Having then gifts differing according to the grace that is given to us...*
—ROMANS 12:6

There was something special about our new church member, Jane. She positively glowed. She never complained and had such a joyful, willing attitude that she amazed all of us. Soon we were asking her to do everything.

One day the president of the Women's Group asked her to present the monthly devotional at their regular meeting.

The young woman stammered, "But I...I...don't speak in public. I mean I never have. I...I...."

The president persisted.

Jane looked down at her feet, her face pale. Another woman came upon the scene. She must have overheard the conversation. She hugged Jane and spoke to the president in a soft voice: "Jane *is* a devotion. She doesn't really need to present one, does she?" Jane sighed and the glow returned to her face.

I suddenly felt ashamed. How many times, I wondered, had *I* pressed Jane, and others, to serve the church without considering their best interests? In my enthusiasm, filling a need had become more important than the person's uniqueness and special talents. In the future I would remember to be more mindful of my fellow church members....

And Jane? Jane still serves in our church — in her own way.

Lord, we are a Body of many parts. Let us respect one another's gifts. —MARION BOND WEST

---

13 *...The true Light, which lighteth every man that cometh into the world.* —JOHN 1:9

On my desk there sits a prism — a small bit of multi-faceted glass that produces no light of its own. Rather, it catches the rays of the sun and pours them out into the world in a kaleidoscope of dancing color.

We Christians resemble the prism, I think. We have no light of our own. But we can take the Light of Jesus and break it into the many hues of love: a loaf of bread for the hungry, a cup of cold water for the thirsty, a smile of welcome for the stranger, a call to the lonely, a visit to the sick or imprisoned, a deed of justice on behalf of the oppressed, a story of Good News to those who need to hear it.

We don't create that light but when we serve as its *prism*, we illuminate others — making their world beautiful too.

Will the world see the Light of Christ reflected through you today?

Lord, let me radiate the colors of Your love in all my actions.
—PATRICIA HOUCK SPRINKLE

14 *I, even I, am he that blotteth out thy transgressions for
mine own sake, and will not remember thy sins.*
— ISAIAH 43:25

"I know John has told me he's sorry but it still bugs me," I
said to my golfing partner. Although golf is one of my favorite
sports, on that day I just couldn't keep my mind on the game. "John
told me he would be careful with my class notes — I can't believe he
lost them!"

"You don't believe in forgiveness?" Tim questioned.

"Sure I do. I've tried to forgive him and forget about it, I really
have. But still, he lost those notes. No one can ever change that." I
sighed, took a few practice swings with my driver and then hit a
beautiful shot to within six feet of the hole. "Wow!" I exclaimed.
"Sure is a lot better than dropping it in the water like I did on the
last hole. I think this is one reason that I like golf — every hole is a
fresh chance."

Tim bent over to tee up his ball. Then he looked up at me and
said, "Guess that makes golf a lot like life."

"What are you getting at?"

"Just that no matter how badly you blow one hole, you can walk
to the next tee with a clean slate. Heck, you really blew that last
hole — just check your scorecard — but that didn't mean a thing on
your drive here. Life is similar. We blow it all the time — I do, you
do, John certainly did. We can't change it — it's on the scorecard —
but because of God's promised forgiveness, we can play on with a
clean slate. A fresh start, you might say."

I looked down the fairway at my ball, sitting next to the flagstick,
then back at the pond. "Hey, Tim, remind me to call John when we
finish the round," I said, smiling. "I think it's time John and I move
on to the next hole."

*Father, we thank You for granting us a clean slate after each one
of our "holes."* — JEFF JAPINGA

JOURNEY OF FAITH

15 Your traveling companion is MOSES
. . . who learned the value of a detour.

—EXODUS, LEVITICUS, NUMBERS, DEUTERONOMY

A journey into freedom — this is the central story of Moses' life, and the central theme of faith. Whatever our "slavery" is, we walk with Moses the uncharted road away from the chains of the past. Let's look at the false starts and seeming dead ends of Moses' pilgrimage and how God uses them for our growth.

To Enlarge Our Vision. Moses personally had escaped the hard lot of his people. Adopted by Pharaoh's daughter, he had been raised in privilege and plenty. But Moses had a dream. Hatred of injustice was deeply ingrained in the man, whether it was an Egyptian brutalizing a Hebrew, or a Hebrew bullying a fellow slave, or a group of men shoving a woman away from a watering trough. And he dreamed, probably, of using his influence at court to outlaw the use of the whip or shorten the working day.

Instead, with one hasty ill-timed deed he finds himself, at age forty, exiled from the people he meant to help. To him it must have seemed that he'd thrown away his chances, given up whatever leverage he had with the policy makers, to come to some God-forsaken wilderness and herd a bunch of silly sheep.

How could Moses know that the trouble with his original dream was not that it was too big but that it was not big enough! That he was not called to improve working conditions in a particular slave labor camp, but to lead an entire people away from slavery forever.

To Give Us Specific Training. God knew — and we know, with hindsight — that the skills of the desert sheepherder, the knowledge of the capricious Sinai weather, the secret of water trapped in the limestone hills, the location of oases, were precisely the know-how Moses would need to lead not sheep, but men, women and children through the wilderness. What must have seemed to Moses years of tedious routine — wasted years in terms of his youthful dream — were in God's all-seeing economy, the perfect preparation for the work that lay ahead.

To Reveal Himself. Moses was a busy man, a man with responsibilities, entrusted with his father-in-law's large flocks. A shepherd's daily trek in that arid land is not a carefree ramble but a purposeful march toward a fixed destination — each night's watering place planned in advance. But he was not performing it with a narrow concentration that shut out the possibility of the unexpected and the holy. *He turned aside.*

And it was only then, from the burning bush, that God spoke to Moses by name, revealed His own nature, and showed Moses the true work to which he was called. When we, in our busy lives, hurry by with tunnel vision, we miss meeting God in the burning bush.

To Temper Our Faith. So Moses returned to Egypt and — after harrowing confrontations with Pharaoh — led his people to freedom. But what a strange roundabout route they took! Their destination — our destination — is the Promised Land, where the good things of God are waiting. But God did not lead them by the "way of the Philistines" — or the shortest route — one where they might face a battle around any bend before they were toughened and disciplined by the wilderness experience.

If there are times when *our* lives don't move in a straight line, perhaps it's because a faith that encounters no obstacles is one that crumbles with the first opposition.

To Give Us Another Chance. On the very threshold of the Promised Land, God's people panicked. They clamoured only to return to the slavery and safety of Egypt. A year-and-a-half in the wilderness had not sufficed for basic training: the final detour was to last forty years before they would be battle ready.

It was a devastating blow to Moses, and yet it corresponds to our own experience. While any part of us longs to return to Egypt...to the old dependent, enslaving patterns...God holds back. The qualities nurtured and strengthened on desert marches, will prove us fit for life in His kingdom.

> *Lord, let me learn the lessons of the wilderness through which You are leading me this month...so that I will be prepared to meet the future!*
>
> —ELIZABETH SHERRILL

16   *Honour thy father and thy mother...*   —EXODUS 20:12

I met her at a writers' conference, a little old lady of seventy-five, maybe a bit more, still lively as a cricket.

"How's the conference going for you?" I asked her.

"Oh, marvelous," she said. "I'm so glad I came — even though I had to fight my children to get here!"

That seemed strange. "What caused the fighting?" I asked her.

"*Smother* love," she said promptly. "It usually refers to parents who are overprotective of their children. But believe me, it can work both ways. My children love me, but they seem to think I'm made of glass. 'Don't do this, Mama! Don't do that, Mama! You shouldn't drive all that way, Mama! What if you get sick? What if you get lost?' Why, if I listened to them, I'd never do anything. So I just told them, 'I'm going!' And here I am!"

Smother love in reverse...are you guilty of it? Honoring parents and elders certainly means giving them love and respect. But it means giving them freedom too...even if it involves some risk.

Father, I release my parents to Your protective care.

—ARTHUR GORDON

17   *The eternal God is thy refuge, and underneath are the everlasting arms...*   —DEUTERONOMY 33:27

In high school Dorothy was voted "The Most Likely to Succeed." And succeed she did. The Perfect Wife. The Perfect Mother. The Chairperson Most in Demand. And then suddenly she was threatened with a nervous breakdown. She began to make the rounds of psychiatrists' offices, without finding any relief. In desperation she sought out a retired minister who was also a family friend. To him she poured out her troubles: community demands, problems at home, physical difficulties, the approaching of middle age.

"I just can't cope," Dorothy said to him. "I'm at the end of my rope."

"Good," the minister said firmly, "Then *let go!*"

He pointed out that a rigid telephone pole can snap in a high wind while a willow can move with a gale and survive. "The word for spirit and wind are one and the same in ancient Biblical language," he said. "You need to let the Holy Spirit move freely through your life. Learn to yield to it. *Let go!*"

"Right there and then, in a flood of tears," Dorothy told me later, "I did. I let go. My problems didn't disappear but I found that I could bend with them. I am strengthened as long as I remind myself to let go!"

Dear Lord, when I feel that I must run my world on my own, remind me, please, to relax and Let Go to You! —ELAINE ST. JOHNS

---

18 *Happy is the man that findeth wisdom... For the merchandise of it is better than the merchandise of silver...* —PROVERBS 3:13,14

Eleven-year-old Markita Andrews just has to be one of the all-time-great Girl Scout cookie salespersons. During each of the past two years she has sold over three thousand boxes of cookies. When my eye caught a headline over a news story dubbing her a "cookie monster," I thought, *That's probably just what she is — a pushy little kid who won't take "no" for an answer.* But when I read further, I gained an entirely different impression.

There's no gimmickry to Markita's salesmanship. "It's most important," she says "that you keep on trying." Markita is the mistress of the polite soft-sell. When she sees that potential customers are in a hurry or in a bad mood, she doesn't bother them. She comes back later.

Too often I am apt to associate success in selling with unfeeling aggression but Markita's example has taught me to see it in a new light. When Jesus said that the meek would inherit the earth, perhaps He had people such as Markita in mind.

Lord, may I always be on the gentle side of success — placing people before goals.
—JAMES McDERMOTT

---

19 *I press toward the mark...* —PHILIPPIANS 3:14

My small son is in a state of enchantment every time we take him to a circus. Thrilled at meeting the tightrope walker one day at the circus, he asked her how she managed to keep from falling.

"It's really not very hard," she told him. "The trick is to never look down. From the minute you step onto the rope, look at where you are going, toward the platform at the other end. Concentrate on your goal. If you stop or look down, you are pretty sure to lose your balance and fall. But if you keep your eyes on the goal, your feet go where they are supposed to go."

When the call comes through to step out in a new Christian endeavor, or to meet a challenge I have never faced before, or to keep on going when I'm too weary to move, I recall the tightrope walker's rule: I try to think only of my goal — Jesus. When I keep Him in view, my feet go where they are supposed to go!

Dear Lord, fasten my heart and my eyes on You that I may walk steadily and confidently this day. —PATRICIA HOUCK SPRINKLE

20 Nevertheless he saved them for his name's sake, that he might make his mighty power to be known. —PSALM 106:8

So often when I open the newspaper I find myself reading a depressing headline — words in big letters shouting about a world threat, a crisis, another crime. There is surely a lot of bad news to read about these days.

But one day last January I opened the Sunday edition of our town's paper and read a remarkable headline printed in half-inch letters: "I Asked Jesus Into My Heart." This story followed:

During the night several dogs had begun to bark furiously around the home of a local couple. Usually the dogs' barking signaled that something was amiss, that perhaps prowlers or thieves lurked nearby. But the next morning, the couple discovered that nothing had been taken. Instead, something had been returned. Resting against the front door were two car speakers that had been stolen six weeks earlier. A note was attached to them that read, "I'm sorry that I took your speakers, but now I have repented my sins and asked Jesus to forgive me. I hope you will forgive me too. I no longer take other people's belongings...God has changed me. I'm a new creature since I asked Jesus into my heart. From...'Saved.'"

God is still alive and at work in the lives of His people, changing them into new and loving creatures. That's not usually front-page news but it's there just the same — tiny happenings in small, unnoticed corners everywhere. So we must not despair when we feel bombarded with bad news. You see, there's a lot of Good News in the world — just waiting to be noticed. I thought that tonight when you sit down with your newspaper or watch the six-o'clock news, you might like to remember that.

You *are such Good News, Lord!*   —SUE MONK KIDD

21 *...We glory in tribulations also: knowing that tribulation worketh patience; And patience, experience; and experience, hope...* —ROMANS 5:3,4

It's called *the infiltration course*. A part of Army basic training. It is one of the tests new soldiers are given, in which they are required to crawl through an obstacle-littered field while live ammunition is shot overhead.

Why are soldiers put through such a regimen? So that on the battlefield in the face of gunfire, they will be prepared to handle it without fear.

Sometimes during the course of our lives I think we are put through "infiltration courses" — trials and tests that tear at us. We don't understand why we have to undergo such painful experiences. But in retrospect we discover that we have survived the ordeal and a new-found strength has prepared us for future conflict. And as Christians, a deep assurance wells up in our souls that with God on our side, we can face the future. That's the benefit and enduring blessing of spiritual infiltration courses.

Train me, Father, and prepare me for the future. —FRED BAUER

22 *And Jesus... said unto her, Martha, Martha, thou art careful and troubled about many things: But one thing is needful: and Mary hath chosen that good part, which shall not be taken away from her.* —LUKE 10:41,42

There was a house and within its walls there dwelt two sisters. When the Visitor came, one sister filled the house with rituals customary to such an occasion and she prepared and served meals. She tried to be the perfect hostess. The other sister abandoned her usual ways and went to the Visitor, sat down, listened and learned many things as a student from a teacher.

The issue is, whose *house* is it once Jesus enters?

The issue is, whose *life* is it once Jesus arrives?

The issue is, once Jesus is present, *who* sets the agenda?

The issue is, are we busy *for* Jesus or are we abiding *with* Jesus?

Will I spend today busying myself with service *for* Jesus — or will I walk through this day *with* Jesus, allowing Him to instruct me?

In the Bethany of my soul, am I a Martha — or am I a Mary?

Dear Lord, don't let me get so busy this day in serving You that I fail to abide with You. —PATRICIA HOUCK SPRINKLE

23

I can do all things through Christ which strengtheneth me. —PHILIPPIANS 4:13

"I have always had the most wonderful students!" Mrs. Hooten exclaims whenever we see her. She was my husband's teacher when he was a boy and she was also our son's grade-school teacher. She was dearly loved by both of them.

"What made your students so wonderful?" I asked her one day.

"Treat students like winners and they achieve; treat them like losers and they fail," she explained. "If a child is naughty or bored, his time is being wasted. We must discover what he enjoys doing, what his talents are and then help him to develop them. If we do that, the lessons take care of themselves. The poet James Whitcomb Riley was a notorious failure until a teacher noticed his literary flair, encouraged him and treated him like a winner."

Do you know a "winner" who could use some encouragement from you today? How about yourself? You know, all of us are God's "winners," created with talent that's just waiting to be tapped and developed.

With You and for You, Lord, I will nourish the talents You have given me. —ZONA B. DAVIS

---

24 *He that regardeth the day, regardeth it unto the Lord...*
—ROMANS 14:6

The minister to Queen Victoria completed his sermon on the return of our Lord to this earth when he saw that his Queen was in tears. He hurried to her side to inquire if he had offended her with any of his words.

"Oh, no!" the great lady said. "I am only sad because I am afraid I shall die before His return. How I yearn to live long enough to remove this crown of England from my head and lay it at the feet of the King of Kings!"

I have no crown to wear, yet I too look forward to laying all that I have at my Lord's feet. But I don't want my thoughts about the future to dampen my spirits today. There's plenty of work to be done in His name right here and now.

Lord, keep me mindful of the present for I don't want to be too "heavenly" minded and no "earthly" good. —DRUE DUKE

25 *Consider the lilies of the field, how they grow; they toil not, neither do they spin: And yet I say unto you, That even Solomon in all his glory was not arrayed like one of these.* —MATTHEW 6:28, 29

There is a poetry contest held in Spain each year wherein the third-place winner receives a silver rose, the second-place winner a gold rose and the first-place winner a real rose.

I used to puzzle over those awards — a real rose as the *top prize*. Yet the more I think about it, the more fitting it seems. For no matter how great the artistry of man, not a one of us can create the exquisite perfection of a delicately perfumed and velvet-petaled rose. Only the genius of the Master Creator can produce such glorious beauty and magnificence.

What better prize could one receive, then, than a gift from the Hand of God Himself?

Lord, help me not only to see, but to also appreciate Your great glories. —MADGE HARRAH

26 *I will walk within my house with a perfect heart.* —PSALM 101:2

I decided to plan an unusual shower. Tired of games and puzzles, I wanted the occasion to be really meaningful and so I invited the bride's Sunday school teacher, Bernie Cantrell, to share some words with us on "How To Have a Christian Marriage."

In speaking about the virtues of a godly wife, Bernie told us that her grandmother had had seven aprons — one for each day of the week. Every morning she arose early and put on a fresh apron. Bernie explained that the apron served as a symbol — an avowal of eagerness to serve and help other members of the family. At this both of my daughters glanced across the room at me. I didn't have any aprons. Nor was I always eager to serve my family — especially by cooking. After the shower, I somehow felt that Bernie's message had been meant for me as much as for the young bride-to-be.

I began to look at aprons in stores, cautiously at first. Some were quite beautiful. Each one seemed to have its own personality, Finally I bought one, a pretty calico with ruffles. That evening as I slipped it on, I felt as though I were slipping into a pleasant attitude about fixing supper. I found something inexplicably delightful about wearing the apron.

Now I've begun to collect aprons…maybe someday I will even have seven, like Bernie's grandmother.

Help me to clothe myself, Father, in Jesus' name, especially when I must do humdrum chores for others. —MARION BOND WEST

---

27 *The law of truth was in his mouth…* —MALACHI 2:6

I belong to a writers' critique group. Since I'm tempted to see only the positive aspects of a fellow writer's work — plus the fact that I don't want to hurt anyone's feelings — I don't always tell the whole truth at our meetings. I discussed my dilemma with a friend.

"You're there to help," she said firmly. "First, of course, describe what you do like; then if you have a suggestion for improvement, say so. In that way you will be people-*helping* instead of people-*pleasing*."

She was right. At the next session, although filled with trepidation, I tried to speak up in all honesty. And you know, I received gratitude from my fellow writers. Now they are being helped as much by me as I am by them.

Today I'm finding it easier than ever before to be candid with others — whether they be friends, family members or members of my church. They appreciate my honesty. And — honestly — I appreciate theirs too. It helps.

Today, Lord, enable me to dare to be honest with others in the only way that counts — with loving kindness.   —DORIS HAASE

---

28 *...Add to your faith... brotherly kindness; and to brotherly kindness charity.*   —II PETER 1:5,7

Last year on a sunny May morning a friend introduced me to the perils and joys of white-water canoeing. In midday we stopped to have the lunch that Sandy's wife had prepared for us. He took out two plastic bottles and asked me, "What'll it be, apple juice or a double whammy?"

"What's a double whammy?"

"It's Sue's special mixture of grape juice and apple juice," Sandy replied. "Would you like to try it?"

"Well, sure," I said. He tossed me the bottle. The concoction was really delicious and I drank it all.

That evening when we reached home, Sue greeted us with, "Hey, Sandy, how was the double whammy?"

"Uh..." Sandy said, "I decided to have some apple juice instead."

"What!" Sue exclaimed in mock horror. "Did someone hold you at knife point?"

I got the picture. The double whammy had been Sandy's drink of choice but he had graciously given it to me. A small thing, you might say. But I believe that one way to recognize a Christian is by noting his small, selfless acts. Come to think of it, Sandy's generosity wasn't all that small. You should have tasted that double whammy!

Before this day is over, Lord, I'm going to quietly put another's interests ahead of my own.   —JAMES McDERMOTT

29

The fruit of the righteous is a tree of life…

—PROVERBS 11:30

While paging through a travel magazine, I saw a picture of what I thought was a grove of trees. *How can so many trees grow that close together without stifling each other,* I wondered? Upon reading the caption I learned that this was not a *grove* of trees but *one tree* — a banyan tree.

It seems that as the banyan tree grows its lower branches become so thick and so long that the trunk cannot support them. The branches bend low, touch the ground, take root, and an offspring banyan tree is born. This process repeats itself and the trees thereby create a forest, each offspring connected to another.

This kind of growth reminds me of the spread of Christianity. Could it be that our separate acts of Christian love — feeding the hungry, treating the sick, educating the ignorant, helping the underprivileged — are like the branches of a banyan tree, spreading out, taking root and producing new Christians? I like to think that wherever we may be, we can sow our acts of kindness and love so that they multiply.

Lord, let my life be like a tree that sets new roots — spreading out to create a forest covering the world for You. —GLENN KITTLER

30

The Lord watch between me and thee, when we are absent one from another.

—GENESIS 31:49

It was Memorial Day. Driving rain and bad roads had kept us from making the hundred-mile trip to visit my father's grave, but Dad had been on my mind all day. The dark door that slammed when he died seemed to be locked tighter than ever, and I felt

156

completely cut off from him. As the day drizzled on, the grayness outside became a grayness within me that I couldn't shake.

Later in the day, suddenly, a single word shot a beam of light across my mind. It was a word that my father used to put at the end of his letters to us when he was on a ship in the South Pacific during World War II. The word was *Mizpah*. It means: "The Lord watch between me and thee, when we are absent one from another."

Slowly a shaft of light began to shine through that dark door that separated me from my father; I understood that God's promise to "watch between us when we are absent one from another" is a *forever* thing.

As I pause this day to remember my absent loved one, Lord, I thank You for being the link between us for eternity.
—MARILYN MORGAN HELLEBERG

---

31 *Resist the devil, and he will flee from you.* —JAMES 4:7

There are many harmless ways to get rid of frustrations so that neither man, beast nor object need suffer.

A friend who has no garden of her own came to our house one afternoon and asked, "Do you have some weeds I can pull up?"

She explained that she was feeling angry and frustrated and that she was always able to dissipate such feelings by the labor of pulling up weeds. She weeded our garden well and in the doing she taught me a lesson: When frustrated, you can do something useful, not destructive.

Don't waste the hot steam of anger. Vent it constructively.

Let my negative feelings lead me to positive outlets, Father.
—ZONA B. DAVIS

Praise Diary for May

1 _____

2 _____

3 _____

4 _____

5 _____

6 _____

7 _____

8 _____

9 _____

10 _____

11

12

13

14

15

16

17

18

19

20

21

22

23

24

25

26

27

28

29

30

31

June

*Blessed be the Lord, because he hath heard the voice
of my supplications.* —PSALM 28:6

Thank You, Lord, for quiet moments,
Little "sabbaths" in the day,
For the feeling of contentment
When I meditate and pray....

Thank You, Lord, for Your commandments,
Words to take me down life's roads,
Words of wisdom, words of guidance,
Words that lighten all my loads....

Thank You, Lord, for stars to reach for,
Plans and goals I'm dreaming of,
Thank You, Lord, for quiet moments
When I know Your peace and love!

—ALICE JOYCE DAVIDSON

PATTERN FOR A BLESSED LIFE
Blessed are the merciful: for they shall obtain mercy.
—MATTHEW 5:7

1

Mr. Clark once cheated my doctor father out of a considerable sum of money. Dad was not a vengeful kind of man but the injustice rankled and he couldn't put it out of his mind.

Then one night Mr. Clark was brought into the hospital emergency room, hemorrhaging critically. He looked up at my father and said, "I wouldn't blame you if you'd let me bleed to death, Doc."

My father's reply was, "What's your blood type?" It was the same as his. Without a moment's hesitation, Daddy donated his own blood. That act of mercy probably saved Mr. Clark's life but it also healed my father of the torment of unforgiveness. Later Daddy told me that he felt closer to God on that night then he had ever felt before.

If someone has wronged you, perform an act of mercy for him. God will heal you both.

I will devote this month, Lord, to healing old hurts, performing an act of kindness or mercy every day.
—MARILYN MORGAN HELLEBERG

2

. . . Except the Lord keep the city, the watchman waketh but in vain.
—PSALM 127:1

Some years ago an assignment from *Reader's Digest* took me to the little town of Taizé (pronounced *Tay-zay*) in southern France. There a community of monks, some Catholic, some Protestant, live together in simplicity and pray for Christian unity.

There was great spiritual power in that little Burgundian village, and I wondered how to put it into words. I needed a symbol of some kind, but couldn't seem to find one.

Then one evening at dusk as I wandered down a road, an old French peasant came along wearing farmer's boots and a black beret. We exchanged greetings, and since he seemed tolerant of my faltering French, I decided to ask him the question that was troubling me: What was the real meaning of Taizé?

He looked at me thoughtfully for a little while. Then he pointed to the sky.

"Up there," he said, "is God." He pointed downward. "Down here below are His people. Over there on one side, but not too far, are the Catholics. On the other side, but not too distant either, are the Protestants." He paused, his brown eyes watching me closely. "Now, if you draw a line up and down, and another line from side to side, what do you have?"

"You have a cross," I said slowly.

I remember how his weatherbeaten face broke into a smile. "Ah, *m'sieu*, that is Taizé!"

Lord, help me reach up to You — and out to my fellow man.
                                                            —ARTHUR GORDON

---

3   *Heaviness in the heart of man maketh it stoop: but a good word maketh it glad.*   —PROVERBS 12:25

In her television shows animal-trainer Barbara Woodhouse tells people that the way to a dog's heart is through verbal kindness. "They love to hear 'What a good dog,'" she reports. "All dogs like to be told they are beautiful."

Of course Miss Woodhouse is right but she doesn't need to stop with animals. All people, even those who seem to go out of their way to be unlovable, like to hear others say that they are good and beautiful.

There are only two rules for becoming an expert compliment-giver — first, that your praises be specific and second, that they be sincere. One cautionary note: Don't pay compliments unless you are prepared to receive them, because they are likely to follow.

Lord, help me to see the positive things in life, and give me the words to express my appreciation. —FRED BAUER

---

4   *... Make you perfect in every good work to do his will, working in you that which is well-pleasing in his sight...*
—HEBREWS 13:21

Did you waste the day or lose it?
   Was it well or sorely spent?
Did you leave a trail of kindness,
   or a scar of discontent?

As you close your eyes in slumber,
   do you think God will say:
"You have earned one more tomorrow
   by the work you did today"... ?

If I had to earn each tomorrow by the work I've done each day, I would have been a goner long ago. How good it is of God that He doesn't issue us another day *if only* we hand in a good report for the past one. But if it were so, I think I might give more attention to the needs of others; look more diligently for opportunities to serve; express love with greater compassion.

So why don't I do these things anyway, knowing that they would please God?

Jesus, help me to do the things I should do — every day.
—ZONA B. DAVIS

5   *For my thoughts are not your thoughts, neither are your
ways my ways, saith the Lord.*   —ISAIAH 55:8

He was a gifted boy and he had grown up to be a pagan.
His mother, a devout Christian, was brokenhearted.

In his adult years he decided to leave his home in North Africa
and travel to Italy to give further study to his profession, the
practice and teaching of rhetoric. His mother opposed the idea,
fearing that if they were separated her son would never be converted. She prayed with all her heart that God would not allow him
to drift out into the pagan world and thus sever his last tie with the
Christian faith. Despite her objections, he boarded a boat bound for
Italy. Her prayer denied, his mother lost hope for her wayward son.

When the young man arrived in Milan, it was suggested that he
study the widely known rhetorical skills of a man named Ambrose,
who happened to be the Bishop of Milan. So the young student
found himself, of all places, in the church, studying the form of
Ambrose's sermons. Slowly their content began to speak to him.
And there in Italy he was converted. His mother's prayers at long
last were answered.

We know him today as *St. Augustine.*

When God denies my prayer requests, perhaps I should remind
myself that I cannot see things from God's view. For sometimes
when He says "No," He has not finished. He simply has a better way
in mind for me.

Teach me, Father, to trust Your "No" answers, too.

            —SUE MONK KIDD

6 *And whosoever shall compel thee to go a mile, go with him twain.* —MATTHEW 5:41

Last year in our travels, Norman and I had the good fortune to spend the night in one of Washington, D.C.'s best hotels. The next morning, in chatting with the manager, I complimented him on the hotel's service, which had been noticeably efficient and warm.

"Thank you," he said. "We do make an effort. We even have a name for it among ourselves. We call it 'Plus One Service.'"

Then he explained that the staff had been instructed to add one additional courtesy to each duty they performed. For instance, if a guest requested his key at the desk in the evening, the clerk would not only reach for it, but ask if a wake-up call was desired. When the operator called in the morning, she would not only tell the visitor what time it was, but give a quick report of the weather. If the guest telephoned for breakfast, Room Service would ask if the guest wanted a newspaper as well; and when the tray arrived, in addition to the food, it held a tiny vase with a bright flower in it.

"Always thinking about that extra something keeps us on our toes," the manager said. "It not only makes for better service, but somehow or other I think it makes us better people. It's kind of a secret of successful living, isn't it?"

Yes, I thought to myself, *but it's not really a secret.* Upstairs in my hotel room, lying open on the bureau, was a Book (another facet of the hotel's thoughtful "extra something"). In it Jesus Christ makes His own recommendation for "Plus One Service." It's there in Matthew 5:41.

Jesus, today I'll try to add to my service: plus one...plus two...plus three... —RUTH STAFFORD PEALE

7 *Take heed that ye do not your alms before men, to be seen of them...* —MATTHEW 6:1

When a biographer was preparing a book on the life of the Duke of Wellington, his research provided him with ample data on the Duke's achievements. But the writer could find nothing to indicate what the man himself was like. Then he came across the Duke's checkbooks. And there the stubs, showing how the Duke had spent his money, gave him the answers he sought.

The checkbooks portrayed a man who, although very frugal, used his personal funds to help others who were going through bad times. Listed on the stubs were the names of old acquaintances who were in financial trouble as well as the Duke's entire command of soldiers when once their military pay did not arrive on time. A generous and compassionate man in his public life, the Duke was equally generous and compassionate in his private life.

I have just flipped through my checkbook, wondering what a biographer might learn from it. More important, how does God see me through the way in which I spend my money?

Have you studied your check stubs lately?

You said, Lord, that we were to give You the first tenth of everything. Guide my use of the rest. —DRUE DUKE

8 *For the word of God is quick, and powerful, and sharper than any two-edged sword...* —HEBREWS 4:12

My friend Linda was puzzled to see her six-year-old son, Mel, sitting with the Bible on his lap. He was running his finger over the open pages.

"Mel, what are you doing?" his mother asked.

Not looking up, he answered her: "Didn't you tell me that there was power in the Word of God and that it was available to anyone?"

"Yes," she said, becoming even more curious, "but you can't read."

"But there's power in the Word?" he questioned.

"Certainly, Mel. But you have to be able to read about it. And why are you turning the pages so fast?"

"Well, I need some power in my life in a hurry. I'm touching the words in the Bible and the power will have to go in my fingers and then into me. It has to. I believe it will."

Linda left her determined son to his "reading" of the Word. For almost an hour he sat there patiently turning page after page, feeling the hundreds and hundreds of words with his finger. Feeling and believing.

One night as I read my Bible, I too needed power in my life in a hurry. Remembering little Mel, I read one page while I allowed my fingers to *feel* the words on the opposite page. I smiled, knowing I was taking the Bible a little too literally. But then, having the childlike faith of little Mel once in a while reminds me to trust the power of the Word Who became flesh and dwelt among us.

Lord, when I read Your Word today, let me know Your presence and feel Your power. —MARION BOND WEST

---

9   *Let every one of us please his neighbour...* —ROMANS 15:2

The sun was setting as I parked the rented moving van in front of the apartment building. My wife and I were exhausted after the eight-hundred-mile drive to our new home. But now the really hard job began — unloading the truck.

When we raised the rear door of the van, a set of golf clubs tumbled to our feet and golf balls scattered wildly all over the road. I sank to the curb, not knowing whether to laugh or cry.

"Hey, do you need some help?" a voice called from a passing car.

"Well, I sure wouldn't turn it down."

"Okay, let me take my car home — it's just around the corner. Maybe some of the neighbors can come back with me."

Five minutes later six young men were cheerfully helping us move our belongings into our new apartment. Within half an hour the big truck was empty.

"I'd offer you some lemonade or cookies or something, but —" I began, almost apologetically.

"Wouldn't think of it," one of the young men interrupted. "Do just one thing though. If you see someone else moving in down the line, you help him."

Lynn and I watched our six Good Samaritans walk off down the road toward home.

I sighed, "Do unto others..."

"...is what faith really means," Lynn concluded. And the following week when a rented moving van rolled up to an adjacent building, not six but seven neighborly hands were there to help unload.

Thank You, Father, for hands that work in the service of love.
—JEFF JAPINGA

---

10   *My tongue shall speak of thy word....*   —PSALM 119:172

"It all started with Aunt Susan," a friend told me. "You know, she's eighty-seven now and her eyesight is failing. I was just wishing I had the time to run over there and read one of these wonderful *Guideposts* devotionals to her. *Then*, I thought to myself, *Why not call her on the phone?* I did, and she listened while I read to her for a few minutes.

"'Well,' said Aunt Susan, 'that must have been written especially for me.' So I began to call her every day and read a devotional to her. Now she says that it helps her through the day. And I have begun to read to several shut-ins. It makes life's problems easier to deal with, they tell me. But," she smiled, "it helps me the most of all."

Is there someone who could be helped with a *Daily Guideposts* phone call from you?

Today, God, I will set aside five minutes to change a friend's day.
—ZONA B. DAVIS

---

11 *For whether we live, we live unto the Lord; and whether we die, we die unto the Lord: whether we live therefore, or die, we are the Lord's.* —ROMANS 14:8

Mother died during the night and I went to the hospital to pick up her suitcase. While I was at the nurses' station, the head nurse told me that a Mr. Lewis, who had been operated on early that morning, wanted to see me. She pointed out his room to me.

"If he's asleep," she said, "wake him up. He desperately wants to talk to you."

He was asleep, a thin man in his late sixties with a post-surgery pallor. "Mr. Lewis?" I whispered, highly reluctant to awaken a man barely five hours out of surgery.

He awoke instantly and smiled when he saw me standing there.

"I had heart surgery today," he said in a soft voice. "And last night I was afraid of dying. Restless, I got up and walked around. I saw a light on in your mother's room and when I looked in, she invited me to enter. For fully twenty minutes she cheered me up.

"'Don't worry,' she reassured me. 'You look like a tough old coot!' For the first time in months, I laughed. Then after my surgery today, I heard that she...." Mr. Lewis paused, his hands fluttering over his bed covers like aimless sparrows.

"I just wanted to tell you how sorry I am...and how very grateful I am...to have known her."

"And Mom —" I asked. "Did she laugh too?"

"Yes," he replied. "We both had a good laugh."

"Well, then, Mr. Lewis," I said, "I think she was grateful to you too."

Father, teach us not to hold to our lives with tenacity but, like Mother, with generosity toward others. —JAMES McDERMOTT

---

12   *Give us this day our daily bread.*   —MATTHEW 6:11

When I was a little girl, my grandmother went to the phone each morning and ordered her groceries. Soon afterward the grocer's truck delivered the order for the day.

Today when I go to the grocery store, it's to buy for a whole week. Sometimes two. I tend to be nervous when my well-stocked pantry runs low.

The Israelites knew the feeling. When food ran out in the desert, they yearned for the well-stocked pantries of Egypt. But God gave them manna one day at a time. *Daily* bread.

Sometimes when problems drain me and I doubt that my supply of faith will hold out, I think of God's provision of manna to the Israelites.

Do you suppose that's why God chooses to give us *daily* bread — so that we may be *daily* aware of Him?

Dear Lord, teach us to pray for our daily bread, with trust in You for our tomorrows. —PATRICIA HOUCK SPRINKLE

13 *And he said, Lay not thine hand upon the lad, neither do thou any thing unto him: for now I know that thou fearest God, seeing thou hast not withheld thy son, thine only son from me.* —GENESIS 22:12

The story is told of a man who had the highest mountain in the country right outisde his back door. Ever since childhood he had dreamed of climbing it and finally, at the age of forty-seven, he did. He almost reached the top, whereupon he became so excited that he threw up his arms in joy and thereby lost his balance. As he was tumbling down the side of the mountain, he grabbed onto a small tree growing out of the cliff and clung to it.

Looking up, he shouted, "Is anybody there?" A firm voice responded immediately. "Yes, Henry. This is the Lord. Now if you want to be helped out of your predicament, just follow these simple directions. First, let go of the branch."

There was a long pause.

"Is anybody *else* there?"

A preposterous story? Yes, but it made me stop to consider my own faith. How do I respond to God's commands? Do I try, like the mountain-climber, to find a way that seems better to me? Or am I able to obey God with utter confidence and follow His lead?

I want to obey — to let go of the branch — to trust....

Lord, what now? I await Your holy command. —DORIS HAASE

14 *But grow in grace, and in the knowledge of our Lord and Saviour Jesus Christ.* —II PETER 3:18

A real, live American flag blossomed on the front lawn at the home of Mr. and Mrs. Edward Torbeck in Altamont, Illinois.

Measuring ten feet by twelve feet, each of its thirteen stripes bore
the name of one of the thirteen colonies and the date upon which
the colony had joined the union. Underneath the flag were the
words, "God Bless America," and a colorful border of growing plants
completed the unusual scene.

One Sunday afternoon we took guests to see the remarkable and
beautiful work and when we arrived, we found that many others
were already there, admiring the lovely creation. Among them was
a small boy with his parents.

"Did that flag just grow like that?" he asked.

"Oh, no," his father explained. "Mr. Torbeck planted it — and
then God made it grow."

How true. Just like our nation. Our founding fathers planted it —
and we must never forget that it is God who blessed it and helped it
to grow.

*Heavenly Father, bless the seeds of the good will we sow today.
Help them to blossom tomorrow.*　　　　　—ZONA B. DAVIS

JOURNEY OF FAITH

15 Your traveling companion is SAMUEL
... *who listened as he walked.*　　　—I SAMUEL 1-16

He was a circuit judge, tramping endlessly between district seats: from Bethel to Gilgal to Mizpah, then back to his wife
and children in Ramah.

Samuel's route would have taken him regularly by the ruins of
Shiloh: that heap of rubble there had been the temple where the
sacred lamp burned before the Ark. There was the gate — the only
part of the wall still intact — where the old priest Eli used to sit. It

was here that Samuel's astonishing career began — in Shiloh early one morning.

He hears a voice call to him in the cold predawn, jumps from his mat on the floor and *runs* to respond. The voice calling to Samuel is God's. But it sounds no different from human voices, and he runs to the only human being nearby — the old priest Eli.

But Eli has not called. Samuel returns to his pallet and the voice calls again. Once more Samuel goes to see what Eli wants; once more he is told to go back to sleep. Still a third time the urgent voice summons him; it never enters Samuel's head that this could be a word from God.

To me, this is an immensely reassuring story. I tend to imagine that spiritual giants have an easier time discerning God' voice than I do. But they are as hindered by their preconceptions — until corrected — as we are. If we do not — not *really* — expect God to speak, we will miss Him when He does.

God called Samuel by name. In the Bible, a person's name stands for his uniqueness, the essential qualities that make him himself. God's word for each instant in time, always has a name attached. It is not only *logos* — true for all time and people — but *rhema*, true today for you in particular. It comes in terms of what interests, distresses, frightens or excites you at that moment; it will "have your name on it." Listen for His *rhema* in the voice that is closest, clearest, most natural.

To believe that God speaks, and speaks to you personally, is still not the whole story. When Samuel appeared a third time at Eli's bedside, insisting that someone had called his name, he realized that the lad was hearing God.

"If it happens again," he told him, "reply, 'Your servant is listening!'" Not "Your curious bystander," or "Your scholarly investigator." Your *servant*, ready and waiting to do Your will — as soon as he knows what it is! Presenting ourselves to God as servants, we offer our obedience, not opinions or best judgment. And when we engage to carry out God's design, He will unfold it for us.

The message which followed pinned Samuel to his mat. Could he be hearing right? Was he really to tell his venerable and beloved master Eli that he and his entire family were going to be destroyed by God? No wonder Samuel stayed put the rest of the night. *Samuel was afraid to tell the vision to Eli.* But it is Eli who teaches Samuel: *however perilous the assignment God gives us, it is far more dangerous not to fulfill it.*

Samuel must have remembered that lesson when later he was instructed by God to go to King Saul and inform him that God was taking the kingdom of Israel out of his hands. You see, he had given unwelcome news to Eli on the day he *first* heard God's voice.

> *Whatever the task to which I'm called this hour, this day, this month, God, I will in faithfulness obey when You first call me.*

—ELIZABETH SHERRILL

---

16 *The rich and the poor meet together: the Lord is the maker of them all.* —PROVERBS 22:2

Recently I attended a luncheon given in the home of a friend. During the meal one of the guests mentioned a woman who had just lost a teenaged son.

"She needs the comfort of God's word," said the guest, "but I don't believe that there's even one Bible in her home."

Our hostess left the table and soon returned with some money in an envelope. "It sounds like a good place to use my 'inasmuch' fund,'" she said, handing the envelope to the guest. "Please buy a Bible for that family."

When we asked her what an "inasmuch fund" was, she replied, "Do you remember the verse in Matthew —'Inasmuch as ye have done it unto one of the least of these…'? Well, from time to time I put aside a little extra money just so I'll have it handy to give when I hear of someone with a special need. I can't take credit for the idea — I heard about it from someone else. But I've found that it really helps at the most unexpected times." She smiled and added, "Maybe it helps me most of all."

Because of my friend, I now have an "inasmuch fund" too. And it's an active account.

Thank You, Father, for reminding me that I am my brother's keeper. —MADGE HARRAH

---

17 *I will instruct thee and teach thee in the way which thou shalt go: I will guide thee with mine eye.* —PSALM 32:8

When I first came to New York looking for a job, I attended Marble Collegiate Church and one Sunday I heard Norman Vincent Peale deliver perhaps the greatest sermon I had ever heard. Discouraged after many weeks of unproductive interviews and about to give up on a long-held dream, I was particularly receptive to Dr. Peale's challenging words.

"The Lord expects you to make the most of the talents He has given you," Dr. Peale preached. "What He wants you to do is to take your gifts, develop them and attack life with wholehearted enthusiasm. If you do, you cannot help but succeed. So go out and give life your best. *Be Somebody*."

His words could not have come at a better time for me. I needed to hear them like a drowning person needs air, and they helped me through an uncertain time. And I *did* find the job I wanted.

If you have a dream that is lying fallow, one that you cannot seem to get off the ground, don't turn in your wings until you have exhausted every possible avenue that might lead to your success. Often many have given up just one step, one day, one phone call, one letter, too soon. Pray about your heart's sincere desire. Ask for and follow God's guidance. If you put yourself in the center of His will, you cannot fail and you are sure to *Be Somebody* in the sight of the One Who counts most.

Show me Your plan for my life, Lord, and give me the courage to follow it. —FRED BAUER

---

18 *... Thou shalt love the Lord thy God with all thy heart, and with all thy soul, and with all thy mind.*

—MATTHEW 22:37

"Hey, I like you!"

My seven-year-old nephew Doug was speaking to Ronnie, a youngster whose family had recently moved into the house next to ours. I was delighted. There weren't many children of Doug's age in our neighborhood and I was hoping that he and Ronnie would get along well. Ronnie's parents seemed like nice people — a little standoffish though.

Then as I watched Doug and Ronnie play together, I wondered. Maybe it wan't Ronnie's parents who were standoffish after all.

I felt a little foolish when I knocked on their door a short time later. "Sue, uh, there's something I'd like to tell you," I said when Ronnie's mother appeared.

I hadn't planned what I would say and the words tumbled out all at once: "I just wanted to tell you — *Sue, I like you!* I'm glad to have you for a neighbor."

"Why thank you," she said with a warm smile. "I've been wanting to say the same thing to you but I didn't quite know how to."

It was then that I decided that if I like someone, I'm going to say so. Right to the person's face. Childish? Maybe. And maybe that's a nice way to be.

Lord, I like You! —PHYLLIS HOBE

19 *But we have the mind of Christ.* —I CORINTHIANS 2:16

When I went with my son John to buy a necktie for his dad for Father's Day, there were several racks loaded with ties. I flipped through them quickly and instinctively, saying, "No, he wouldn't like that one. Not that one. No. Ah! Here's one he'd like!"

John looked at me in astonishment. "How did you know which one he'd like?"

I was hard pressed to answer except to say, "I guess I just kind of put on *Dad's* mind and saw with *his* eyes as I looked at the ties." (By the way, Rex loved the tie.)

Perhaps the ability to discern the will of God comes in the same way. People who spend time with the Lord daily gradually develop an inner sense of His will. Then when decisions need to be made, they are able to make them easily. Intuitively, they know what He would have them do in each situation. As in marriage, it's the *daily companionship* that creates the kind of knowing intimacy. It's a goal I want to strive toward. How about you?

Lord, live with me and in me, that I may see.
—MARILYN MORGAN HELLEBERG

20 *...As newborn babes, desire the sincere milk of the word, that ye may grow thereby...* —I PETER 2:2

"Five, four, three, two, one...." A huge roar went up from the crowd. We had won the conference basketball championship in the final game of the regular season. Now we were looking forward to having a week off before the first round of the state tournament.

Down in the locker room Coach gathered us together. "Congrat-

178

ulations," he said. "We did it! Practice is scheduled for Monday morning before school. Conditioning and drills."

A loud groan went up as Coach turned and walked away. I followed him into his office.

"I'm not starting a mutiny or anything," I said, "but why, with a whole week before our next game, and with a team we've beaten twice, do we need more conditioning practice? How will running laps and lifting weights make a difference now?"

"Probably won't," Coach answered.

"So why the practice then?"

"I saw you in church this week, right?" Coach said. "And in youth group you said you prayed and had devotions daily. Why daily?"

"Well, because I'm a Christian. And that's how you strengthen your faith — through prayer, devotions, church, youth group.... "

"Strengthen your faith?" Coach queried. "But why? You seem to be getting along quite well these days."

Suddenly I smiled at him. I understood. Coach wanted us to practice so we would increase our skills even though the next test might not demand all our abilities. But should the team need it, we would have a reserve from which we could draw, just as I might need a stronger faith to draw on in coping with unexpected difficulties.

That night before devotions, I turned the floodlights on our driveway and practiced free throws for half an hour. Someday....

Help me never to be content with the status quo, Father.

—JEFF JAPINGA

---

21 *... Is a candle brought to be put under a bushel, or under a bed? and not to be set on a candlestick?* —MARK 4:21

I have a forty-year-old, sixteen-foot wooden sloop that gives me a lot of pleasure. Her sails are many times mended, her rigging is haphazard, and she's a "leaker." Yet when the wind is fair, she sails like a dream.

Last summer I ran across one just like her in an out-of-the-way boathouse. This one had been built at about the same time as mine, but she had never been launched. The little boat was beautiful — her decks gleamed, her unstepped mast and rigging were pristine. But as I marveled at her perfection, I felt a twinge of sadness. She had never known the joy of a single breeze, she had never experienced the purpose for which she had been built.

Suddenly I loved my old "leaker" even more. I could picture her tugging at her mooring, eager to sail. Battered and bruised, she had a glorious history.

It made me think. Sometimes when I'm a bit too cautious with myself, I'm like that pristine sloop. I fend off a friend who needs help with moving a couch (I have a back problem); I can't help dislodge a neighbor's car (it's snowing); I can't get to the polls (it's raining)....

Sure I'll save myself some wear and tear — just as that little sloop that was never put to the test — but I'll also miss out on the countless small joys of everyday living, the joys that make me feel alive and useful.

Lord, help me to remember that as long as I rush to greet it, it's a glorious life.   —JAMES McDERMOTT

---

22 *... And to love his neighbour as himself, is more than all whole burnt-offerings and sacrifices.*   —MARK 12:33

After the Great Fire of London in 1666, the talented architect, Sir Christopher Wren, redesigned most of the churches that had been destroyed. Saint Paul's Cathedral is perhaps the most famous of all. The largest cathedral of the Church of England, it is a magnificent work of architecture that took thirty-five years to build — a towering structure of carvings, columns, arches and spires.

Sir Christopher Wren is buried inside the Cathedral, beneath a plain and simple slab. Barely noticeable and void of trappings, his tomb bears only this inscription: "If you seek his monument, look around you."

Perhaps this is an appropriate epitaph for my life and yours. For most of us our only monument will be the deeds that we undertake here on earth. Look around you — at what you are doing for loved ones, for your neighbors, for your community.

Keep me busy, God, in building the only true and lasting monuments on earth — works of love. —SUE MONK KIDD

---

23 *Therefore all things whatsoever ye would that men should do to you, do ye even so to them...*
—MATTHEW 7:12

Every day I race through New York City's Pennsylvania Station, fighting my way through crowds of people, hoping to catch my commuter train before it leaves. Usually I do.

One evening I passed two men who were struggling with some suitcases and I couldn't help but overhear their animated conversation.

"But I don't need your help," the first man was saying. "I have two suitcases and two strong arms. Why do *you* have to carry one of *my* suitcases?"

"Because," the second man replied, "then you'll have a free hand in case someone *else* needs help."

I laughed to myself at the corny logic — after all, why couldn't the second man just as easily help someone else? But then I thought about it on the train. It began to make sense. We can't help others if our hands are full. But if we allow another to help us, we will always have a free hand with which to help someone else. And if we help someone else, that person will have a free hand, and so on.

I had been having trouble with my car and pride had prevented me from consulting one of my neighbors who is a mechanic. *But if I let him help me,* I thought as the train sped along, *I'll have a free "hand."*

When I got home, I picked up the phone. "Joe, I've got a problem.... "

I think there's no better day than today, Father, to begin some chain reactions.
—JEFF JAPINGA

---

24 My flesh and my heart faileth: but God is the strength of my heart.... —PSALM 73:26

On the morning that I was to appear on a television talk show, I awakened in my hotel room with an acute case of the flu. The hotel maid, much concerned, asked if she could pray for me. She knelt by my bed and in a torrent of words, like a stream flowing over stones, she prayed. Then she arose. "You can get up now," she announced confidently.

I barricaded myself in the bathroom, hoping that she would leave, but when I emerged, there she was, waiting to help me dress. "I can't..." I muttered, still feeling weak.

"*God* is able," she said firmly.

Fully dressed now, I staggered out the door to seek refuge in my mother's suite down the hall. The woman followed part way and called after me, "*God* is able!"

Flustered, I told Mother what had happened. "So said John the Baptist..." she said.

"But she believes He can raise *me* up..." I protested.

"*Don't you?*" asked my mother.

I did the show. And now — whenever something I must do is threatened by my weakness — I always remember: "*God* is able!"

Thank You, Father, for strengthening the weak and making firm the faltering. —ELAINE ST. JOHNS

---

25 *O Lord... Thou compassest my path... and art acquainted with all my ways.* —PSALM 139:1,3

After twenty-four years of marriage, Jerry and I decided to renew our marriage vows. On the day of the ceremony I reminisced about our life together.

Shortly after our wedding we discovered that we had vast differences. Jerry liked to eat. I didn't like to cook. He's a born mathematician. I can't balance the checkbook.... Why, we didn't even know each other then, although we had been acquainted for six years! Those feelings we had for one another — were they truly love? How can you "love" someone about whom you know only the good things?

But we clung to each other when one of the babies almost died. We comforted each other when one of our teenagers went through a rebellious period — and we rejoiced together when that child "came home" again. And we argued and then learned to say "I'm sorry" and "Forgive me."

Later, as we set out to "go get married," I asked, "Do you remember when we used to talk for five hours without stopping?"

Jerry nodded.

"You like silence, don't you?"

He nodded again.

"I'm learning to be quiet."

"Wonderful." He leaned over and gave me a kiss and held my hand as we drove off. We rode along in a comfortable silence.

I was deeply content. Learning to love someone — whether it be a spouse, a child, a friend, or even God — means that you allow yourself to be known, truly known, to the other. And the reward is in the knowing that you are loved, truly loved, just for being yourself!

Thank You for knowing me, Father, and for loving me.
—MARION BOND WEST

---

26 *… This people draweth nigh unto me with their mouth, and honoureth me with their lips; but their heart is far from me.* —MATTHEW 15:8

Prior to the pastor's message at church one evening, the song leader directed us in the singing of several choruses. Then he asked us to "turn to page three hundred and sixty-three."

After the leafing of pages ceased and he was sure that everyone had found the announced number in the hymnals, he asked, "Now, can anyone tell me the name of the previous song — the one we just finished singing?"

None of us could remember!

I don't know about the rest of the choir but I was startled — and humiliated — to realize that I had merely been reciting empty words because my mind had been on other matters.

It taught me a lesson. Today when I go to church, I give God my *whole* attention — whether I'm singing, praying or praising Him.

Lord, when I sing Your praises with my voice, my heart will accompany my words. —ISABEL CHAMP

27 *Come ye yourselves apart... and rest a while.* —MARK 6:31

The only difference between the words, *a part* and *apart*, is a single space, and yet they seem to be opposite in meaning. *Apart* speaks of separation, while being *a part* of something indicates unity. Can there be a connection between the two?

I think Jesus advised His disciples to "Come ye yourselves *apart*... and rest a while" in order that they might become aware, on a deep level, that they really were *a part* of all that is.

The difference is but a single space. And yet it's only when I keep that space, when I go *apart* daily to be alone with God, that I can effectively serve as *a part* of the Body of Christ.

"Come ye yourselves apart... and rest a while." His words are for you and me today.

Thank You, Jesus, for my time apart with You; that I can be a part of You. —MARILYN MORGAN HELLEBERG

---

28 *It is good that a man should both hope and quietly wait...* —LAMENTATIONS 3:26

Why won't he look at me?

For a month I had been working as a volunteer at a home for retarded children, and Jim — one of the children assigned to me — wasn't responding at all. Each time I visited, he simply stared at the television.

I tried everything. I showed him brightly colored balls, urged him to jump rope, offered him a bicycle to ride — but he only turned away. I worried incessantly about him... he was so alone, so friendless.

JUNE 1983

Then one day I brought my dog Trooper to work with me. Jim's eyes brightened the moment he saw the dog. Trooper sniffed all around Jim's room, the way dogs will, and once acquainted with his surroundings, he curled up at Jim's feet in front of the television set.

I left them together and went on to do other things.

When I returned an hour later, Trooper was peacefully curled up in Jim's lap, lying there quietly as Jim gently patted his head and whispered into his ear. They were friends!

Now why haven't I been able to draw some of that love from Jim? I asked myself. Because I had tried to force my friendship on him rather than simply let him be, as Trooper did, until he reached for me.

Father, teach me to be still that I can receive love as well as give it.
—PHYLLIS HOBE

---

29 *Commit thy works unto the Lord, and thy thoughts shall be established.* —PROVERBS 16:3

A friend told me a little story about a vacation she and her family spent at the beach.

One morning she arose very early, hoping to sneak away quietly for a solitary walk along the shore. Suddenly she heard her six-year-old's voice, "Wait, Mom! I'll go with you."

She was somewhat irritated — now her plan for a few moments of solitude was spoiled. But she followed her son as he ran ahead. He brought her a beautiful sand dollar. He made her laugh with delight at the sandpipers darting in and out with the tide. He showed her a little hole in the sand and dug up a clam. Soon, she told me, she was happy for his company — through his eyes she had seen special and wonderful things that she would have missed otherwise.

I suppose that when our plans are changed, it is natural for us to feel disturbed. At first Simon Peter and Andrew must have felt that way. They wanted to get on with their fishing when Jesus interrupted them. At first they didn't understand but then not only did they accept the new turn of events, they dropped everything and started out on an astounding adventure that changed the course of their lives.

Today if your plans are "interrupted" — will you be ready for the *adventure?*

When I keep my eyes on You, Lord, my disappointments turn to joy.   —DORIS HAASE

---

30 *He giveth power to the faint; and to them that have no might he increaseth strength.*   —ISAIAH 40:29

Wherever I went I seemed to meet her — at the supermarket, at the post office, at the church circle. On top of that, Hazel also lived next door to us. I was slightly annoyed by all this proximity.

In addition, her big dog was abrasive. When Hazel was at home, Blacky ran loose (always into my yard). When she wasn't at home, Blacky's continual barking just about drove me wild.

One morning at breakfast I told the family of my bout with what I termed "Hazelitis" — it was after a sleepless night of tossing and turning. "The Bible says that I'm to love my neighbor as myself. If it were just some other neighbor, I wouldn't be having such a hard time. *What* can I do?"

My husband answered, "You must give the problem to the Lord."

"I've tried to do that but I can't seem to let go," I told him.

At about that time, my son — who has always seemed more serene than most twenty-year-olds — said, "Mom, I've discovered that sometimes even the 'letting go' must be given to God."

JUNE 1983

Ah...I saw anew what I must do. And silently, I thanked God for giving me such a wise son!

Father, You lift my burdens. You always do for me those things that I cannot do for myself. —ISABEL CHAMP

Praise Diary for June

1
_____

2
_____

3
_____

4
_____

5
_____

6

7

8

9

10

11

12

13

14

15

16

17

18

JUNE 1983

19

20

21

22

23

24

25

26

27

28

29

30

July

I will hear what God the Lord will speak: for he will speak peace unto his people... —PSALM 85:8

You gave us
  messages of peace
    and we ignored them.
You sent us
  messengers of peace
    and we deplored them.

Now we come before You, Lord....

Help me take
  one small step
    toward understanding others.
Help me, Lord,
  to realize
    that all men are my brothers!

—ALICE JOYCE DAVIDSON

PATTERN FOR A BLESSED LIFE
Blessed are the pure in heart: for they shall see God.
—MATTHEW 5:8

1

Since everyone had told me beforehand that our speaker was a beautiful person, I was surprised to see that she was really quite plain, not especially attractive at all.

She called our attention to John 1:9: "That was the true Light, which lighteth every man that cometh into the world," and reminded us that the light of Christ is available to each of us. Then she said that every time she feels worried, or tempted, or depressed, she closes her eyes and visualizes the face of Jesus until she can *feel* His love radiating within her.

As she continued to speak, I saw a lovely golden glow envelop her and by the time her talk was finished, my first impression of her was gone. She *was* beautiful.... and I think I know her "beauty secret!"

Lord, help me to keep my heart centered in You through each day in July so that Your beauty may shine through me.

—MARILYN MORGAN HELLEBERG

2

...The substance of a diligent man is precious.
—PROVERBS 12:27

The other day I went to buy a surf-casting reel for one of our daughters who has suddenly become an enthusiastic — if inexperienced — angler. The salesman showed me various spinning reels, including the kind where the line slides off the end of the spool so easily and automatically that even a beginner can look like an expert.

192

"Where are the old conventional reels?" I asked him. "The kind where you have to apply just the right amount of thumb pressure or risk a dreadful backlash?"

"I have one or two," he said, "but there's not much demand for them any more. Takes too much patience and skill to handle them. People don't want to bother."

I thought about that for a minute. "Give me one of the old type," I said. "I'll exchange it if I change my mind."

When I presented the reel to my daughter, I explained that it could be exchanged for a spinning reel should she prefer that.

"Does this kind catch more fish?" she asked.

"No," I said.

"Does it get more distance?"

"Not really."

"What's the advantage then?"

"It requires some skill."

"Oh!" She looked thoughtful; then she smiled. "In that case, I'll keep it."

I smiled too.

Lord, when life seems to be too easy, help me to seek the challenging way, please. —ARTHUR GORDON

---

3   *Finally, brethren, pray for us...* —II THESSALONIANS 3:1

If you drive north along the California coast in Big Sur country, you will come upon a sign on your right that says something like this:

We are contemplative monks. If you are hungry, if you are ill, if you are troubled, if you are lost, please come in and

193

let us try to help you. Otherwise, dear friend, please leave
us to our prayers, all of which are for you.

As often as I have seen that sign, the words always strike me
afresh and set my mind at ease. There is a certain comfort in
knowing that others are praying for me. And then I am stirred to
add a few prayers of my own.

Prayer: A gift that ever rewards... the giver and the receiver.

Lord, help me to express my concern for others, even strangers.
—GLENN KITTLER

---

4 *O earth, earth, earth, hear the word of the Lord.*
—JEREMIAH 22:29

The Fourth of July... Independence Day... the glorious
beginning of our beloved country. Have you ever tried thinking of it
as Dependence Day too? The men and women who founded our
nation did. Let me give you an idea of what I mean:

· When the Pilgrims stood on the deck of the *Mayflower* in 1620,
they prepared the first written constitution of our land. Their
Mayflower Compact opened with these words: "In the name of
God, Amen," and then went on to state that the hazardous voyage
to the New World had been "undertaken for the glory of God." And
they signed the document "solemnly and mutually in the presence
of God."

· The farsighted men who gathered in Philadelphia in 1776 signed
a proclamation that read in part: "...all men are endowed by their
Creator with certain inalienable rights...."

· The Great Seal of the United States depicts the Eye of God
above a pyramid.

· Our national anthem ends with these words: "...and this be our
motto — In God is our trust."

· And the coins in your pocket — take one out and examine it. Look at that strong, impressive word, "Liberty." Now look at the four words that are always nearby — "In God We Trust."

On this day I pray that you and I and all of those who follow us will continue to celebrate the Fourth of July independently dependent upon Him!

O Father, strengthen us, that Your Word may be heard across the land. —NORMAN VINCENT PEALE

---

5 *...And where I am, there shall also my servant be...*
—JOHN 12:26

Whenever I face a particularly difficult or unpleasant task and my motivation level is hovering near empty, I try to remind myself of a little story that I heard years ago.

An American tourist was walking down a street in India when she came upon a young missionary nurse who was washing the legs and feet of an old man who had leprosy. The tourist was repelled by the sight.

"I wouldn't do that for a million dollars!" she exclaimed.

The young nurse looked up at her and smiled. "Neither would I," she said. "But I *would* do it for Christ."

For Christ. That is the only motivation for any task we ever face. Somehow, when we perform our earthly chores in His name, they are not chores but acts of love. If you face an especially hard or unpleasant job today, why not try to do it for Christ?

Help me to become a servant just for You, Jesus.
—SUE MONK KIDD

6   *Finally, be ye all of one mind, having compassion one of another, love as brethren, be pitiful, be courteous: not rendering evil for evil, or railing for railing: but contrariwise blessing; knowing that ye are thereunto called, that ye should inherit a blessing.* —I PETER 3:8,9

The middle-aged woman had experienced a drinking problem for years. None of us paid much attention to her; in fact, we were careful to avoid her. Then one day my wise friend Angie invited her to join our small prayer group that met once a week.

"Will you come?" Angie asked her.

The woman hesitated. "But I can't come to a God-meeting smelling...like...like...bourbon. What would the other ladies think?"

Angie smiled and replied, "Oh, we all smell of something. One of us has a problem with gossip. Another criticizes her husband. And another has a problem with unforgiveness. God knows how we all 'smell,' but He still loves us. Won't you come?"

The stunned woman understood. She began to laugh even while crying a little. "Yes, oh, yes, I'll come. Thank you. Thank you."

True, we were uncomfortable at first. But the more we opened ourselves to our new member, the more we came to love her. Oh, she still has some tough problems to overcome. I guess she's a lot like the rest of us.

No one is exempt from Your forgiveness, Heavenly Father, not even the self-righteous. Help us love one another.

—MARION BOND WEST

7   *. . . Walk worthy of the vocation wherewith ye are called.*
                                         —EPHESIANS 4:1

Recently I traced my ancestral roots and I learned that I was descended from one of the signers of the Declaration of Independence. That little bit of information made me feel proud. And secretly I gloated over finding such an illustrious ancestor in my background.

Then in a history book, I came across a reply Abraham Lincoln gave when asked about the identity of his grandfather.

"I don't know who my grandfather was," the great man said quietly. "I am more concerned to know what his grandson will be."

Make this my concern, Jesus: to be all You've created me to be.
                                         —DRUE DUKE

---

8   *Beloved, follow not that which is evil, but that which is good.*
                                         —III JOHN 1:11

One summer my godson David and I were driving high in the Rocky Mountains when we came to a sign that read, "Continental Divide."

"The great watershed," David said to me. "From here the waters flow toward either the Atlantic or the Pacific."

Watershed, I said to myself, and at that moment I recalled my grandmother's favorite expression, "Watershed Moments."

"In a split second you can often decide which way things are going to go," Gran would explain, "to the good or to the bad."

An example of a Watershed Moment? Say you're waiting for someone who's late, your wife maybe, and she well knows that you have plans for dinner and an evening on the town, but her tardiness is throwing a shoe in the machinery. You're annoyed. Even angry. Then she comes into sight — that's the Watershed Moment.

Will you welcome her with a blast because she's late? Or will you tell her how glad you are to see her? What you decide in that one moment, that Watershed Moment, could set the tone for the whole evening.

Every morning we awake to a Watershed Moment. With a full day awaiting us, we can decide which way things are going to go. We can choose to fill our day with faith, thanking and praising God for all that comes our way. Or we can choose to cling to worry, anxiously questioning every little thing, only to be weighed down by fear and doubt. *This* very moment could be your Watershed Moment. Which way will you flow?

Toward You, O Lord.   —VAN VARNER

---

9   *That the trial of your faith, being much more precious than of gold that perisheth, though it be tried with fire, might be found unto praise and honour and glory at the appearing of Jesus Christ...*   —I PETER 1:7

Last summer my youngsters had their first look at the amazing redwoods in California's Sequoia National Park. While most people are impressed by the size of the trees (over two hundred and fifty feet tall and thirty-six feet in diameter) and their age (estimated to be up to thirty-seven hundred years), my twelve-year-old Daniel thought the trees' fire resistance (attributable to a unique type of spongy bark) was most fascinating.

Our guide pointed out trees that had been either decapitated by lightning or ravaged at their bases by raging forest fires. In each case the trees had survived, fed by a root system that nourished them through skeleton bases. Daniel was awestruck. And so was I — but for another reason.

The trees reminded me of some Christians I have known who possess a Sequoia-like faith. They have been through the fires of adversity, suffered scars that would have destroyed lesser souls, known hardships that tested them to their very marrow. But because they were rooted in God's love, they have not only weathered their trials but continued to grow in spiritual strength.

Few things offer greater testimony to the sustaining grace of our Heavenly Father than do the victories of those people who have survived life's vicissitudes by placing their full trust in Him. They stand out among others like gigantic redwoods — fire-scarred, yes, but unbowed.

Lord, let my life be a witness to faith that is rooted in You, enabling me to withstand life's hardships and trials. —FRED BAUER

10 *...I have learned, in whatsoever state I am, therewith to be content.* —PHILIPPIANS 4:11

I first met Ruth one Sunday evening when I volunteered to take her to her shelter-care home after church services. The home was adjacent to a busy highway and I asked her, "Does the noise of the traffic bother you?"

"Oh, no," she said quickly. "I like living by the highway and watching the people pass by. I like to wonder where they came from and I try to imagine where they're going. I thank God that He gave me plenty of imagination."

Later Ruth was moved to another room where a wing of the building cut off her view of everything but an enormous, spreading tree. "Maybe you should ask for a different room," I suggested.

"Oh, no," she said, "I like this one. That big old tree has many stories to tell me...about storms that it has weathered, and lightning and cold snows and singing birds and frisky squirrels. I do thank God for the gift of imagination!"

Then Ruth was transferred to another shelter-care home in town. "You've lost your big tree," I sympathized.

"Oh, this is fine," she told me. "I can watch the children playing outdoors...it brings back such wonderful memories. Also, there's a senior-citizens center only two blocks away and I often go over there to visit friends and enjoy a cup of tea."

"Well, let's hope you won't have to move again," I told her with a sigh.

"Oh, that's all right — Jesus always moves with me," she smiled, her blue eyes shining. "He brings me my *imagination.*"

Father, wherever I may be, I look for signs of You — and I am content.
—ZONA B. DAVIS

---

11 *And the Lord spake...as a man speaketh unto his friend.*
—EXODUS 33:11

Macy and Ree were playing "business office" in kindergarten. Macy was "taking dictation" from her friend — mostly orders for chocolate bars to fill all the shelves of the bookcases.

"Now," said Ree in her most businesslike voice, "we'll write a letter to God."

Macy's curls bobbed in approval. "What shall we order?"

"Oh, let's not order anything today. Let's just talk to Him."

I think the Lord would truly appreciate such a letter. What a joy it must be to Him to have His children come to Him ordering nothing, but saying instead:

Dear Lord, there is nothing I need today. I've come only to talk.
—JUNE MASTERS BACHER

12

And whither I go ye know, and the way ye know.

—JOHN 14:4

Sir Robert Baden-Powell, founder of the Boy Scouts of England, once told my grandmother, Juliette Low, founder of the Girl Scouts of America, that every organization should have a motto or slogan that reflected the ideals behind it. For scouting he thought that a good motto might be the South African word *ipesi*, or *whither*, meaning "to what destination?" or "to what place?" Each letter of *ipesi*, he said could stand for an important characteristic:

> *I* for imagination
> *P* for persistence
> *E* for excellence
> *S* for selflessness
> *I* for inspiration

Whither? A good one-word question to ask ourselves from time to time. Whither *are* we going in this journey that we call life? What ultimate destination are we hoping to reach? Are we on the right course? *Ipesi?*

Lord, show me The Way.

—ARTHUR GORDON

13

. . . Be ye therefore wise as serpents, and harmless as doves.

—MATTHEW 10:16

When my son was six years old, I took him on a tour of the Metro-Goldwyn-Mayer studio. There George was introduced to Leo, the Metro lion, whose great head and vast roar precedes all M-G-M pictures.

I turned briefly to greet Leo's trainer, and when I turned back, I saw that George had thrust his hand into the cage and was stroking the lion. I stood frozen with terror while the trainer's calm voice instructed my son to withdraw his arm. When I could speak, I quavered, "It's incredible that he wasn't afraid of the lion." Leo's trainer replied, "You can thank the Lord for that. Because he wasn't afraid, the lion wasn't afraid of him."

"Fear," he went on, "breeds fear." George had been safer than most adults would have been because Leo sensed that he was harmless.

"Harmlessness," said the trainer, "is the great safety valve."

Harmlessness. My small son was safe because he posed no threat to the huge beast. Would I have been safe? Am I? In my relationship with others, do I send out danger signals of fear and aggression? Am I quick to criticize or judge others, or am I — *harmless*?

Let love so flood my heart, dear Lord, that it casts out fear and all else within me that would threaten my neighbor.

—ELAINE ST. JOHNS

---

14   *Study to shew thyself approved unto God...*
—II TIMOTHY 2:15

When I was in high school, I had a German teacher who called the first three weeks of every semester "basic training." No matter at what level of German we were, no matter how vehemently we complained (and we complained a lot), he would always spend those three-week periods in a review of basic grammar and vocabulary. Every single day he would drill us.

"I want German to be in here, not just up there," he would tell us first pointing to his heart, then to his head.

It took me a long time to understand his motive — in fact, it wasn't until I faced a tough college-placement exam in German that I began to grasp it. For although I made mistakes in my translation, found that I had been given the basic tools to carry me through the most difficult sections of the test.

As a Christian, I have often found myself complaining about the basic training that God demands of us — to live under His authority, to learn and use the grammar and vocabulary of the Christian life. But maybe when I have instilled my faith "in here, not just up there," I can begin to move the mountains that the Bible tells me my faith can move.

Help me, Father, to take the time, to make the effort, to build a faith that's real. —JEFF JAPINGA

JOURNEY OF FAITH

15 Your traveling companion is *ELISHA*
... *who walked behind another.*

—II KINGS 19:16-21, II KINGS 2-9

There are two figures on a heat-shimmering road of Palestine, and Elisha is the second. A few steps ahead of him strides Elijah, Elisha's teacher, inspirer and guide. It is a relationship that suggests our own need for a spiritual companion who travels the road ahead of us.

Elisha's farm lay in the loveliest part of Palestine, the fertile, abundantly watered valley south of the Sea of Galilee. Here in this secure and pleasant setting Elisha had expected to live out his days.

Suddenly in the very act of turning a furrow — just as we might be putting the dishes in the dishwasher, typing a paper for school, boarding the train for work — a mantle is placed on his shoulders.

Elijah's gesture was clear at once to Elisha. Clear and terrifying: *Someday you are going to wear my cloak.* Elisha, the farmer, succeed the famous prophet Elijah? Whatever calling you and I have from God could scarcely be more daunting than Elisha's.

Even Elijah seems appalled at the extent of the sacrifice he has proposed. "Go back!" he cries. "For what have I done to you?" Elisha, however, needs no more time. His "I will follow you," springs from his heart. Elisha drops his plow without even finishing the field.

Elijah meanwhile has not even broken his stride. The old prophet is already on his way; Elisha has to run after him with his resounding, "Yes!"

And what happens when the leader in whose footsteps we are walking, steps aside and hands *us* the staff? When *we* in turn must lead others? Elisha's experience was dramatic — and instructive.

It was general knowledge that old Elijah's earthly ministry was nearing its end: a group of fifty men from Jericho followed the two companions that final day as far as the banks of the Jordan River. There Elijah rolled up his old goatskin mantle — the one he had symbolically thrown across Elisha's shoulders so long ago — and struck the surface of the stream. Awed, the fifty witnesses watched the waters part and the old man and his younger companion cross over.

Out of sight of the curious crowd, Elijah turns for the last time to his faithful follower, Elisha. "Ask what I can do for you," he invites, "before I am taken from you."

Elisha answers without hesitation, "Let me inherit a double share of your spirit!"

Elisha asks for a spiritual inheritance — in an abundance that will let him continue his master's ministry.

And now Elisha is alone. He returns to the Jordan to find the fifty onlookers still waiting, full of misgivings, no doubt, about the new man's ability to fill the post. Elisha's heart is pounding as he rolls up the mantle which is now his, and strikes the water with it as he has seen his master do. "Where is the God of Elijah?" he cries. And the water was parted to the one side and to the other, and Elisha went over.

It is the last time he calls on "the God of Elijah." He has stepped out on the power of God, Himself.

> *Lord, thank You for the leaders who encourage me. Give me the wisdom to know when my apprenticeship is over and the risky moment of trust is here.*

—ELIZABETH SHERRILL

16   *And now, Lord, what wait I for? my hope is in thee.*
                                —PSALM 39:8

"Let's plant some trees out back!"

It seemed like a marvelous idea when my neighbor Alice suggested it. The land behind our adjacent houses was level and there was absolutely nothing to shield us from the sun on hot summer days.

So we ordered six young trees from a mail-order catalog after having read the promise, "You can plant them yourself!" True enough — but it simply wasn't as easy as it sounded. Digging a hole big enough to accommodate a ball of tree roots is — well, a lot of digging. By the end of the day, our muscles protested every move we made. But as we stood there studying the spindly little saplings, we were mighty proud of our work.

We still didn't have any shade. We would have to wait for that — and wait we did. In the meantime we saw the trees through storms that threatened to uproot them from the ground and heavy snows that bent their slender branches almost flat. We braced them with posts when they began to tilt and we watched helplessly as they struggled through drought.

Usually I'm not a very patient person but for some reason I haven't minded waiting for the trees to grow. I learned something important from planting them: Not everything in life is "instant." It's comforting to know that something wonderful is going to happen — in time.

Maybe that's what hope is really all about.

Father, You are our hope, now and for ever.   —PHYLLIS HOBE

17 *... But whosoever drinketh of the water that I shall give him shall never thirst; but the water that I shall give him shall be in him a well of water springing up into everlasting life.* —JOHN 4:14

"*Resurrection plant,*" my encyclopedia says, "any of several annual and perennial fernlike desert plants requiring little water to survive.... When deprived of moisture, the resurrection plant contracts into a small ball and may be borne by the wind until it settles near water and, unfolding, renews itself."

I remembered that plant one morning after a frenzied work week. It was a Sunday and since I really *needed* church, I hurried off to the service. The sermon was titled: "Come...and Be Renewed!"

Yes, the resurrection plant and I have much in common. Water restores it to life and enables it, unfolding, to "renew itself" — and the Living Water of Christ's Word does just the same for me! Do you need to be "resurrected" today? Seek Him to fill you. Come...and be renewed!

Lord Jesus, like the Samaritan woman at the well, let me drink from the fountain of Your Word and never know thirst again.
—DORIS HAASE

18 *For whom the Lord loveth he chasteneth...*
—HEBREWS 12:6

U.T. (Brad) Bradley was my college crew coach, widely known in rowing circles as the "dean of small-college crew." He was much-loved by nearly all those he coached.

At first I wondered why. He never had a good word for any of us. He was sardonic and quick to spot a fault. He seemed to know nothing about feelings. He would take a boy from the varsity boat and replace him with a junior varsity oarsman without an explanation to the demoted or a compliment to the promoted. He would practice starts until our hands were bleeding, wind sprints until we nearly fainted.

One spring vacation while training, a crew of Marines came to our lake to practice, and their coach challenged our varsity to a race. Brad told him, "You'd be better off racing our J.V." The Marines were insulted and I could see why. Lean, hard, and each over 6'4", they outweighed our motley J.V. crew by about forty pounds a man.

When we lined up for the start, the Marines were breathing fire, and the race was as grueling as you could imagine. But at the finish line we were first, by a whisker. Brad ordered his coaching launch over to the Marine boat, and looking fondly at our spent and gasping crew, he growled, "I admit they don't look like much... until they get on the water." All at once that comment, that flicker of a glance, made me understand what Brad was all about.

Another coach might have gone a little easier on his oarsmen. But Brad was not that kind of a coach. He was the kind who cared about excellence, and he persevered until we realized the best that was in us. He cared more about what we felt about ourselves than what we thought of him.

And we loved him.

Father, if it sometimes seems that You are being hard on me, let me remember that it's because You love me and want to bring out the best in me. —JAMES McDERMOTT

19 *Call unto me, and I will answer thee...* —JEREMIAH 33:3

My son's voice on the other end of the phone sounded somewhat uncertain. Fearful. "Mama, I forgot my lunch money. Will you bring me some, *now*? We eat in a few minutes."

"Why didn't you take money?" I asked in a somewhat irritated tone.

"Mama, aren't you going to bring it?" I could see him in my mind, standing in the school office with people watching, listening. I was his only hope.

Of course I was going to bring him the money. He was my responsibility. I was the person he should have come to. Never mind that he'd forgotten his money.

"I'll be there in five minutes," I answered.

I grabbed a dollar and drove the short distance to the school. On the way back, thoughts from God eased into my mind.

"You *wanted* to meet his need, didn't you? He was fearful to ask, but you met his need. Now tell Me what you fear to ask of Me. Your loving Father will meet your needs, child. You are My responsibility."

Father, here I am again with that request I've been afraid to ask of You.... —MARION BOND WEST

20 *Withhold not good from them to whom it is due, when it is in the power of thine hand to do it.* —PROVERBS 3:27

When our daughter was in high school, she had the privilege of dancing in Paul Green's patriotic outdoor musical, *Faith of Our Fathers*; and later, as a student at William and Mary College, in his famous outdoor drama of the Revolution, *The Common Glory.* Whenever we saw her after a performance, we would ask, "Well, how did it go?"

"Oh, so-so," she would sometimes shrug. "The audience sat on their hands." Or she would rush in, elated: "They loved us. They started to clap during the first act, and we gave them everything we had. Applause makes so much difference."

Applause makes so much difference. And it takes only one pair of hands to start. Let somebody begin clapping in even a single dark corner of a theater and suddenly everybody else joins in; little bonfires of enthusiasm burst forth throughout.

For the cast, results can be electrifying. Something that doesn't cost a cent at the box office sends everyone home smiling, for it has produced an outstanding show.

To hear praise, to be encouraged. What a difference they make in every performance of life — whether in the theater, at work, or at home. When people are doing their best to please you, don't be afraid to applaud. It often takes courage — yes, Christian courage — to be the first to clap approval in public or to say, "Good for you, that's wonderful!" to a child, a co-worker, a friend. But what a glow it puts in the heart, and how bright are its results.

Surely God never wants us to "sit on our hands" when we could be using them to reward and inspire others.

Lord, don't let me ever be too shy or too indifferent to express my appreciation, whether with words or a pair of clapping hands.
—MARJORIE HOLMES

---

21   *Give us day by day our daily bread.*   —LUKE 11:3

Not long ago I stayed overnight at the home of Barbara and Peter Jenkins, the young couple who walked clear across America. Barbara is a fragile-looking brunette beauty who was going to school in New Orleans when Peter came "walking" through. They fell in love, got married and he persuaded her to hike with him the remaining three thousand miles to Oregon.

Everyone asks Barbara how she did it, especially since she became pregnant during the last stages of their journey.

"Well," she says with a smile, "I know it's an obvious answer but I did it one step at a time. I particularly remember one day when we were nearing the border of Louisiana. I had blisters the size of silver dollars and aching muscles and a terrible sunburn. When Peter took out a map and showed me how far it was to Oregon, I burst into tears. Looking at the whole distance, it just seemed impossible that I could go on. It was only when I learned to focus on one day at a time, one mile at a time, *one step at a time*, that the impossible became possible."

If you're facing a task that seems too big for you, break it into smaller pieces. Tell yourself that you can handle the small piece that lies just ahead. Then tackle it. After that go on to the next small piece, and the next, and the next, until — suddenly — one of them is the last.

Life is a series of steps, Lord. Help me to take it one at a time.
—ARTHUR GORDON

---

22 *Let no corrupt communication proceed out of your mouth, but that which is good... that it may minister grace unto the hearers.* —EPHESIANS 4:29

Recently I saw a stage production of the play, *The Elephant Man*. It is the story of Englishman, John Merrick, who was tragically deformed. To my surprise, the actor playing Merrick appeared without make-up. Yet, because of the reactions of his fellow actors to his "grotesque" appearance, we in the audience soon "saw" his defects, too, even though they weren't actually there.

Not long after that, I heard gossip about an acquaintance, and I believed it. It suggested an ugly flaw in her character and whenever I saw that person, she seemed deformed to me and less trustworthy.

Then I learned the rumor wasn't true. The next time I met her, she was just as beautiful as she'd been before the rumor started. My "belief" in the rumor had made me "see" her supposed flaws.

Right then I made a resolution — not only would I try not to gossip, I would try not to *listen* when others gossiped.

Today, Lord, let me speak and hear only those things that are helpful or kind. —MADGE HARRAH

GOD-GIFTS FROM THE SEA

From out of a summer vacation with her family at the seashore, Sue Monk Kidd shares with you eight special days of spiritual discoveries — God-gifts from the sea.

23 *To every thing there is a season, and a time to every purpose under the heaven...* —ECCLESIASTES 3:1

On the first night of my vacation I took a solitary walk on the beach. In the distance pier lights shredded the darkness with long, yellow beams. Waves spilled loudly on the shore.

After a mile or so, I sat down and gazed into the depths of the starry night. I became aware of a great rhythm about me, as though my hand had inadvertently slipped upon a pulse beating deep in the universe. The stars wheeled in precise pattern, the moon and the tides came and went without skipping a beat and the wind moved like a breath. Night and day, wind and tide, current and moon — it was a magnificent dance to silent music, choreographed by God Himself.

I wondered. Hadn't God designed the world within me as He had designed the world around me — to be lived in rhythm with Him, to be danced to the silent music of His will? And then I had to face the hard question: *When my life seems off balance, restless and fragmented, can it be that I am out of step with God?*

I stood up and began the walk back. Could I discover God's rhythms? Of course I could — if only I fixed my eyes and my heart on the Choreographer.

Lord, may my dance always be in harmony with You.

—SUE MONK KIDD

---

24 *But it is good for me to draw near to God...*

—PSALM 73:28

I cupped the small conch to my ear. Sitting very still, I listened for the sound within its labyrinths. Then I heard it — the faint and haunting echo buried deep inside, the whispering voice of the ocean.

And sitting there with my back to the world's clamor, I realized that I was hearing one of the sounds hidden deep within our universe.

Are these tiny, secret sounds like little messages? I wondered later. Like the "still, small voice" of God? How often God's voice is like the sound buried deep inside the conch shell. Only when I turn aside and become still, cupping my ear to the ground of God's being, can I hope to hear His gentle whisper.

Today might be a good day to try...

Teach me to spend time alone with You, Lord... listening.

—SUE MONK KIDD

25 *Now the God of patience and consolation grant you to be likeminded one toward another...* —ROMANS 15:5

She came uninvited to the sand dune where I sat making notes in my journal. She was old and used a cane. I had seen her before, meandering along the beach in her floppy straw hat. Like the predictable sweep of a clock's hand, she would wander up to anyone, hoping for a chat. *Now here she was, on my sand dune.*

"It's too pretty a day to work," she said, nodding at my notebook.

"I suppose," I replied, trying not to be drawn in.

She leaned on her cane and began to chatter away...about her late husband, about the grandchildren she rarely saw. I listened with a polite kind of patience, glancing once at my watch. Finally she took her leave and headed across the dune. And as I watched her go, I knew that she was a lonely woman who had only wanted to share a friendly moment.

Far down the windy beach the woman disappeared, the moment to care gone with her. I felt ashamed. Oh, it was fine to express my love through large service projects, as is my wont. But love should run like an underground stream through *every* minute. Love is for the unscheduled, unexpected times...for all the sand-dune moments.

I looked up into the blue sky and made a promise to God and myself: I would climb the sand dune tomorrow. And wait.

Lord, show me how to love — especially during the "sand-dune" moments of life. —SUE MONK KIDD

26 *Whereby are given unto us exceeding great and precious promises: that by these ye might be partakers of the divine nature...* —II PETER 1:4

I was leafing through one of several books about the sea that I had brought along for my children to read at the beach.

There are 85,000 varieties of sea animals! the little book said. Creatures with ten legs. A scallop with two rows of blue eyes. A whale as long as a boxcar. A grasshopper fish that jumps along the ocean floor.

The ocean — the great brewing pot for God's imagination.

"What are you reading?" my son asked.

"*Your* book," I replied, holding up a page that showed a little boy on the beach surrounded by all sorts of marine life — anemones, sea turtles, an electric eel. "Just look at these creatures God made!" I said. "Which one do you like best?"

He studied the picture, his face breaking into an impish little grin. "The boy!" he answered.

I was surprised. *Of course, of course,* I thought. Of all the creatures God made, His imagination reached a height when He made man. I lowered the book and studied the people on the beach. Perhaps I needed to look at the human family with new eyes, to see each person as the marvelous creature he is...and most of all, as a tiny portrait of God's Own image.

Lord, help me to appreciate anew Your world of wonders — and especially Your human creation. —SUE MONK KIDD

27

...As I have loved you, that ye also love one another.

—JOHN 13:34

One afternoon as my husband and I lay sunning on the beach, I noticed a middle-aged couple sitting on a towel with a poodle wedged between them. The man stroked the dog and absently gazed at the sea. The woman traced in the sand with her finger, from time to time cocking her head to see the effect. Later, when I looked again, they were holding hands.

The hours passed. The tide crept away. The couple with the dog left. My husband and I dragged the children from the water and headed back to the cottage. Passing the spot where the couple had sat holding hands, I noticed the woman's sand tracing. It read, *I love you.*

Three sandy words stared up at me — words that I was sometimes too complacent or too busy to say. And they reminded me of the need to put love into words. *I love you.* Simply saying the words ...writing them...unleashing them...somehow makes life warm and special, full of potential. They had made a couple suddenly hold hands on a crowded beach...and feel cherished.

The waves broke into wide smiles across the shore. In the distance the children danced after my husband and I chased after them...my heart full of the words on the sand, whispering...

I love You.

—SUE MONK KIDD

28

Through God we shall do valiantly...　　—PSALM 108:13

We were crab hunting that morning when my husband gave a shout and pulled up his crab net. Inside, two blue crabs flopped about. Before I could stop him, eight-year-old Bob reached into the net. Four fearless claws leaped up at him, ready to stand their ground and do battle. Bob yanked his hand back and said, "They're not like the little hermit crabs that hide in their shell when they see you coming. These ocean blue crabs come right after you!"

I had to smile. Maybe the ways of crabs aren't so different from the ways of humans. Sometimes when a big problem or threat reaches into my life, my first instinct is to become like a little hermit crab — to run and hide, to bury myself in fear. How silly and useless that is!

There on the backwater beach it was good to remember that I have a choice. I can also plant my feet with courage and say, "With God's help, I'll go after this problem, no matter how insurmountable it seems."

Lord, help me to respond to life's crises with courage.

—SUE MONK KIDD

---

29 *And we know that all things work together for good to them that love God, to them who are the called according to his purpose.* —ROMANS 8:28

I was awakened by a crash of thunder and a torrent of rain slamming against the beach house. The windows rattled and lightning filled the room with stuttering light. Outside, black waves rose up and roared. I lay awake all night, marveling at the fury of nature. Finally near dawn the storm abated.

After breakfast I walked down to the beach. The shore was strewn with beauty: rare shells from far out on the ocean floor, sea-polished pieces of driftwood, rumpled chains of seaweed. I could only imagine the joy the children would have in filling their buckets today.

I bent down and picked up a delicate pink shell. How wonderful it is that such exquisite treasure can come from a squalling storm. Like the storms in my life perhaps? Does God bring something good from them too? Are there hidden treasures in wait in the after calm? Precious peace, untarnished faith, priceless reassurances of His love…God-given gifts?

I carried the pink shell back to the cottage — a reminder to search for the treasure after the storm rather than stare at the heavens and ask "Why?"

Lord, help me discover Your good gifts when the storm abates.
—SUE MONK KIDD

---

30 *I will not leave you comfortless: I will come to you.*
—JOHN 14:18:

It was our last morning at the seashore. It was early and I stood gazing from the balcony of the little beach cottage. The vast ocean stretched before me. It seemed to roll across the whole earth, swallowing even the mightiest mountains in its wake. I shivered at the loneliness of its deep, shadowed depths.

A line of pelicans swooped low over the water and dropped like a single dipper into the sea. It was then that the familiar Bible verse surfaced from my memory: "If I take the wings of the morning and dwell in the uttermost parts of the sea, even there shall thy hand lead me and thy right hand shall hold me." *Even there!*

Yes, in every place of my life God is available, at any moment. Even here, with the vast, mysterious sea stretching before me, causing me to feel small and insignificant. No matter how deep a problem may be, or how shallow the need…*even there* God is with me. *Even there.*

The words echo deep within me — on lonely days, problem days or just plain ordinary days. On days when I'm far, far away from this beautiful, vast sea.... *Even there...even there.*

Thank You, Lord, for the assurance that there is nothing in life that I need face without You...the most wonderful God-gift of all!
                                                            —SUE MONK KIDD

---

31 *...I have prayed for thee, that thy faith fail not...*
                                                            —LUKE 22:32

          I sat transfixed in front of the television set, watching the 1981 New York marathon. Although Alberto Salazar was more than halfway through a race of more than twenty-six miles, he was running each mile faster than I had ever run just one. Mile after mile he ran, his face resolute and determined; somehow he ignored the pain and exhaustion that his body must have been feeling. And when he finished in two hours, eight minutes and thirty-four seconds, Salazar had broken the record.

"How does he do it?" I wondered out loud.

The next day a reporter asked him the same question. Salazar's answer was not related to superior training or to an intense desire to win or even to a physical advantage. Rather, he spoke of his family, its origin in and eventual escape from Cuba, and the coaches who had worked so carefully with him. In the toughest stretches, Salazar said, when it hurt to run, he thought of those people. "Had it not been for them, there's a good chance that I would have eased off." In that case, there would have been no record.

I found Salazar's comments to be comforting for I too have gained strength in times of difficulty or stress through the knowledge that the prayers of my family and friends were with me. Interesting, isn't it, that in a world as complex as ours, a simple prayer of concern from you is often the key to another's success.

Father, please keep my friends from failing. —JEFF JAPINGA

Praise Diary for July

1

2

3

4

5

6

7

8

9

10

11

12

13

14

15

16

17

18

19

20

21

22

23

24

25

26

27

28

29

30

31

August

For thou, Lord, wilt bless the righteous... —PSALM 5:12

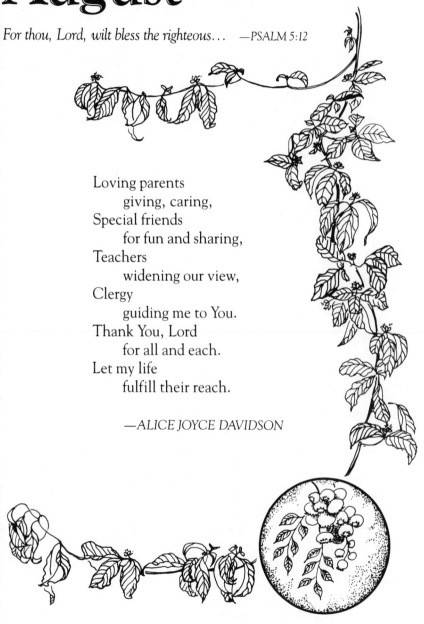

Loving parents
      giving, caring,
Special friends
      for fun and sharing,
Teachers
      widening our view,
Clergy
      guiding me to You.
Thank You, Lord
      for all and each.
Let my life
      fulfill their reach.

—ALICE JOYCE DAVIDSON

PATTERN FOR A BLESSED LIFE
Blessed are the peacemakers: for they shall be called the children of God. —MATTHEW 5:9

1

My friend Anna seems to be at peace with God, with other people and with herself. When I asked her how she achieved her serenity, Anna replied, "I think it's because I become a little child every night."

Since Anna is over seventy years old, I asked her what she meant.

"Well, I just kneel before my Heavenly Father and lay my problems, one by one, in His lap. If I'm feeling guilty about something, I ask His forgiveness and then *accept* it. If I'm worried about anything, I hand the problem to Him and let go of it. If I feel lonely or rejected, I tell Him so and He enfolds me in His Fatherly arms. Always, after letting go, a deep peace settles over me," Anna concluded.

Every August night, Father, I will come to You as a little child — letting go, trusting You, knowing that I am loved unconditionally. Oh, how blessed I am to be Your child.

—MARILYN MORGAN HELLEBERG

2 *Confess your faults one to another...* —JAMES 5:16

I once asked a successful marriage counselor if he had any special technique or approach that he used in difficult cases.

"Well," he said, "I have yet to meet a warring couple where the fault is entirely on one side. So I start out by talking with the husband and the wife separately. To each of them I say, 'I know you have a lot of grievances and complaints about your marriage partner, and no doubt many of them are valid. But tell me, is there anything in your own performance that you regret, anything that you've done or failed to do that you feel sorry for? If there is, I wish you'd tell me because it will help me see the whole picture more clearly.'

"Most people are basically fair-minded. Almost always I get an honest answer. Later I bring the partners together, and in a calm moment I ask each of them to repeat exactly what they shared with me. That single admission of being at fault, of accepting their own mistakes, is usually the beginning of a break-through. Never under-estimate the power of confession. It is the soothing balm that heals the wounded."

Give me courage to confess my failings, humility to start anew.
—ARTHUR GORDON

---

3 *Be ye therefore ready also: for the Son of man cometh at an hour when ye think not.* —LUKE 12:40

John Wesley was once asked what he would do if he learned that this was to be his last day on earth. Without hesitation Mr. Wesley enumerated the things that made up his daily routine — Bible study, prayer, visiting the sick, preaching. For him, nothing would have to be readjusted.

I have often wondered how I might answer that question. If I knew that at dusk today I would meet my Master face to face, how many things would I be doing differently?

What about you? How many rearrangements would you need to make?

Lord, bless this day's schedule. May it please You. —DRUE DUKE

4 ...Love...seeketh not her own... —I CORINTHIANS 13:5

My new friend Anne invited me to a get-together in her home. My husband was away on an extended business trip and I really didn't want to go out. Feeling down, I just wanted to stay home. But Anne insisted — and I reluctantly agreed.

It was a wonderful party! Someone played the piano and we sang. Everyone seemed friendly and engaging and I began to feel better. Soon I didn't want to leave, for Anne's attentiveness and warmth toward all of us had permeated the house.

Later, as several of us were getting our coats to leave, I noticed on a table in the foyer a photograph of a beautiful little blonde-haired girl.

"That's Anne's child who was killed in an auto accident almost twenty years ago," said one of the women next to me. "Anne has this annual get-together on the anniversary of her daughter's death to cheer up others and to forget about her own loss."

Suddenly I felt small. My "problem" had made me want to withdraw and be self-indulgent. Anne, in her loss, was reaching out to others.

Help me, God, to be other-centered when I'm tempted only to center on myself. —MARION BOND WEST

5 Order my steps in thy word: and let not any iniquity have dominion over me. —PSALM 119:133

Have you ever climbed up an extension ladder? It's a scary and fascinating experience. When you begin, the ladder seems wobbly and unsteady, as though it would topple at any minute. But if you boldly climb higher, one rung at a time, you discover that the weight of your body combines with gravity to steady the ladder. The higher you climb, the safer you feel!

Have you ever climbed up the ladder of faith? It's a scary and fascinating experience. At the beginning you feel very shaky and insecure, wondering if you will topple. But if you boldly climb higher, one day of trust at a time, you discover that the weight of your trust in God combines with His love for you and you are thereby steadied.

Faith is very much like an extension ladder, I think. The higher we climb, the safer we feel!

Lord, I am taking one step at a time — higher and higher — up the ladder of faith. —PATRICIA HOUCK SPRINKLE

---

6 *As cold water to a thirsty soul, so is good news from a far country.* —PROVERBS 25:25

Along with my black coffee, I absorbed the black headlines in the morning paper.

"I'm sick of bad news," I complained later to a friend. "Day after day after day it's the same thing, all terrible. Just once I'd like to read a paper that carries good news."

"There is one," she said.

"Tell me where and I'll go out right now and buy a copy," I replied.

She laughed. "You have it already. The Bible."

"Oh, you!" I said, shrugging off her words.

But then I got to thinking about it — she's right, the Bible *is* full of good news, news that never goes out of date and always brings hope.

Now each morning before I read the news in the paper, I take a few minutes to read the Good News in the Bible. Though the black headlines in the newspaper still concern me, I don't get as depressed any more. Now, with a prayerful attitude in my heart, I bring the Good News of Jesus to my morning paper-reading and nothing ever looks so bleak.

Father, You are the Messenger of Good News for me and the world. —MADGE HARRAH

---

7   *But when ye pray, use not vain repetitions, as the heathen do: for they think that they shall be heard for their much speaking.* —MATTHEW 6:7

"'And this...we beseech Thee, Most High, King of Kings, in the name of Your most holy and divine Son, our Master, Jesus Christ our Lord, Amen.' Well, what do you think — will that be okay for the prayer breakfast?" I was practicing the words on my wife.

"Sounds a little pompous to me," Lynn observed. "It's hardly you."

"I know, I know, but all those important people will be there. I can't say something corny — what will they think?"

I felt a tug on my sleeve. It was Evan, the two-year-old son of our neighbor for whom we were babysitting that night. "Lynn prayed with me before," he said. "Now it's your turn and then I'll go to sleep. Okay?"

"Okay, Evan," I agreed. He raced ahead of me and was sitting on the edge of his bed, his hands folded in his lap, when I got there. He closed his eyes tight. "Jesus...Amen!" That's all — just "Jesus, Amen." After giving me a hug, he dove under the covers.

"Well?" Lynn asked when I returned to the living room.

"I'm impressed," I muttered.

"Evan's prayers simply say what's on his mind, right?" Lynn said with a gleam in her eye.

And she *was* right. I had been trying to show off, trying to impress others.

I crumpled up the piece of paper I had been writing on, pulled out a clean sheet and put my dictionary and thesaurus away. And then I asked my heart of its own concerns and wrote what I myself truly felt. Not impressive. But real. Like "Jesus...Amen!"

Father, teach us to pray. —JEFF JAPINGA

---

8 *Come unto me, all ye that labour and are heavy laden, and I will give you rest. Take my yoke upon you...For my yoke is easy, and my burden is light.*
—MATTHEW 11:28-30

A few years ago I drove with some friends along the banks of the Nile River at Cairo and marveled at the scenery. It reminded me of a picture page from one of our Bibles. Camels, laden with straw, were reflected in the green-hued water. At the river's edge a sapling — denuded of limbs and foliage — had been pulled down and a bucket attached to its top so that water might be dipped for people living along the banks.

Nearby, a water buffalo was yoked to one end of a crude pole. It plodded in endless circles around a center post to which the other end of the pole was attached. This process worked a water wheel, emptying its paddled contents into the furrows of a cornfield beyond.

What primitive procedures these people endure, I thought as I snapped my camera, taking picture after picture.

But when I saw the color slides projected on my home screen several weeks later, I noticed something that I hadn't observed at the time. In the background, behind the laden camels and the bucket device, there loomed high-powered electricity poles...and I realized with a jolt of surprise that the people weren't using the power!

Do you sometimes miss God's power? And — like the water buffalo — do you just keep plodding around in circles? Take a new look. You may be surprised by what you discover....

Father, You are the Powerhouse for all my needs. —ISABEL CHAMP

---

9   *...A virtuous woman...she looketh well to the ways of her household, and eateth not the bread of idleness.*
—PROVERBS 31:10, 27

I don't care very much for daytime television but sometimes when I visit a friend or a relative who does, courtesy bids me to watch it too. There is one thing in particular about daytime shows that I find extremely annoying: the middle-aged woman who identifies herself as "just a housewife." Why "just"?

My friend Cal Farley, the founder and long-time director of *Boys Ranch* in Texas, once said to me, "The reason a lot of youngsters are having problems today is that Mom is not in the kitchen when they come home from school." It's true that many mothers have to go to work nowadays to help support the family but it's also true that this does not diminish the importance of their role in the home.

St. Theresa of Avila, one of the most influential women in Christianity and eventually the spiritual mother to thousands of nuns, nevertheless took her turn in the convent's kitchen.

"Christ," she said, "is among the pots and pans."

Lord, help us to perform all of our tasks happily and proudly for You. —GLENN KITTLER

10 *...Rejoicing in hope; patient in tribulation; continuing instant in prayer...*
—ROMANS 12:12

When the Nazis invaded France, Margot DeVingy, along with her little girl and a group of refugees, fled through the dangerous, snow-clogged passes of the Pyrenees toward Spain. Whenever a member of the little band despaired or fell down sobbing "I can't go on," Margot would say: "It's *your* turn to carry the child." Everyone wanted so desperately to save the little girl that by taking turns in carrying her and by asking for God's help, each found new strength with which to go on. And they did go on until eventually they reached safety.

Now, in times of discouragement, grief, failure or disappointment — times when I want to give up — I remember the story of Margot and the refugees and I tell myself, *It's your turn to carry the child.*

I find that my weakness turns into strength, my doubts into hope, my fears into faith. And I can go on.

Father, thank You for the gift of faith to carry me through the hard times.
—ZONA B. DAVIS

11 *What then? shall we sin, because we are not under the law, but under grace? God forbid.*
—ROMANS 6:15

Psychologists often refer to the "divided self" that resides inside each of us. That is a very insightful expression because it is indeed true that each of us does have two sides and by my reckoning, they are those age-old battlers, good and evil. Aligned with the former are the positive virtues — selflessness, kindness, thoughtfulness, helpfulness, generosity, faithfulness, love. On the negative

231

side — selfishness, cruelty, jealousy, distrust, bigotry, greed, doubt, hatred.

Although most of us like to see ourselves only in the former light, we are a mix of strengths *and* weaknesses, pluses *and* minuses, good *and* not-so-good. But fortunately, if we are followers of Christ, we have a Saviour Who understands our good intentions and inconsistent behavior, a Saviour Who is willing to forgive our sins of both omission and commission.

But, oh, how it must please Him when our divided selves quit warring and we choose light instead of darkness.

Lord, give me a united self, one that reflects Your peace.
—FRED BAUER

---

12 *... For, behold, the kingdom of God is within you.*
—LUKE 17:21

My father always believed in me more than I believed in myself. When I was growing up, I would ask his advice on matters that seemed beyond me. "Daddy, do you think I can climb that tree?" I asked when I was small, pointing to an enormous oak.

He nodded right away. "Sure you can," he said.

When I was fourteen, I asked, "Daddy, do you believe I could make the basketball team?"

He thought it over for a moment. And then he said, "You can do it."

But I particularly remember a day when I was seventeen. I let him read my English theme and then, trying to sound nonchalant, I said, "Daddy, do you suppose... maybe one day I could be a writer?" I waited, swallowing hard.

He smiled at me. "You can do it," he said. "You can."

Maybe we all need somebody like my father. Someone to affirm our capacities. Someone to help us reach just a little higher than we might ordinarily reach. For God has given us far more potential than most of us ever dare to use. And the key of affirmation often helps to unlock it. My father knew that. And today — with my own children now, and with my family and friends — I want to use that key, too.

Help me always to draw out the very best in others.
—SUE MONK KIDD

---

13 *And he shall purify the sons of Levi, and purge them as gold and silver, that they may offer unto the Lord an offering in righteousness.* —MALACHI 3:3

The children and I went shell-hunting when we visited my parents in Florida several years ago. We filled our ice-cream buckets with pretty coral, an amazing variety of little shells and some smoothly polished stones. Some of the stones looked like shining crystal, some like golden gemstones. A few were sky blue. I put many of these glistening bits in my bucket, and when we got back to the house, Mother explained that they were merely pieces of broken glass from discarded bottles. Sand and water and wind had transformed these pieces of trash into gleaming beauties.

It made me think of all the sharp and broken parts of my life — those harsh words I would take back if I could, the disappointments that still sting, the mistakes I can't correct. Maybe it's time for me to toss them all out, like broken bottles. I wonder.

Tonight I'll offer all the sharp edges of this day to my heavenly Father. Who can tell what special treasures these throwaways may become?

Lord, take the jagged pieces of this day and smooth away the cutting edges. —MARILYN MORGAN HELLEBERG

14 *To him who alone doeth great wonders: for his mercy endureth for ever.* —PSALM 136:4

I was at the dinner table with Anne Shelley and her family in Sherman Oaks, California. Sixteen-year-old Anne was recounting the extraordinary events she had written about in her prize-winning story (*Guideposts* Youth Writing Contest). She had told about the night that her left arm was severed from her body by an airplane propeller. It might have been a horror tale — but it wasn't.

At the time Anne was a young woman with a fully matured faith in God. On the night of her accident her deep belief that God is wholeness gave her insuperable strength. Her confidence never flagged. "God," she prayed as she lay on the airport runway, "I want my arm back." She believed that it would be restored to her. And it was.

Time played a crucial part; if there was the least medical possibility of reattaching her arm, haste was of the utmost importance. And so it *just happened* that a man who witnessed the accident had the presence of mind to run to a telephone that *just happened* to be nearby. He called the fire department that *just happened* to be across the street from the Burbank Airport. He was clear-minded and specific in his directions so the firemen who rushed to the scene brought just the right equipment to take care of Anne — and her arm. At the hospital where Anne was taken, it *just happened* that the doctor at the receiving desk was helping out that night — normally he was at another hospital — and he *just happened* to know of the very surgeon who could perform the delicate operation. It was July and many physicians were away on vacation, but it *just happened* that the very surgeon was at home — and available to rush to the hospital.

"What a startling series of coincidences," I said as I watched, still in awe, as Anne shifted a fork from one hand to the other.

Anne's mother looked across the table at me. Her next words reassured me of the depth of God's presence not only in that family,

234

but in the whole world. "Coincidences?" Mrs. Shelley asked. *"There are no coincidences."*

Today, Jesus, grant me the wisdom to take nothing for granted.
—VAN VARNER

JOURNEY OF FAITH

15 Your traveling companion is *GIDEON*
... who was stronger than he knew. —JUDGES 6-8

Gideon is a timid young farmer living in the fledgling nation of Israel. The chosen people had established a foothold in the Promised Land — but enemies pressed in from all sides.

For thousands of years, bands of nomads would sweep over the desert, strike settled communities, and vanish again into the wilderness. The Midianites, a tribe of nomadic Bedouins, invented camel warfare — swifter and more unpredictable than anything the mind of man had yet imagined. Against these attacks there was no known defense...except to flee to the mountains and hide.

But the Midianites had no intention of settling down. They wanted only to steal the fruit and grain and livestock. Having camped like locusts on the captured farms for a few weeks, they would move on, leaving no sustenance in Israel.

Gideon and the others would creep down from their mountain hideaways to start again from scratch, pulling their own plows, restaking the trampled vineyards until at harvest time the whirlwind attack would come again.

Things reached rock bottom. *Then* they turned to God. How often we too try every escape route before we try prayer!

God's response to the Israelites' cry for help was a word spoken in the ear of Gideon. But Gideon didn't believe that the individual conversing with him was God.

What this ill-informed stranger was saying made absolutely no sense: *"The Lord is with you, you mighty man of valor."* These statements seemed as implausible to Gideon — as they do to us: *The Lord is with me? Me, a mighty man of valor?*

Valor was not exactly Gideon's hallmark. At the very moment he hears these words he is hiding from the Midianites at the bottom of a wine press!

This might of Gideon's, of yours and mine...is a might we do not know we have, and therefore cannot use, until God shows it to us.

> *Today, God, speak that special word that describes me to you. Whatever the quality, I will accept it as true and live it this week.*

A sword for the Lord and for Gideon! This was the rallying cry that aroused the victimized Israelites to go on the offensive against Midian. Note the order of the names.

God wants there to be no mistake about where the might and victory come from; he wants us confident, not cocky; valiant, not vain. And so He instructs Gideon to send all but three-hundred men back to their homes. With this handful He — and valorous Gideon — ends the Midianite scourge forever.

> *In the conflicts I face this month, I will adopt Gideon's battle cry as my own: A sword for the Lord and for _____!*

—ELIZABETH SHERRILL

---

16 *Forasmuch as ye are manifestly declared to be the epistle of Christ ministered by us, written not with ink, but with the Spirit of the living God; not in tables of stone, but in fleshy tables of the heart.* —II CORINTHIANS 3:3

Before me is today's mail. I reach for the bundle with anticipation and fan it out across my desk. Bills...a sweepstakes' offer...a charity solicitation...a fund-raiser notice.... And then in the midst of all the clutter, one letter gleams bright and true. It is a letter from home, addressed to me by name and in a familiar handwriting. It tells me...

that my parents are alive and well,
    what they have been doing recently,
        and that *I am loved.*

The world is full of impersonal messages. People crave a letter from home, addressed to them by name and in a familiar handwriting. They need to know...

that their Heavenly Parent is alive and well,
    what He has been doing recently,
        and that *they are loved.*

You and I are letters from Christ to the world. We can be messengers of His love today.

Dear Lord, thank You for letting us serve as Your letters to today's lonely world. We will share Your Good News.

—PATRICIA HOUCK SPRINKLE

---

17 *Now the God of hope fill you with all joy and peace in believing...* —ROMANS 15:13

The other teachers said that he *wanted* to fail. We knew that he was bright, that he could do as well as anyone else, if not better. But he refused even to try and no one could reach him — not with praise, not with disciplinary threats, not with well-meaning offers of assistance.

One day I had him stay after class and I told him, "You leave me no choice. I'm going to have to fail you. Doesn't that matter to you?"

"Not really," he drawled, leaning back in his chair with that slight mocking smile of his.

With that I ran out of hope and I let him go. He ambled out of the room jauntily. "Oh, Lord," I said out loud. "What did this to him? Please, God, *do* something!" I put my head down on the desk...and unexpectedly found myself in tears.

I don't know how long I had been sitting there when I felt a hand on my shoulder. I looked up. He had returned. "I didn't know ...that...that anybody cared that much," he said. The mocking smile was gone. "If I try, will you help me?"

"You'll have to work very hard," I replied. "Both of us will."

"Then let's get started," he said. "Right now."

He did work hard and he did do well — in all of his classes. And finally he even became one of our best students!

But maybe I learned even more than he did. I learned that God answers prayer. That despair is contagious...but so is its antidote, hope.

When I despair, Lord, I know that soon You will raise me with Your hope.　　　　　　　　　　　　　　　　　　　　—PHYLLIS HOBE

---

18 *And the Lord said unto Moses, Wherefore criest thou unto me? speak unto the children of Israel, that they go forward...*　　　　　　　　　　　　　　　— EXODUS 14:15

A friend of mine had been carefully studying the life of Moses. "Here was Moses, praying," he told me, "when all the time the children of Israel were trapped between the Red Sea and the pursuing Pharoah. God said to Moses in effect, 'Move! I have promised to support you.'"

I saw the message: There are times when prayer cannot be used as a substitute for effort.

Once I heard my minister rebuke a misguided young man who had asked for prayers for an increased income. "God," the minister said, "does not put money in your bank account by a conjuring trick."

I must remember that there are times when God does *for* us what He can only do *through* us.

Father, teach me to shoulder my part. Do not let me attempt to accomplish by supplication that which can be done only by my own action. — ELAINE ST. JOHNS

---

19 *But we have this treasure in earthen vessels, that the excellency of the power may be of God, and not of us.*
—II CORINTHIANS 4:7

My mother's newest purchase from the city dump was a squat-looking pot she had bought for fifty cents.

"Exactly like the one Grandmother kept by the fireplace," she beamed.

"Maybe, Mama, but —" *It was ugly,* I thought. But when Mother rotated a scratch pad gently over the painted surface of the pot, she let out a squeal of delight. It was my turn to gasp. The pot was copper. *Real copper!*

How true to life, I thought. All around me there are persons like that poor pot. Persons who have been cast into the dumps of despair. Once created in God's image, they are now layered with ugliness, thought to be worthless, and cast aside. They need somebody who cares enough to believe in their hidden beauty. To polish them. And let them shine.

Lord, whose spirit can I help shine with a new glow?
—JUNE MASTERS BACHER

20 *... Pour out thine heart like water before the face of the Lord...* —LAMENTATIONS 2:19

A little boy was playing happily on the beach, digging a hole in the sand. Carefully he finished it off with a smooth collar and then, picking up a drinking cup, he busied himself with dipping the cup in the ocean and emptying it into the hole. He had made trip after trip when his father asked, "Son, what are you doing?"

"I'm pouring the ocean in the hole," he answered, "but the water disappears." With that the boy plunked himself down next to the sand sculpture in perplexity.

The incident in the sand gave me a message.

Isn't God's forgiveness rather like a container—a cup that we fill with our failures, disappointments and anger? Then He empties it, allowing our troubles to seep away. And His cup is never filled...for His forgiveness and His love for His children know no bounds.

Father, I give You another cupful today...let my errors seep away as I am filled with Your love. —ZONA B. DAVIS

21 *Pray one for another, that ye may be healed.* —JAMES 5:16

My friend Joan called me from the hospital on the night before her surgery and asked me to pray with her.

"But first," she said, "do you mind if I pray for a couple of other people?"

She prayed for her neighbor's son, whose wife had left him, and then she prayed for the lady in the other bed. Only then did we pray about Joan's upcoming surgery.

Later, when she was fully recovered, Joan explained. At age seven, when she accepted Jesus as her Saviour, the first thing her pastor told her was: "Now you have a job to do. Other people need your prayers and Jesus is waiting to hear them."

"How thrilled I was!" said Joan. "Since then, praying for others first has always made me realize that I'm important to the Lord and to other people."

I think Joan's rule is a good one — interceding before self-pleading. Praying for others opens a channel through which blessings can flow — to them *and* to you.

Help me to accept my responsibility as an intercessor, Lord.
—MARILYN MORGAN HELLEBERG

---

22 *He giveth power to the faint; and to them that have no might he increaseth strength.* —ISAIAH 40:29

Every one of us at one time or another faces something difficult, something we want to do, should do, but are afraid to do. Once I met a circus trapeze artist who told me a little true story that has always helped me whenever I hesitate to attempt a hard task.

A youngster came to him seeking lessons in becoming an aerialist. The veteran obliged, starting the lad with the basics on the lower swings, then gradually increasing the height. Finally the day arrived when he told the boy: "Now, Tony, the time has come for you to get up on the high trapeze. I've taught you everything I know. Go up there and perform."

Well, Tony went up. But just before he reached out for the bar that swung his way, he froze. "I'm afraid I can't do it!" he shouted and came back down, ashamed.

The veteran aerialist put his hand on the boy's shoulder. "Go back up, Tony. You *can* do it," he said. "Throw your *heart* over the bar, and your *body* will follow."

Strange-sounding advice? Maybe. But the boy understood. Tony obeyed and his triumph followed.

Throw your heart into victory and the rest of you will follow its lead. Whenever a problem stands in your way, think of yourself as, with God's power, spiritually rising above it. Your physical self, which is secondary, will follow.

Dear Jesus, give me a victorious attitude to meet the challenge ahead. —NORMAN VINCENT PEALE

---

23 *In every thing give thanks: for this is the will of God in Christ Jesus concerning you.* —I THESSALONIANS 5:18

My Hawaiian vacation had been perfect until this last stop. I was looking forward to one final tropical swim but now my heart sank before the barren stretch of jagged, volcanic rock.

"It's certainly not a place for swimmers," my son commented. "But put on a happy face, Mom. Let's trust that God has something better in mind and look for it."

At his insistence we hiked along the shore. Waves foamed white against ebony stone. We explored small caves, saw unusual volcanic formations and discovered a tidepool where purple sea anemones clung to the bottom. Several tiny crabs skittered sidewise and miniature tropical fish darted about. We had a great day after all and I forgot all about the swim I had wanted.

My son taught me a valuable lesson that day. Now whenever things go wrong, I try to:

1) Put on a *happy face.*

2) Trust that God has a *better* plan.

3) *Look* for it.

The Master Planner never lets me down.

Keep me alert to Your plan for me today, God...it's the best.
—DORIS HAASE

24 *...Eye hath not seen, nor ear heard, neither have entered into the heart of man, the things which God hath prepared for them that love him.* —I CORINTHIANS 2:9

"Death is the veil which those who live call life;
They sleep, and it is lifted...."

The first time I read those lines, written by the poet Shelley, I did not understand them. They seemed to compress an idea of such enormity into so few words that my mind simply bounced off them. I had to read them again and again.

But once I understood the meaning, I never forgot it. This life, Shelley is saying — the life that we are living this very minute, the life that seems so vivid and precious to us — is really blocking our vision. When we die, that veil "which those who live call life" will be lifted and we will see such unimagined magnificence that by comparison our present life will seem a temporary death.

Eighteen centuries before Shelley wrote his poetry, St. Paul expressed virtually the same idea: "Now we see through a glass, darkly; but then...."

What excitement, what hope, what promise in those two simple words: *but then!*

But then — *our eternal life with You, dear God.*
—ARTHUR GORDON

25 *For wisdom is better than rubies; and all the things that may be desired are not to be compared to it.*
—PROVERBS 8:11

To me reading is like a breath of life itself...I don't understand how people can live without it. For years I have passed along articles to my children — bits of poetry, a human-interest story, an example of courage — but like most children, they resist the very material their parents so urgently want them to read!

There must be a way, I told the Lord one day, that I can get my children's attention to these articles without seeming to nag.

I was praying about the problem as I cleared off the breakfast table. I picked up two cereal boxes and began to close them when I happened to glance at the back of one of them. Junk reading. Memory of the children hunched over a cereal box and reading intently flashed across my mind. "I've got it! Thank You, Lord," I whispered. Quickly I took two of the articles that I wanted my children to read and carefully I taped them to the backs of the cereal boxes before I replaced them in the pantry. It was almost impossible to tell that the boxes had been tampered with.

It worked! Today — without urging or nagging — the children regularly fill their minds with healthful reading from the backs of cereal boxes. Just today one of the boys said, "Hey, Mama, did you read this neat thing about our state senator on the back of the cereal box? He's something else!"

Father, for the gift of words — to teach, inspire and comfort us — we thank You.
—MARION BOND WEST

---

26   *... Knowing that of the Lord ye shall receive the reward of the inheritance: for ye serve the Lord Christ.*
—COLOSSIANS 3:24

In his book, *The Invisible Pyramid*, the late Loren Eiseley recalls a spring night in 1910 when his father took him outdoors and pointed to Halley's comet streaking across the starlit sky. His father told his young son that only if the boy lived to be an old man would he see this phenomenon again.

"I'll be gone," the father explained, "because Halley's comet comes only once in every seventy-five years."

The fact that Dr. Eiseley, noted naturalist and anthropologist, died several years short of his reunion with the famed comet (which will reappear in 1985) is another reminder of life's transience. In truth we are all strangers passing through a strange land, and our journey will be over someday. Fortunately, our success in life does not depend upon how long we live or how much wealth or power we accumulate but rather on a spiritual measure that is succinctly expressed by the Prophet Micah in an Old Testament admonition. It follows the question: "What does the Lord require of thee?" The answer: "To do justly, and to love mercy, and to walk humbly with thy God" (Micah 6:8).

Lord, my relationship with You is life's most satisfying — and only real — success. —FRED BAUER

---

27 *Thou therefore endure hardness, as a good soldier of Jesus Christ.* —II TIMOTHY 2:3

Deserted and quiet, the surface of the olympic indoor pool resembled a taut blue sheet stretched across the cement. Four weeks earlier I had taken up a regular swimming program, beginning with only a few laps and intending to work up to a full mile of sixty-four, nonstop laps. But despite all my efforts, I could not get beyond twenty laps. It seemed that I had reached an invisible wall and now I was thinking about giving up. A mile seemed an utterly impossible goal.

As I slid into the water, another swimmer plunged in beside me and began her workout. Long after I had stopped, she swam up and down the pool, back and forth.

"Where do you get such endurance?" I asked her later.

"Once when I thought I couldn't possibly go another lap," she replied, "I somehow hung on for just one more. That was when I discovered my second wind. It was like shifting into a different gear that allowed me to go the distance."

I was fascinated. Was there really such a thing as "second wind"? The next time I hit my "wall" of twenty laps, I determined to hang on and to keep on swimming despite my fatigue. Sure enough, I found a second wind! That was the day I reached the half-mile mark. Not long afterward I was swimming my "impossible" mile.

Is there a lesson here that can apply to my whole life? I think so. For when a problem rises up like a wall and it seems that I cannot go beyond it, when discouragement invites me to give up, I like to think of the second-wind capacity that God gave all of us. I am reminded to never give up too quickly; I seem to hear these energizing words of hope within myself: *If you just hang in there a little longer, you'll make the distance.*

Lord, give me a determined spirit, a second wind, when facing "impossible" situations. —SUE MONK KIDD

---

28 *... There are some which walk among you disorderly, working not at all, but are busybodies.*
—II THESSALONIANS 3:11

Sundays of my girlhood I visited my close friend Margaret. Even though we ran to her house or mine as fast as we could from church, there never seemed to be enough time to get all our playing and talking finished, and we didn't want to part when our respective mothers called us.

"Come halfway with me," Margaret begged one Sunday.

The little bonus visit was so much fun that the following Sunday we extended it. When my friend walked halfway with me, I in turn walked back part of the way with her. We dallied longer and longer.

Then came the Sunday that our back-and-forth trips went on and on, and it was sundown when I finally reached home. My mother was displeased.

"Half the way home will *never* get you here," she scolded.

Memory of the incident stayed with me. I lettered a little sign that has helped me put an end to my dillydallying too long — even with the pleasant things in life — when there is a responsibility I need to fulfill. "Half the Way Home Will Never Get You There," it says.

And that is especially important when You *call me, Lord!*
—JUNE MASTERS BACHER

---

29 ... *They have escaped the pollutions of the world through the knowledge of the Lord and Saviour Jesus Christ...*
—II PETER 2:20

While science was never my forte in school, I shall never forget reading about Dr. René Dubos, the world-renowned microbiologist, well known for the profound humanity he brought to his subject.

Especially concerned with pollution, Dubos made a profound statement that forever changed my thinking: "The most deplorable aspect of existence in American cities may not be murder, rape or robbery but the constant exposure of children to pollutants, noise, ugliness and garbage in the streets. This constant exposure conditions children to accept public squalor as the normal state of affairs and thereby handicaps them mentally from the beginning of their lives."

It is a profound principle, really, that we are affected most by the *conditions* of our immediate environment. Often I find myself complaining about crime and fearing the violent actions of others. But perhaps the criminal on the street is *me* — and the conditions that I accept. If I am willing to tolerate ugliness in my city, my home, my soul — will my children accept that wrong as right?

Is the example you have set for your children today one that you hope they can follow? Fortunately we have a Heavenly Father Who has given us the supreme guide to good living — the guide we can pass along to future generations forever.

Father, thank You for Your guiding light. Help us to follow it in all that we do. — JEFF JAPINGA

---

30 *...The God of all comfort; Who comforteth us in all our tribulation, that we may be able to comfort them which are in any trouble...* —II CORINTHIANS 1:3,4

I felt so helpless as I sat in the hospital waiting room. Down the hall my eight-year-old niece battled an illness that no one had been able to diagnose. Her temperature was 104° and all efforts to bring it down had been to no avail.

As I looked at my sister-in-law and my brother, I saw their lips move in prayer and wished that I could *do* something. Yes, I had prayed, and was continuing to pray. Still, there comes a time when you feel that you simply have to *do* something.

I looked up then and saw Jeannette, my friend and neighbor, coming toward us. She reached into a tote bag and handed each of us an orange cut into small sections, wrapped in plastic. It seemed odd to me that we sat there eating oranges but we had been too distressed to think of food. Jeanette's oranges ministered to our spirits as well as to our bodies.

Then two of the doctors joined us. My niece's temperature was subsiding. With that news we all held hands and prayed...and cried.

Before I left the waiting room, I gathered the orange peels and wrappings and put them in a wastebasket. And as I did so, I realized that Jeanette had taught me a lesson: There's always something we *can do* in a crisis. Even though we may think it very small, it can seem very big to someone else.

Lord, help me to remember the little things that people need... I know that You will take care of the big things. —PHYLLIS HOBE

---

31 *...Being reviled, we bless...* —I CORINTHIANS 4:12

When our teen-age grandchildren were small, our visits to their home always brought a chorus of "Can we go home with you?" or "Can we come and stay the night?" We loved having them.

At bedtime Marinell, the youngest of the three, liked to snuggle down in the big, extra-long bed that had been her father's and listen to me read a story. When her eyelids became heavy, we said our prayers and then I would wind up the little plush puppy that played "Lullaby" as she drifted off to sleep.

One night when saying her prayers, she said, "God bless Mama; God bless Daddy; God bless Paul Mark; God bless Grandma and Grandpa."

"You left out Stokes," I told her.

"I'm not going to 'God bless him.'"

Surprised, I asked, "Why not?"

"Because he wouldn't let me have the marbles."

"But we must forgive our enemies," I reminded her.

"He's not my enemy, he's my brother," she said firmly.

"Then *I'll* ask God to bless him," I told her. "God bless all brothers."

As I tucked her in, I heard a small voice murmer, "God bless Stokes."

Later, after I had kissed Marinell good night and left the room, I thought of the lesson: Were I to look at all people as my *brothers* and no one as my *enemies*, there would be far more thanks and blessings in my prayers.

Heavenly Father, remind me that peace does not begin with other people, but with myself. —ZONA B. DAVIS

Praise Diary for August

1

2

3

4

5

6

7

8

9

10

11

12

13

14

15

16

17

18

19

20

21

22

23

24

25

26

27

28

29

30

31

September

O Lord, thou hast searched me, and known me.
Thou knowest my downsitting and mine uprising,
thou understandest my thought afar off.

—PSALM 139:1,2

Give me, give me, give me!
    Position, rank and power....
The hunger, Lord, for things
    Can fill our waking hours.

I'm well aware, Dear Father,
    I catch the fever too,
I concentrate too much on things
    And not enough on You.

But when I pause to meditate
    On what means most to me,
YOU are my mind's contentment,
    My soul's tranquility.

—ALICE JOYCE DAVIDSON

PATTERN FOR A BLESSED LIFE

Blessed are they which are persecuted for righteousness'
sake: for theirs is the kingdom of heaven.

—MATTHEW 5:10

1

In his book, *The Persecutor*, Sergio Kourdakov tells about the terror and suffering he inflicted on Russian Christians when he was a member of the secret police. Day after day he observed the courage and devotion of the believers, even in the face of torture and the threat of death.

Then he began to realize that they possessed something that he didn't have. Eventually Kourdakov joined those whom he had once persecuted so cruelly, becoming a loyal and devout Christian.

That valiant group of believers forces me to face the fact that I take my religious freedom for granted. If someone like Kourdakov were to step into my life today, would he be so moved by the love I show to others that he would want what I have? What can I do to make it so?

Thank You, Lord, for my freedom to worship You. I will make a
special effort during September to show love to my brothers and
sisters in Christ. —MARILYN MORGAN HELLEBERG

2

. . . Ye shall know the truth, and the truth shall make you
free. —JOHN 8:32

When my daughter was a sophomore in high school, she ran for class president and lost — by one vote.

"That vote was my own," she said. "I voted for the other candidate because you taught me that no 'lady' votes for herself. But, tell me this, Mom — if I hadn't thought I would make the best class president, I shouldn't have run, right? And if I did think so, then not voting for myself didn't make me a lady but a liar. Oh, I don't blame you," she added softly. "You taught me the best you knew, probably the same thing someone taught you. But I wouldn't do that again."

At that moment I saw something magnificent happen. Kris may have lost an election but she won maturity. She had seen a truth that freed her from false behavior. And in freeing herself, she showed me the courage I needed to act on my own beliefs. As we are promised, the truth — and the truth only — can set us free.

Lord, don't let past conditioning or present assumptions prevent me from being true to myself. —ELAINE ST. JOHNS

---

3   *And he dreamed, and behold a ladder set up on the earth, and the top of it reached to heaven…*
—GENESIS 28:12

Whenever I've talked with Gloria Gaither of the talented song-writing, song-singing Gaither Trio, I've always been impressed with her insights. She has a poet's ear and eye for seeing beneath the surface and the ability to put lyrical wings on the most earthbound things. One of her secrets is to listen to children, especially her own, because she has discovered that children speak truths that are for the most part unclouded by adult sophistication.

Gloria recalls that one day a few years ago her son Benjie ran into the kitchen.

"Come outside, quick!" he exclaimed.

Reluctantly she followed him. Her son pointed at twin contrails left on the evening sky by speeding jets. Normally white, the two parallel streams had assumed the crimson glow of the Indiana sunset.

"It's a red ladder to God," Benjie said admiringly.

Gloria, touched by the scene and Benjie's description of it, hugged him and thanked him for showing her something she would have otherwise missed.

How often in our busyness we miss the red ladders of life. Ladders of beauty and opportunity that could turn ordinary days into memorable ones, mundane experiences into heavenly ones, casual relationships into lasting ones. People who have not forgotten how to be children are the ones most adept at climbing those magical rungs.

Keep me climbing higher, God, and higher....   —FRED BAUER

---

4 *The Spirit itself beareth witness with our spirit, that we are the children of God.*   —ROMANS 8:16

Monday's child is fair of face,
Tuesday's child is full of grace,
Wednesday's child is full of woe,
Thursday's child has far to go,
Friday's child is loving and giving,
Saturday's child has to work for its living,
But the child that's born on the Sabbath day
Is fair and wise and good and gay.

What fun we had learning that little nursery rhyme the year I was in the fourth grade! We'd greet each other with the question, "Whose child are you?"

It became doubly exciting when we encountered a "twin."

"Whose child are you?" someone would ask.

"I'm Friday's child," I would reply.

And what a joy when that person cried out, "I'm Friday's child too!" I still remember the warmth and closeness I felt toward my new friend.

Today I'm going to say, "I am Jesus' child!" What a joy it will be to find a "twin"!

Jesus, I'm so glad You've given us to each other.

—JUNE MASTERS BACHER

---

5 *For we are labourers together with God...*

—I CORINTHIANS 3:9

At the mention of Labor Day I immediately think of large factories with long assembly lines, blue shirts and bulldozers, sooty miners, teachers in classrooms, people operating power looms and sewing machines, mechanics under hoisted cars, hammers and tools; workers harvesting food; I think of doctors and nurses, firemen and police officers.

All who labor are so vital to our on-going world that it's only fitting that we set aside a special day for paying homage to their efforts.

But what about Christ? He had a shortage of laborers. Jesus told His disciples, "The harvest truly is plenteous, but the laborers are few."

Are you ready to roll up your sleeves and go to work as one of Christ's "laborers" for love in the world today?

Yes, Lord, I'm ready to do my part.   —ZONA B. DAVIS

6

Be still, and know that I am God... —PSALM 46:10

I believe one of the beautiful mysteries of God's world is the unexpected power in silence. For years I walked my dog in Central Park at the same hour a neighbor walked hers. Then one tangy autumnal morning she came up to me and said, "I'm leaving tomorrow. I'm going back to live in France again. I doubt that I shall ever return."

"I'm sorry," I said. "I shall miss you."

"And I you," she said. "You've been a wonderful friend." She reached up and kissed me on the cheek, then walked away.

The odd thing about that encounter is this: It was the first conversation we had ever had. Those were the first words we had ever spoken to each other.

And yet she and I *were* friends, good friends. Every morning we had sent out signals of friendship through a glint in the eye, a nod, a smile. She and I liked the way we cared about our animals, the way we both drank in the glories of mornings in the park. We trusted each other, and all without a word being spoken.

What incredible things are accomplished silently! We don't hear the gravitational pull on the oceans, but its force is awesome. We don't hear the rays of the sun, but they cause seeds to sprout and the earth to green. And sometimes, I think you'll agree, it is even possible to hear a silent sound. In the quiet of a church, for instance, there is no better place for hearing the Voice of God.

Heavenly Father, in silence I will seek You now. —VAN VARNER

7 *Beloved, follow not that which is evil, but that which is good.* —III JOHN 11

My husband and I were driving through heavy fog on our way to a party aboard the *Queen Mary*. We had never been to the Long Beach Marina before. As we wound our way past warehouses and docks, we noticed that one car in particular had been in front of us for most of the time.

"He's probably going to the same place we are," I suggested to my husband. "Why don't you follow him?"

He did. When at last both cars came to a stop in a dead-end street, the man got out and walked back to us.

"Say, do you folks know how to get to the *Queen Mary?*" he asked....

"Before I ever follow anyone again," my husband commented after receiving directions from a gas-station attendant, "I'm going to be very sure he knows where he's going!"

A good resolution, not only for traveling but for living. Each day we have many opportunities to do good or evil...to be patient or irritable...to show kindness or selfishness. Before setting the course, however, we must make very sure that we're headed in the right direction.

Dearest Jesus, help me always to follow You! —DORIS HAASE

8 *For whosoever shall do the will of God, the same is my brother, and my sister, and mother.* —MARK 3:35

While I was going to college, I had a summer job in a Chicago bank where I became close friends with one of my co-workers. He was Protestant and I was Catholic.

259

One day as we were traveling by bus to his home for dinner, we passed a large church.

"Watch all the Catholic men in the bus tip their hats," I whispered to him.

Sure enough, as the bus rumbled past the church, men seated here and there throughout the bus tipped their hats, some of them without even looking up from their newspapers.

My Protestant friend asked, "Why do they do that?"

I answered. "It's just a way of saying hello to God."

After we reached our stop, we had a few blocks to walk before coming to my friend's house. As we approached a church, my friend pointed toward it and said, "Here's where *I* go to church. Do we say hello?"

"Of course we do," I replied — and we tipped our hats.

In the same block there was a building that, judging from the Star of David on the door, was a synagogue. Neither my friend nor I said a word. We simply tipped our hats.

Heavenly Father, Creator of us all, we acknowledge to You that we are brothers.
　　　　　　　　　　　　　　　　　　　　—GLENN KITTLER

---

9   *For we are his workmanship, created in Christ Jesus unto good works, which God hath before ordained that we should walk in them.* —EPHESIANS 2:10

One of our family's all-time favorite pets was a dog named Scampy. He was a black-and-tan, rag-eared mutt, part cocker, part Schnauzer, part whatcha-ma-call-it. When he was six months old, he was hit by a car and suffered a broken hind leg, which was put in a splint. Gangrene developed and the veterinarian recommended euthanasia. My children, however, full of love and affection for

Scampy, lobbied for amputation and their tearful motion, put to a vote in a family council, was carried.

To my pleasant surprise, Scampy adjusted beautifully. Like a tricycle with the wheels reversed, he developed excellent balance and although running in unorthodox motion, he moved amazingly fast. Squirrels scattered when he flew off the back porch as though propelled by a pogo stick.

Friends of the children called him Hopalong or Tripod or Crip, among other names, but Scampy had a couple of advantages over people: He didn't understand their jibes and he didn't know that he was handicapped. He lived on courageously for many years, doing the best with what he had. People who can do the same are, I am convinced, the winners in life.

Father, help me focus on what I am — and what I've got; not what I wish I had — and what is not. —FRED BAUER

---

10 *A merry heart doeth good like a medicine...*
—PROVERBS 17:22

Can laughter heal? The personnel of DeKalb General Hospital near Atlanta, Georgia, think so. There, a new room has been opened — a room especially for laughter — in the cancer section of the hospital.

A nurse in Atlanta had read an article about the opening of such a room in a Houston hospital. She had also heard about a man who overcame a crippling illness by taking large doses of vitamin C — mixed with heavy doses of laughter. He had spent many hours of each day in viewing comedy films. *Well,* she thought, *the idea might work here too.*

So "The Lively Room" — named after its doner, Mr. Lively —

was born. The room has been carefully decorated. There's a player piano and a video discplayer, with reels of musicals and comedies. "It's laugh or cry," a cancer patient who often visits "the laughing room" commented. "Laughter is so helpful to cancer patients," she added.

And laughter, the Bible tells us, is beneficial to any condition — whether it be poor health or poor spirit. Job, with all his problems and pains was told that "He will fill your mouth with laughter" (Job 8:21). And in Proverbs 14:13 we read, "Even in laughter the heart may be in pain."

Why not try one of the Bible's most delightful prescriptions for good health today?

We thank You, Father, for the healing gift of laughter.
—MARION BOND WEST

---

11 *... And what is the exceeding greatness of his power to us-ward who believe...* —EPHESIANS 1:19

When our five-year-old grandson Stokes spent a weekend with us, he was eager to participate in everything we did.

On Saturday afternoon my husband rolled out the lawn mower and began to cut the grass. "Let me do that, Grandpa," Stokes begged. "Let me do it."

"Okay," Plaford told him. "Put your hand on mine." Stokes did and away they went around the lawn.

When they had finished, Stokes came in the house and proudly announced, "I mowed the lawn!"

"Great!" I told him. "I must go see how pretty it is." Stokes just beamed.

That, I thought, *is what God tells us when we want to achieve something but haven't the ability to do it on our own. He has given us a standing invitation to "Put your hand on Mine." It is then that we receive the wisdom, direction, inspiration and determination to accomplish those things that we could not do otherwise.*

Lord, I will reach out for Your steadying hand — today.

—ZONA B. DAVIS

---

12   *All scripture is given by inspiration of God, and is profitable...*   —II TIMOTHY 3:16

The sociology test papers had just been returned to us by our teacher; I wasn't at all pleased. I scribbled a note to Ann, who was sitting next to me. "Did you see the test results?" I scrawled angrily. "I got a 57. I guess I can write this class off for this semester."

Ann smiled as she handed me her reply. "*Hear instruction, and be wise, and refuse it not. Proverbs 8:33.* I got a 42."

I scribbled back, "Why does he give such hard tests? I bet everybody did poorly."

"*An inheritance may be gotten hastily at the beginning; but the end thereof will not be blessed. Proverbs 20:21.* I guess we won't forget that material, will we?"

By this time I was smiling. I realized that my attitude had been hasty. "Thanks for the lift — and the lesson," I wrote.

"*A soft answer turneth away wrath. Proverbs 15:1.* Don't thank me, thank God," was the reply.

"Is there any question you *don't* have a verse for?" I queried.

"Yes," Ann wrote back with a twinkle in her eye. "How do I get a date for Friday?"

Quickly I pulled out the small Bible I always carry in my backpack and began paging to Proverbs. "*Many daughters have done virtuously, but thou excellest them all. Proverbs 31:29.* Pizza Friday?"

Father, thank You for Your complete guide to the conduct of our lives — the Bible. —JEFF JAPINGA

---

13 *... For in the wilderness shall waters break out, and streams in the desert.* —ISAIAH 35:6

Have you seen the riverbeds of America's Southwest? Most of the time they are full of dust — they look more like rocky roads than riverbeds. Occasionally a thin trickle of water flows through but only when heavy rains come or the snows melt do those riverbeds gush with torrents of water.

Christians are like those riverbeds, I think. We may not always gush with Living Water. Sometimes we may feel dried up for days and weeks. Then we meet someone who needs a listening ear or sympathy for a minor grief or prayer for a new endeavor, and a trickle of Living Water flows through us as we reach out to another.

Ah — but sometimes, only sometimes — we feel the surge as a flood of Living Water pours through us to quench a mighty thirst, to cause blossoms of joy to bloom in an especially barren existence. And we know it is this for which we have been waiting.

The riverbed doesn't decide for itself how much water it will carry; it can only prepare itself. And when I as a Christian feel dry and arid, I simply need to remember the riverbed, wait — and stay ready. Today the flood may come!

Dear Source of Living Water, I hold myself in readiness this day for Your love to flow through me to others.

—PATRICIA HOUCK SPRINKLE

14 *He hath made every thing beautiful in his time...*
—ECCLESIASTES 3:11

We had anchored in a spot in Long Island's Moriches Bay that in years past had yielded countless fluke and weakfish. But on this day an hour passed with nary a bite.

"Not much of a day," I said to my friend, Bill O'Brien.

"You never know," he said philosophically.

I retreated into my gloom. Another half hour passed, slowly.

"I thought rainy days made for the best fishing," I commented.

"The tide's going to change in twenty minutes," Bill said. "Things will probably pick up then."

Half an hour later I asked, "Well?"

"Take it easy, Jim. Things could be worse," Bill cautioned.

Then, not twenty feet from the boat, a sleek, dark brown head emerged from the water.

"A seal!" we exclaimed in unison.

Hearing our voices, the creature turned his delicate, whiskered snout to us, blinked, gave a little snort and deftly flipped under water. Fascinated, we watched him surface several times before he disappeared into the distance.

"Wow, I've never before seen a seal in the wild!" I exclaimed.

"I daresay we're the first to see one in these waters for thirty years," Bill said. "He was a handsome little feller, wasn't he?"

As suddenly, my day transformed, I realized that I needn't have put such a bad face on it in the first place. As Bill had said, "You never know." We still reminisce about the time we saw the seal, but the important thing about that outing is that it taught me a lesson: Look for the best in each day, rainy or sunny. God gives us each new day — unlike any other — and each has its own wonderful possibilities.

Thank You for today, Lord. With Your help, I'm going to make the best of it. —JAMES McDERMOTT

JOURNEY OF FAITH

15 Your traveling companion is NAAMAN
... who learned that the lowest road leads highest.

—II KINGS 5

Naaman had plenty to be proud of. The general of Syria's army, he was *a mighty man of valor* who had won his nation's independence from the great Assyrian Empire.

And then...Naaman contracted leprosy.

When the first telltale white spot appeared on General Naaman's body he was terrified. He made the rounds of local miracle workers, spending a fortune on incantations and spells, paying inflated prices for amulets of locusts' eggs and foxes' teeth.

Nothing helped. The hideous pale patch spread and multiplied. Naaman, "the Delight" of his people became Naaman, "the Leper."

Now, Naaman was accustomed to moving in the best circles — with kings, generals, high priests. When you need help, go to the top. Right? Meanwhile, beneath Naaman's very nose there was a little slave girl who told her mistress, Naaman's wife, about a prophet in her own land of Israel who had a gift of healing.

Ordinarily the great general would have paid no attention to her: she was a slave, an Israelite, a female, a child — by definition "inferior."

But Naaman was desperate enough to follow the advice of the slave girl, although he still operated through his own channels: power and money. From the king of Syria he secured a letter of recommendation to the king of Israel. He gathered ten embroidered robes, ten talents of silver and six thousand shekels of gold — more than one hundred thousand dollars — and headed for Israel.

And lo, he discovered that his connections and his cash counted for nothing. The king read the letter and was distressed: but *he* couldn't heal leprosy! And the prophet would have none of Naaman's money. As Naaman left the prophet's door, a servant brought the proud Syrian general a message: *Go and wash in the Jordan seven times.* Naaman stormed away as you and I often do when God catches us by surprise. He was offended.

Once more *it was a servant* (not a king or a fellow officer) who spoke the word of God to Naaman: "If the prophet had bid thee do some *great* thing, wouldst thou not have done it?"

Of course Naaman would have! So would we! Some great act of devotion, some deed of heroism or sacrifice. But to just...dunk... dunk up and down in a river? This is what our pride finds hardest. It's too easy. Surely God requires more of us?

Yet it was thus that proud Naaman stepped into the muddy and meager Jordan.

Incredulous, unable at first to grasp what was happening to him, Naaman watched those dread white spots become clean, *like the flesh of a little child.*

Naaman hurried back to the prophet's house. This time he dismounted from his chariot and stood humbly before the door. And this time the man of God came to greet him...as God greets us when we climb off our high horse. By coming with empty hands and by asking in order to receive, Naaman discovered the greatness of God and his own insignificance. It is the way to true faith.

> *Lord, I am grateful that I never cease to need, because need sets me on the road to You.*

—ELIZABETH SHERRILL

---

16 *... Thy sins are forgiven thee.* —LUKE 5:20

When my son John was in the primary grades, he went to a new friend's house after school one blizzardy day and forgot to call home. I phoned all the friends he regularly played with, but no one knew where he was. As the snow continued to fall and drift, and the temperature dropped, my worry intensified. I drove all around his route to and from school, but no John. Desperate, I headed home to call my husband.

As I walked in the door, the phone rang. It was John, sheepish and apologetic. After my initial relief, I was angry and scolded him. He promised never to let it happen again, and I let the matter drop.

Later in the evening he put a note in my lap. It said, in laboriously printed letters, "PLEASE FORGIVEN ME." And I realized that even though I thought I'd forgiven him, I was still angry and had been abrupt with him all night. His spelling error made it clear to me that to *forgive* is to put the whole thing in the *past* tense. And I did.

Lord, when we forgive, help us to make it forgiven.

—MARILYN MORGAN HELLEBERG

---

17 *O the depth of the riches both of the wisdom and knowledge of God! how unsearchable are his judgments, and his ways past finding out!* —ROMANS 11:33

I had left home early in the morning, driven for almost three hours to an unfamiliar city, become caught in rush-hour traffic and lost an hour in looking for a parking space. Then the newspaper files I needed for research on an article I was writing weren't in place — and no one knew where they were.

Once again in my car and maneuvering the crowded city streets, heading homeward, the engine sputtered, coughed and almost quit. "You'd better get to a garage!" another driver called to me. *Yes, but where?* I wondered with mounting panic. *How do you find a garage in a big city like this?*

That's when I told God exactly how I felt. "I just can't take any more, Lord," I said. I could almost hear His reply. "Stay calm. You can take a little more if you have to."

So I crept on, block after block, and suddenly — a garage! "It's five o'clock, lady," the owner said. "We're closed." But he did tell me of another garage a mile away. Maybe, if I hurried…maybe, if the engine lasted.…

Just as I pulled up to the entrance, the car gasped, shuddered and went dead. The mechanic was locking up. He really didn't want to help me — but he did. When I didn't have enough cash, he really didn't want to take my check — but he did. And even though his wife had dinner waiting and he didn't really want to, he thoroughly checked the engine, making certain it would get me home safely.

"I don't know why I'm doing this," he mumbled as he worked. But I knew.

It was God's way of telling me to have confidence in His plans at all times. By enabling me to "take it," He had used my needs for His creation of another Good Samaritan.

If You tell me to do it, God, I will…even though I may not understand. —PHYLLIS HOBE

---

18 *I am the good shepherd, and know my sheep…and they shall hear my voice…* —JOHN 10:14-16

A friend who had just returned from the Holy Land was explaining to me the Eastern shepherd and his ways.

"They don't drive their sheep as we do," he said. "They literally lead them. Each shepherd has his own unique singsong that his sheep recognize and follow. Actually it's difficult to lose a sheep unless it has wandered off and come a cropper — that is, gone over a cliff, been caught in brambles, fallen to beasts of prey. Otherwise a strayed sheep hears his shepherd's call and returns safely to the flock. Of course there are shepherds — and shepherds. Some *will* desert the sheep, go off to town for a bit of excitement —"

"In which case," I quipped, "it's a question of a lost shepherd, not a lost sheep!"

Somehow the little story remained with me. Have I been running

SEPTEMBER 1983

around anxiously seeking a lost shepherd? Or have I been steadfastly
listening for the voice of the Good Shepherd — and following?

*Lord, I accept You as the Good Shepherd, always with me. I
cannot be lost nor can I stray while I heed Your voice.*

—ELAINE ST. JOHNS

SEVEN DAYS TOWARD A BETTER YOU

*Monday is a good day to try something new! Let's call this
week "Involvement Week." Wouldn't it be exciting to work steadily
through the coming week on seven phases of your inner life and
come out a mere 168 hours later noticeably changed — for the
better?*

*So why don't you set aside this week to deliberately increase
your spiritual awareness? Join Arthur Gordon as he takes you
through this seven-day blueprint for Bible-based action.*

19 DAY ONE
Judge not... —MATTHEW 7:1

A temptation that we all face from time to time is the
impulse to say something derogatory or unkind about someone else.

Why are we like this? One reason may be a childish need to feel
superior. Me first. Me best. Pointing out other people's deficiencies
may allow us to feel less uneasy about our own. But that's no excuse.

*So your discipline for the first day of the week is to make a major effort
to go through your whole day — from wake-up to bedtime — without
criticizing another human being.* You might slip and *think* unkind
things, but the discipline insists that you not *express* them. Not a
single one.

So begin with a prayer. Ask God to cleanse and purify your

thoughts. Then each time a critical or disdainful thought about another person enters your mind, put it out. Bite your tongue. Count to ten. Do anything — but do not voice that criticism!

At the end of the day, if you have succeeded, you will feel a deep glow of satisfaction. If you have slipped, take pencil and paper and write down a brief record of each lapse. Pray for the person you judged and ask God to forgive you. Then next Monday read your notes to yourself and start out all over again.

Give me only words of appreciation today, God.

—ARTHUR GORDON

---

20 DAY TWO
Seventy times seven... —MATTHEW 18:22

Can you honestly say that there is no one against whom you hold a grudge or harbor ill will? You're a rare person if you can. Most of us carry some grievance within our hearts because we have been wounded by another at some time in our lives.

But grievances, even those that seem justified, are like barnacles on the hull of a ship, slowing it down, holding it back. Christ Himself recognized this when He told His disciples to forgive not just seven times, but seventy times seven.

Today list the names of persons whom you feel have wronged you, those from whom you are separated by a gulf of anger or resentment. Then choose one person from your list and do something about bridging the gulf.

Make a phone call. Write a note. Go to that person and let him know in your own way that hostilities are over. Your overture may be rejected, and that can be painful. But the fact that you made it is what counts. Inside, you will glow with peace of mind.

God calls it: forgiveness. It's offering another person another chance, isn't it? A chance to heal the relationship, to smooth away the anger, to remove the bitterness. It's the end of estrangement.

I release these hurts to You, God, and forgive.

—ARTHUR GORDON

---

21 DAY THREE
God loveth a cheerful giver... —II CORINTHIANS 9:7

Today in our computerized world, all too often charity becomes remote and impersonal. We give to one needy organization or another, almost as concerned about the tax deduction as with alleviating human misery.

One reason for this may be that we have no direct contact with our recipient. The results of our giving are not witnessed firsthand by us and thus much of the joy of giving is lost.

So the discipline for Wednesday is very specific: Take a possession that you are especially fond of, something that has real value for you, and give it away. Not to a friend who may somehow reciprocate but to a person who needs it more that you do and who cannot repay you.

What you give and how you give it are up to you, but you must make a direct, personal contact, with no intermediary and no hope of reward — not even the pleasure of letting others know how generous you have been. You must tell no one what you have done.

Your secret deed, God in private will reward. For "Give, and it shall be given unto you," the Bible tells us.

From out of my abundance, Lord, I will give.

—ARTHUR GORDON

22 DAY FOUR
Be thankful...   —PSALM 100:4

Each one of us is a debtor, not just to the Giver of life but to the countless individuals who have helped us along the way. Parents who gave us love and protection. Teachers who gave us education and knowledge. Physicians who guarded or restored our health. Friends who offered sympathy or understanding in time of need. Fellow workers who carried the load for us when we weren't capable of carrying it ourselves. The list is endless.

But all too often our debts go unacknowledged. We may feel grateful, but gratitude — like love — isn't much good unless it is expressed. And so the discipline for today — Thursday — is to make a deliberate and concentrated effort to say "Thank you."

Take paper and pencil. Make a list of the ten persons still living to whom you are the most indebted for past thoughtfulness and kindness. Then choose three of them and write each one a note, setting forth the gratitude and remembrance in your heart. One note may be to a former schoolteacher who awakened in you a love of poetry. Another may be to a boss who decided to overlook a mistake you made. Another to a friend who stood by you in a time of trouble.

No matter who the individuals are, a simple "Thank you," even when expressed after many years, will light a glow in their hearts — and rekindle one in your own.

For special friends, Father, and a grateful heart, we thank You.
                                          —ARTHUR GORDON

23 DAY FIVE
Pray without ceasing...
—I THESSALONIANS 5:17

Every dieter is aware of the quick-weight-loss diets in which one of the requirements is to drink eight full glasses of water every day. It sounds easy. Actually, it's not. But without the repetition of this simple act eight times a day, the experts say, the diet won't produce results.

Repetition has its value in developing spiritual awareness too. *The discipline for today, therefore, is to write down a prayer that you find meaningful or a passage of Scripture that inspires you. Don't choose a mere four-line prayer or a single verse of Scripture; choose something with substance to it. Then on eight separate occasions during the day find time to read the passage you have written down and meditate on it for five minutes. Ask yourself: What do the words really mean? What are they trying to say to me? Is the message deeper than I had thought?*

Finding five minutes eight times a day is similar to drinking eight glasses of water — much harder than it sounds. But if you can discipline yourself to set aside those forty minutes and really *use* them, at the end of the day the passage you have chosen will be driven deep into your mind and you will have it forever — it will have become a part of you.

Speak to me, Father, through Your Holy Word, and change me.
—ARTHUR GORDON

24 DAY SIX
A still small voice...
—I KINGS 19:12

This is a noisy and clamorous age; there are few oases of quiet. Yet inner quietude is necessary if we are to listen to "the still

274

small voice" described in the Bible. Saturday, a nonworking day for most of us, is a logical day to seek surcease from the world's din and to reach out for an inner serenity and peace of mind.

The best time to seek quietness is in the early morning, before the oncoming day ruffles the sleep-calmed surface of the mind. Solitude is essential and silence helps. Your surroundings should be familiar. Physical relaxation is a must. Allow yourself fifteen minutes.

Find a comfortable chair. In your imagination summon up a favorite scene that is filled with tranquility: a mountain lake, a lonely beach at sunset, whatever appeals to you. If you feel like reading for a few minutes, choose something that is apart from daily affairs. Poetry is good. The Bible is better. The psalms are uplifting.

Don't try to analyze what you are reading, just accept it. When you feel that you have reached a level of serenity, close the book. Shut your eyes. Try to let go of everything: hopes, plans, dreams, problems, even your identity. Don't expect anything. Just be open. Be receptive. Surrender to the quietness. Let it enfold you, sustain you, restore you. Go as far as you can into the stillness. Then return and face the day.

Is this a form of prayer? Of course it is. The Bible says: "In *quietness* and in confidence shall be your strength." The two go hand in hand.

Thank You for this moment of quiet, Lord, and for Your Presence. —ARTHUR GORDON

---

25 DAY SEVEN
Praise the Lord, O my soul... —PSALM 146:1

Sunday is a day of relaxation from disciplines, which, after all, are a form of work. The wisest Man Who ever lived took one day off in seven. So should you.

It's a day for renewal, for restoration, for revival — and this week, for review.

Go to church half an hour early. There in the stillness, look back over the week just past. How did your efforts go? How successful were you in:

> *Withholding judgments?*
> *Giving up your grudges?*
> *Parting with your possessions?*
> *Expressing gratitude?*
> *Deepening your spiritual awareness?*
> *Achieving inner quietness?*

Give yourself honest answers. Then let go — and open yourself fully to the service that is about to begin. Allow God's peace to descend upon you.

And remember, after Sunday comes Monday. If you want to improve on your performance of the past week, there are always another seven days!

Every day, Lord, I want to grow more and more like You.

—ARTHUR GORDON

---

26 *Now then we are ambassadors for Christ...*

—II CORINTHIANS 5:20

There were several of us in the waiting room when a young woman with a small girl entered. The mother slipped off the child's wraps, smoothed her long, dark hair and handed her a story book. The child ignored the book and gazed steadily at me with large, brown eyes. Then she announced happily, "You're a grandma!" Laughing, I said, "You're right!"

The little girl's observation sparked some soul-searching on my part later. Although I had been sitting there anonymously, my face had apparently said something to her.

I wonder. Does my face communicate a message to all those with whom I come in contact — on the street, in the market place, in a restaurant, in church? What does it say? That I'm happy? That I'm worried? Or indifferent? Doubting?

Maybe if I radiate enough faith, someday someone will announce to me, "You're a Christian!"

Let my face carry Your message of love and hope to those I meet, Father.　　　　　　　　　　　　　　　　　　　　　—ZONA B. DAVIS

---

27 *Rejoice evermore. Pray without ceasing. In every thing give thanks...* —I THESSALONIANS 5:16-18

Although I had been wanting to pray before eating when I dined out in public places, my self-consciousness in restaurants always seemed to overwhelm me. But today as the waitress set a bowl of steaming chili before me, I bowed my head in silence for a moment.

I was about halfway through my meal when a woman at an adjacent table turned to me. "Excuse me, sir, but were you praying?"

"Uh, well...yes, I was," I stammered.

"Would you please pray for my daughter too? She left home a month ago and I don't know where she is. Please, would you ask God to protect her?"

I assured her that I would and then watched a smile cross her careworn face, a smile that buried whatever self-consciousness I had felt earlier. "It helps so much to have others praying with me — I know that with God Jeannie will be okay." Even though her eyes brimmed with tears, the eternal hope in a mother's love shone through.

It's wonderful, I thought as the woman left to pay her check, *what simple prayer can do — every time.* Not only does it open the door to the healing love of God but it turns strangers into friends as they openly share their love for Him.

Keep me ever eager to pray, Father, in deepest solitude or in the midst of throngs.   —JEFF JAPINGA

---

28   *If I then, your Lord and Master, have washed your feet; ye also ought to wash one another's feet.*   —JOHN 13:14

The headmaster of the Connecticut high school that I attended in the middle fifties, George Van Santvoord, had the unique faculty of being gracious in every situation. Whether he was engaged in conversation with the school groundskeeper about azaleas or with a scholar about Latin grammar, he was wonderfully at ease.

One day when a newly hired Spanish professor who spoke no English arrived from out of town, Mr. Van Santvoord was on hand to greet him at the railroad station. He drove the professor into town and then helped him carry his bags into a hotel room. When Mr. Van Santvoord offered his hand by way of farewell, the Spanish professor, confused, dropped a coin into his palm. The headmaster pocketed the money graciously and then briskly turned down the professor's bed before leaving.

This particular gesture has always stood out in my mind as a wonderful lesson in creative living. Mr. Van Santvoord was big enough not to feel offended and resourceful enough to make a little extra effort so that the incident could be handled with good humor later, when the professor realized his mistake. This spirit of regard is in keeping with the leadership quality that Christ exercised — it's called humility. And there's no higher virtue for you and me to strive for than that.

Make me aware, Leader of us all, that a true leader's highest function is to serve. —JAMES McDERMOTT

---

29 *. . . Ye shall be a peculiar treasure unto me above all people. . .* —EXODUS 19:5

"Want to go on a treasure hunt?" I asked my children one lazy autumn afternoon. Earlier I had buried a treasure in the back yard beside a rosebush. It was nothing more than a cigar box containing a couple of improvised certificates redeemable at the ice-cream store. The children jumped up with excitement and dashed off to the back yard.

"Am I getting hot or cold?" Bob called as he climbed up the maple tree.

"Cold — freezing cold," I told him.

"What about me? Am I getting close?" Ann asked, following some clues leading toward the rosebushes.

I smiled. "You're getting warm."

Soon the dirt was flying out of the rose garden as they tunneled into the earth with their sandbox shovels. With more glee than I had envisioned, they discovered their buried treasure.

It occurs to me that perhaps God, with His infinite concern for our welfare, has also buried a treasure — inside each and every person. A gift — a talent — a special ability. And all of life just might be a treasure hunt.

One day when my children are older, I shall remind them of the autumn day when they searched for a treasure buried by the rosebush. And I shall remind them too of the treasures buried within themselves. Treasures placed there by God.

Indeed, we each have a quest.

Father, help me to discover my gifts from You, for You.

—SUE MONK KIDD

---

30 *And, ye fathers, provoke not your children to wrath: but bring them up in the nurture and admonition of the Lord.* —EPHESIANS 6:4

One day while on a business trip in Houston, Texas, I ran across a leaflet in the hotel coffee shop. It had been distributed by the Houston Police Department and was entitled "Rules for Raising Delinquent Children"....

1. Begin with infancy to give the child everything he wants. In this way he will grow up to believe that the world owes him a living.
2. When he uses bad words, laugh at him. This will make him think he's cute. It will encourage him to pick up more "cute" phrases.
3. Never give him any spiritual training. When he's twenty-one, he can decide for himself — cultism, atheism, anything.
4. Avoid the use of the word "wrong." He might develop a guilt complex.
5. Pick up all his strewn-about items — books, shoes, clothes. Do everything for him so that he will be experienced in throwing all of his responsibilities on others.
6. Let him read any printed matter he can get his hands

on. Be careful that the tableware and drinking glasses are sterilized but let his mind feed on garbage!

7. Quarrel frequently with your spouse in the presence of your children. Then they will not be too shocked when the home is broken up later.

8. Give the child all the spending money he wants. Never let him earn his own. Why should he have things as tough as you did?

9. Satisfy his every craving for food, drink and comfort. See that every sensual desire is gratified. Denial may lead him to suffer harmful frustration.

10. Take his part against neighbors, teachers and policemen. They are prejudiced against your child.

11. When he gets into real trouble, apologize for yourself by saying, "I never could do anything for him."

12. Prepare for a little grief. You will be likely to have it!

I think these folks in Houston have said more than I could ever imagine. Let's pray *right now* for all parents and their children.

Father, children are a heavy responsibility. Help us to raise them with love. Help them to learn that those who say "NO" are saying "YES" to You. —GLENN KITTLER

Praise Diary for September

1

2

3

4

5

6

7

8

9

10

11

12

13

14

15

16

17

18

19

20

21

22

23

24

25

26

27

28

29

30

October

*Blessed be the Lord, who daily loadeth us with
benefits...* —PSALM 68:19

For answering my many prayers,
For helping me through trials and cares,
I thank You!

For dreams to dream, for plans to make,
For brand new goals to undertake,
I thank You!

For giving me the zest and will
To keep me reaching higher still,
I thank You, Lord, I thank You!

—ALICE JOYCE DAVIDSON

PATTERN FOR A BLESSED LIFE

Blessed are ye, when men shall revile you, and persecute you, and shall say all manner of evil against you falsely, for my sake. —MATTHEW 5:11

1

"Don't tell me you're going to *another* kook meeting!" exclaimed my visiting relative. "Boy, you've *really* gone off the deep end!"

His remark stung because the "kook meetings" he referred to were my prayer group meetings. By comparison with others, I know that my little persecutions are practically nothing and yet...they hurt.

Jesus warned us about this. He said that should we decide to put Him first, we might not always "fit in." Well, maybe it's not so bad to be a little different. The approval of others can't bring heavenly comfort or secure the Kingdom of Heaven. But trying to live the Beatitudes can. Jesus said so. Compared with the inner joy of living in Christ's presence, human disapproval — even taunting — fades into insignificance.

This month, Lord, I'll put You first. If this brings human disapproval, help me to face it with grace.

—MARILYN MORGAN HELLEBERG

2

The wolf also shall dwell with the lamb...and the calf and the young lion and the fatling together; and a little child shall lead them. — ISAIAH 11:6

Every year on this Sunday the young people of Arroyo Grande, a farming community where I live, gather on the lawn of St. Barnabas Episcopal Church for the Blessing of the Animals.

286

There are 4-H Club members with their "projects": piglets, sheep, calves, horses, in-training guide dogs; wilderness-minded youngsters with brush foxes, jack rabbits, lizards, snakes; toddlers with kittens, puppies, canaries, hamsters. To my city-bred mind it is a yearly miracle that this amalgamation does not result in chaos, if not carnage.

The harmony that prevails is due to the young people themselves. They display affection and consideration without sentimentality, respect and care for their animals and for each other. Their attitude results in the spontaneous courtesy of polite, considerate, helpful acts or remarks — and it is quite apparently contagious. It is this kind of simple courtesy that illuminates the childlike spirit of Francis of Assisi, whose life this day commemorates. In him it reached a perfection, clearly the result of his love for all of God's Creation. By his kindliness he preached easily to the birds, rebuked a deranged wolf, spoke gently but firmly to flies.

These acts were called miracles. And they were. Miracles of courtesy — as possible now as they were then.

Father, let me so respect Thy Creation that I deal courteously with all. — ELAINE ST. JOHNS

---

3 *... A doer of the work, this man shall be blessed in his deed.* —JAMES 1:25

I am told that there is a group of Indians in the Canadian Northwest who have no word in their language for "thank you." It isn't that they are ungrateful or impolite. They simply believe that the best way to respond to kindness is by kindness returned.

I think that these people understand a basic truth many of us forget: namely, actions speak louder than words.

OCTOBER 1983

I'm grateful that we have words in the English language with which to express our thanks. But I'm also aware that on some tongues gratitude can be at times insincere or meaningless. Offhanded "thank-you" words for thoughtfulness that took considerable time and effort can be far too little payment.

Maybe we need to be more active, more demonstrative, more tangible in our thanksgiving. As one ecumenically minded Christian observed, we need less creeds, more deeds.

Give us thankful hearts, God, and help us express our thankfulness.
—FRED BAUER

---

4   *If it be possible, as much as lieth in you, live peaceably with all men.*
—ROMANS 12:18

After Robert Kennedy was assassinated, the mayor of San Francisco made a plea for people to surrender their guns voluntarily. Some two thousand weapons were turned in to be melted down and transformed into a sculpture of St. Francis.

I wept as I watched the dedication and heard thousands of voices intone the saint's immortal prayer: "Where there is hatred, let me sow love...." I even wished I owned a gun so I could offer it for peace.

How foolish I must have seemed to our Lord, for I too had weapons to surrender. What pistol could be more deadly than my refusal to love that "unlovable" person? What rifle could shoot farther than that explosive bit of gossip I passed on? What grenade could be more destructive than that old grudge?

So I would like to propose a peace plan. For each of the next ten days I'm going to take one line at a time of St. Francis' prayer and apply it to a specific situation in my life and surrender my weapon. Will you join me in the name of the Prince of Peace?

288

Lord, make me an instrument of Thy peace,
Where there is hatred, let me sow love;
where there is injury, pardon;
where there is doubt, faith;
where there is despair, hope;
where there is darkness, light;
where there is sadness, joy.
Let me seek not so much to be consoled, as to console;
to be understood, as to understand;
to be loved, as to love;
for it is in giving that we receive;
it is in pardoning that we are pardoned;
and it is in dying that we are born to eternal life.

—MARILYN MORGAN HELLEBERG

---

5 *...And, lo, I am with you alway, even unto the end of the world.* — MATTHEW 28:20

"What is the worst thing that can happen to anybody?"

When the question was posed to my discussion group in psychology class, the students came up with a variety of answers. Terminal illness...the death of a loved one...child abuse....

But the answer of a famous psychologist was very different than ours.

"I was walking through our clinic one day," John Gardner wrote, "and overheard the conversation of three boys. 'My mom yells at me,' the first boy said. 'My dad hits me,' the second said. The third, the most forlorn-looking of the three, slowly raised his eyes. 'My dad doesn't even hit me,' he said. Oh, the worst thing that can ever happen to a human being is to be isolated and ignored."

Immediately I thought of the last promise that Jesus made to us before He ascended — that no matter the circumstances, He will never abandon us. What a Friend we have in Jesus!

Father, for the love that never leaves us, we praise You.

—JEFF JAPINGA

---

6   *And we desire that every one of you do show the same diligence to the full assurance of hope unto the end...*

—HEBREWS 6:11

Once I served on a church outreach committee with a woman who always seemed to accomplish three times as much work as anyone else. Once she drew up a list of the newcomers to our town so that we could visit them and encourage them to join our church. When she handed me my portion of the list, I let out a long sigh. There were enough people on it to man two football teams. I noticed, however, that her list was even longer than mine. *How does she accomplish so much?* I wondered.

Then I caught a glimpse of a sketch of a tiny stick of dynamite that had been penciled at the bottom of her list. Across it was written "TNT."

"What is that?" I asked.

"Oh... that's my little trademark," she said, smiling.

"Dynamite?" I asked.

Now she was laughing. "No, TNT. It stands for 'Today, Not Tomorrow.'"

So that was her secret. And what an explosive effect it had upon the volume of work she did!

I took my list and starting visiting people that very day... putting a little TNT into my life too.

Help me not to procrastinate, Lord, in the work I do for You.

—SUE MONK KIDD

7 *. . . Why are ye fearful, O ye of little faith?*
—MATTHEW 8:26

The phone line hummed as I poured out my worries to a friend. Sounding like the announcer for an old-time radio soap opera, I went on and on with the details until, exhausted, I stopped talking.

"You know," my friend said quietly, "I read somewhere recently that a person who worries has no faith."

I was shocked — and hurt. But later I thought about my friend's words. In all those days when I had been stewing and fretting in the belief that only my personal attention could make everything turn out all right, had I trusted the Lord? What could *I* do about my son's job, my daughter's first year away at college, my husband's physical exam?

There were only two things, I decided, that I could do. I could pray, placing my family in the hands of God. And I could get on with my own work. Worry, I've finally realized, has no place in the life of a busy and "faith-full" Christian.

Dear Lord, I entrust my family to You and myself to this day ahead. —MADGE HARRAH

8 *. . . He that is greatest among you shall be your servant.*
—MATTHEW 23:11

One way in which my father spiced up a column that he wrote for several weekly newspapers on Long Island was to include stories about celebrities. When he first conceived of the idea, he wrote to twelve famous people, asking each of them for a short anecdote.

He sent his queries with the feeling that most of the answers he received would be from the lesser-known people in the group. But he was astounded to get six letters back. Four of them, handwritten, personal notes from Bing Crosby, Mary Pickford, Will Durant and Mary Roberts Rinehart!

"Why would these important people write to me?" my father wondered aloud to me and then went on to answer his own question: "I should have known all along that they were exactly the people who *would* write — the big-hearted people who have distinguished themselves not by ignoring other people's needs but by being sympathetic to them."

Come to think about it, that's one reason why successful people are always so busy. They don't mind obliging others.

Lord, send me someone who needs my help today.
—JAMES McDERMOTT

---

9   *But he was wounded for our transgressions, he was bruised for our iniquities: the chastisement of our peace was upon him; and with his stripes we are healed.*
—ISAIAH 53:5

One Sunday evening in autumn before the church service began, I made my way up three flights of stairs to a little prayer room. It sat like a crow's nest atop the church, a quiet alcove next to the balcony. When I entered, I found the little room caught in that brief, peculiar time just before the sun disappears, when the air is thick and warm and golden. The stained-glass window was at its luminous best. And not a sound floated up to mar the deep peace of the little alcove.

I sat down on the front bench. A gold cross gleamed brightly on the altar before me. I bowed my head, remembering the haunting words that had prompted me to climb the stairs for a few stolen moments alone with God. Words I had read the day before: "God speaks to us every day, but we do not listen." Did He? I wondered if even now God was speaking to me. Had I missed the sound of His coming into my life? I waited, my head bowed, listening to the empty, silent space.

The minutes swept by and the shadows became long and soft-hued. I looked up finally and was startled by what I saw. Directly before me shone the altar cross, and my own image was reflecting from its surface. My eyes stared back at me from the lateral cross-piece. I was captured in the cross with a strangely balanced precision, the reflection as clear and sharp as though in a mirror.

"Are you speaking to me, God?" I whispered into the glowing silence. The last bit of light filtering from the window caused my image on the cross to gleam even more brightly for an instant. Then the air was filled with the unspoken message of redemption — Jesus died for me. For ME. I belonged on the cross, not Him. And yet He took my place.

I climbed down from the prayer loft, believing. Yes, God speaks. For He came to me through my own face shining in the center of a cross.

Jesus, today let me be worthy of Your sacrifice. —SUE MONK KIDD

---

10 ... *We will give ourselves continually to prayer, and to the ministry of the word.* —ACTS 6:4

Veronica lives on a small disability income and so when her black-and-white television set broke down, I offered her my old one. All it needed were a few minor adjustments.

"Oh, I'm too busy these days to watch television," she told me.

"Busy doing what?" I asked, my curiosity aroused.

"Well," she explained, "when I was sick, many people helped me and encouraged me and I found that I had no way to repay them. So I decided that I would pray every day for each one individually, asking God to watch over them, to heal their sicknesses and to meet their needs.

"Then the whole thing snowballed and now they ask me to pray for their friends and their families too. My list just keeps on growing!"

Funny, I had wanted to give Veronica a gift; instead, she gave one to me — the gift of prayer. Today my own list is steadily growing as I put her wonderful idea into practice.

As I pray for others, Lord, I find that I come ever closer to You.
— DORIS HAASE

---

11 *Mark the perfect man, and behold the upright: for the end of that man is peace.* —PSALM 37:37

The day I received word that Evelyn had died, God taught me an important lesson through a little thing — a lopsided turkey made from colored construction paper. My little boy came home from nursery school waving it aloft and shouting, "Look, Mama! I made it for you, for nothing except that I love you."

By no stretch of the imagination was his turkey perfect. No respectable turkey mama would have even acknowledged that it *was* a turkey. Yet I was delighted with it because it was done "for nothing" — except love.

I had been trying to write a letter to Evelyn while she was ill — a perfect letter — and now she was gone. With tears streaming down my cheeks, I understood too late that Evelyn would have treasured *any* word from me — sent "for nothing" but love.

A lopsided paper turkey has made me notice something about God's world. Flowers aren't perfect, nor all trees, nor all turkeys. God concentrates only on perfection in His *perfect love*.

Do you look for perfection in your job, your home, your children, your actions? Let's follow our Heavenly Father's example and strive for God's *perfect love*.

Dear God, Who loves so much and so well, teach us daily how to love more perfectly. —PATRICIA HOUCK SPRINKLE

---

12 *For God hath not given us the spirit of fear; but of power, and of love, and of a sound mind.* —II TIMOTHY 1:7

It is madness to sail a sea that has never been sailed before, to risk falling into black nothingness in search of a land that might be only a dream. If Christopher Columbus had listened to the voices of doom that proclaimed his madness, he might never have weighed anchor. And yet it was this very madness that led him to discover a new world.

By his standards, I am much too sane. I tell myself I'm too old to learn to ski, and I longingly watch the rest of my family enjoying the thrill of the slopes. If I think my opinion might be scoffed at, I hesitate to risk saying what I believe.

Do I have to let fear or lack of confidence or the opinions of others limit me? No. Like Columbus, I too have a sturdy ship and a true compass. The name of my ship is Faith, and the Bible is my unerring compass.

If you face a challenging task today, let the triumph of a man named Columbus inspire you to set sail in Faith. Guided by your

Scriptural compass, you're bound to discover new worlds of achievement.

We can risk new things, Father, because we are supported by the ocean of Your love.   —MARILYN MORGAN HELLEBERG

---

13 *I will praise thee; for I am fearfully and wonderfully made...*   —PSALM 139:14

The popular radio and television preacher, Charles Allen, tells a story about a teacher and a six-year-old boy. When the teacher asked his name, the boy replied proudly that it was George Washington.

"That's a very special name," she responded. "I certainly hope that you will grow up to be just like George Washington."

"I can't help being like George Washington," the boy answered with uncontestable logic, "because that's who I am!"

And so it is with each of us. As long as we are ourselves and don't try to be somebody we aren't, we are sure to be somebody special. That's because God has blessed each of us with our own skills and personality. He has endowed each of us with a uniqueness that gives us our individuality. We miss the mark only when we get it into our heads that we have to be like someone else because we think our gifts are inferior.

It has been said that on Judgment Day we will not be asked why we weren't like sombody else — say, Moses, Einstein or even George Washington — but rather, *were we true to ourselves?*

Thank you, God, for my individual gifts. Help me to use them in ways that are uniquely mine.   —FRED BAUER

14 *Thou shalt not make unto thee any graven image...*
—EXODUS 20:4

A few years ago I read about a team of excavators that unearthed a round metal medallion on which the following was inscribed in an ancient language: *To the bearer of this belongs all the power and privileges of the king of Babylon.*

When I read this, I thought, *What protection that pocket piece must have provided its possessor!* Yet today its value lies only in its antiquity. The might of the one in whose name it was issued has long since vanished — his empire gone, his power shattered.

Today my medallion is not carried in my hand or in my pocket, but in my heart. It provides me with the protection of a King Whose kingdom shall never end, Whose mercy and power are eternal and Who loves me enough to give His life for me.

I need no counterfeit symbols, Jesus, for I have You and Your eternal love. —DRUE DUKE

JOURNEY OF FAITH

15 Your traveling companion is *JONAH*
...who ran in the opposite direction. —BOOK OF JONAH

I feel comfortable with Jonah. He took one look at the journey God was sending him on — and fled! Ordered to travel northeast from his home in Galilee to the city of Ninevah on the Tigris River, he headed instead southwest — to Joppa on the Mediterranean. Once there, taking no chances that God might

297

discover him, he found a ship and headed as far away as possible: to Spain — the absolute limits of the known world.

Lying in his bunk, he doubtless pulled the covers over his head. It was probably the loudest "No way!" ever uttered to a command of God; and it shows me a lot about myself. Jonah was to discover, as I do, that each time I am disobedient, God still leads.

Jonah's flight from God brought him where it brings us all: over our heads and in deep water. Each of us has our own method of avoiding God's claim on our lives, whether it's the fourteen-hour desk sprint of the workaholic, or the television addiction of the escapist...or even the nonstop good works that are not His work for us.

Sooner or later the dodges fail. The ship is nowhere in sight and we're sinking beneath the waves. But the dunking is for our benefit. God wants us out of the boat so that we can enter into a relationship with Him. As the water closed over his head, Jonah said, *"I remembered the Lord."*

Who would imagine, in Jonah's adversity, an enormous fish arriving and swallowing him up — a fish with a belly large enough for a man to live in! Who can imagine the means God will use in *your* predicament? All we can know about His provision is that it will surprise us.

Someone once said that Jonah was the first person to prove that the world was round: traveling a long way, he returned back where he started.

But not quite. The shore where the great fish deposited Jonah was a lot further from Ninevah than his original starting place in Galilee. Now he has a longer road to go. He must have reflected as he trudged ruefully along, that had he followed God's directions in the first place he would have been there by now.

But he hadn't obeyed, and neither, much of the time, do we. The great news of Jonah is that we can never stray so far that He cannot bring us back.

> *Lord, when I run from Your purpose, start me on*
> *my journey back.*

—ELIZABETH SHERRILL

16 *By faith Noah, being warned of God of things not seen as yet, moved with fear, prepared an ark to the saving of his house...* —HEBREWS 11:7

Recently I interviewed a young man who had piloted a small plane that crashed in Southern California a couple of years earlier. Not only did he survive but he was able to hike down the mountainside through heavy fog and find help for another survivor.

"I started out in an easterly direction," David recalled, "but I heard a voice say, 'That's the wrong way!' Even though it wasn't an audible voice, I heard it plainly in my mind. I reversed my steps and later I learned that the first route led through miles of wilderness. I thanked the Lord. His warning saved our lives."

Have you ever heard that warning voice? "Call your mother." "Send that letter." "Don't speak in anger!" I have but there were times when, like the people of Noah's day, I refused to listen.

Communication with the Lord is a pure blessing. He will always guide us wisely but we must first be willing to listen — and then to *follow.*

Let me hear Your voice, Lord, and at all times obey it.
—DORIS HAASE

17 *Follow after charity, and desire spiritual gifts...* —I CORINTHIANS 14:1

With a sigh I put the phone down and went in search of an audience. For an hour I had listened to a grumbling old man describe his various ailments and complain that no one ever came to see him. I started my own complaints as I reached the den.

299

"If you see him once a week, he asks why it wasn't twice. If you take him a bar of candy, he wanted a bag. He makes me feel so defensive about everything I do for him that —"

I stopped. My husband and a friend were too engrossed in television football to have heard a word I said. "Another fumble!" our friend cried, pounding the sofa arm. "I tell you, a good defense isn't enough. You have to have an offense as well."

I was stunned. Can God speak through a frustrated armchair coach? Leaving the men to their game, I went off alone to ponder the possibilities of a campaign of caring, an Offense of Love.

After several friends and I discussed the matter, we arranged a birthday party for the elderly man, cleaned his apartment and offered to wind up some affairs. We began a program of offering love *before* it was demanded. Gradually the old man became genuinely appreciative. And, more important, we found that we came to truly care for him; in fact, we mourned him when he died.

Is there someone in your life who keeps you on the defensive by making demands? Why not try an aggressive campaign of caring? We found that in love, as in football, the best defense is a strong offense!

Dear Lord, today help us love before *we are asked.*

—PATRICIA HOUCK SPRINKLE

---

18 *The Lord is nigh unto all them that call upon him, to all that call upon him in truth.* —PSALM 145:18

When my husband was transferred, we had to move clear across the country. For a month we lived in a hotel until we found a new home.

We didn't know a soul in the community. Although we attended a church for three Sundays in a row, we still felt like newcomers. So when several couples in the congregation offered to help us on moving day, we did the silliest thing. "No, thanks, we don't need any help. We'll be all right," we said shyly — at the same time dreading the hard work that we knew lay ahead.

On moving day we got up extra early to be at our new house when the movers arrived. "Burt, what on earth are all those cars doing here?" I exclaimed as we rounded the corner. Half a dozen cars were parked outside our house. Before Burt could answer, all the car doors opened and out stepped couple after couple from our new church. Not only that, they had brought all the makings for a picnic!

I never imagined that moving could be such fun. By the end of the day everything was in its place and we felt — at home. And among friends. And we were so glad that they hadn't paid any attention to us when we declined their offer to help.

Sometimes I do the same thing with God, who is always standing by, ready to help. "No, thanks," I'll say. "I can manage." But then I'm grateful when He just goes ahead and steps in anyway — because there's never a time when I don't need His helping hand.

O Lord, when I turn down Your offer to help, please ignore me!
—PHYLLIS HOBE

19 *... Rise up, and stand forth in the midst...* —LUKE 6:8

I frowned at the local newspaper. It had sponsored a writing contest for children. I liked the idea, but felt that the Halloween Scary Story Contest had elicited such gruesome responses from the children that it had been a mistake.

How sad, I thought. *Why encourage our children to dwell on such negative things? Why hadn't the paper chosen a holiday with a more inspiring theme? Somebody ought to do something!*

OCTOBER 1983

I couldn't get the contest out of my mind. I complained about it constantly.

Finally my husband said, "Write to the paper."

"They won't pay any attention to *me*," I said. But just to quiet him, I did write and suggested they sponsor another contest. I offered holiday themes: "Why I'm Thankful This Thanksgiving," "My Valentine to the World," "Why I'm Grateful to My Mother on Mother's Day," "Why I'm Grateful to My Father on Father's Day," "The Price of Liberty" and, for a back-to-school theme, "The Kindest Teacher I Ever Knew."

To my astonishment, the paper published my letter. Others wrote in agreement.

My husband grinned at me. "See? *Your* letter, *your* opinion, *your* phone call can make a difference."

The next time I think that *Somebody ought to do something*, I must remember — *I* am somebody.

Father, if I'm the one person who can make a difference, give me the courage to act.   —MARION BOND WEST

---

20   *I am the living bread... if any man eat of this bread, he shall live for ever.*   —JOHN 6:51

A teen-age friend of our daughter's was always thin, her petite frame never carrying more than ninety pounds. As a result, we didn't notice that she was becoming even thinner until we learned that she was suffering from *anorexia nervosa*, a psychosomatic malady manifested in loss of appetite so severe that it can lead to death by starvation if not dealt with in time.

In this young woman's case, the doctors determined that she was frightened of the responsibilities of impending adulthood, of going off to college and being away from home. In other words, she was

302

afraid of growing up. Fortunately, her problem was correctly diagnosed, therapy was begun and a reversal in her condition obtained before there was permanent physical damage.

I have come to believe that there is a spiritual parallel here — an individual may suffer loss of appetite for the things of God. It occurs when people lose sight of His love and turn away from the responsibilities of the mature Christian. Then spiritual malnutrition sets in.

Let's not ever be afraid of growing up! Find nourishment in His Word, today.

Father, I want to be a mature Christian, one who grows in good health with You.   —FRED BAUER

---

21 *Now then we are ambassadors for Christ...*
—II CORINTHIANS 5:20

I had cruised the parking lot for nearly fifteen minutes, looking for a parking space. *The movie has probably already started,* I grumbled to myself, checking my watch.

Suddenly I spied a car pulling out of a space just in front of me; patiently I backed up a few feet to let it out. The driver waved in thanks as he pulled away; but just as I put my car into gear, another car scooted into the space.

I laid on the horn and shouted a few choice remarks to the man behind the wheel. Then abruptly I stopped when I looked at the car's license plate — I LV GOD. It did not relieve my anger at the driver, not did I consider him any less boorish, but it did make me conscious of how often our actions do not reflect the beliefs we profess. Take the words I had just shouted out the car window — hardly Christ-like words.

I'm glad that man took my parking space. Because now, whenever I see a personalized license, I recall the I LV GOD plate. And I ask myself: *Do my actions match that tag?*

Forgive us, O God, for the times we fall short of our calling.
—JEFF JAPINGA

22   *Every man according as he purposeth in his heart, so let him give; not grudgingly, or of necessity: for God loveth a cheerful giver.* —II CORINTHIANS 9:7

One Saturday toward the end of October I received a letter from the pledge chairman of our church.

When I read his suggestion that I make a "significant increase this year," I bridled. I complained to Judy, my wife: "I thought our yearly pledge was already pretty 'significant.'"

Plus that, I had just put into the mail several checks to needy organizations that we regularly support.

I was still grumbling over the letter as Judy and I sat in a bus that was taking us to a museum exhibit. Stopped for a traffic light, I glanced out the window and saw a bum who was eating his lunch on a park bench. He had spread a clean newspaper neatly on his lap. On it were a plastic-wrapped loaf of bread, some luncheon meats and cheese. As I watched, he took the last bite of the sandwich he had made. Then he reached into the bread bag and removed two more slices of bread, after which he carefully tucked away the bag inside the depths of his voluminous overcoat. He repeated the process with the cheese and the luncheon meats.

"Look," I said to Judy, "he's making himself a second course."

But, no — he wasn't. Meticulously he broke the food into small pieces and, with a grand flourish, distributed it to the by now rather large audience of pigeons and squirrels gathered at his feet.

"God loves a cheerful giver," Judy said, giving me a big smile.

"So He does," I replied, more than a little contrite.
I increased my pledge.

Help me to remember, Lord, that the spirit of my giving is as important as the gift itself. —JAMES McDERMOTT

---

23 *Now therefore perform the doing of it...*
—II CORINTHIANS 8:11

"The 'get-at-its' are ready for distribution," read the announcement in my church bulletin. "Pick up a fistful after church in case you had planned to come to choir practice and just can't *get-at-it*...or planned to serve on the nominating committee, attend a prayer meeting, teach a Sunday-school class, come to Bible study but, alas, just can't *get-at-it*."

The announcement struck home. Just this morning my husband had wanted to wear his pale yellow shirt, but the button was missing. I *had* planned to tack it back on but — well, I couldn't *get-at-it*. I owe some letters, and the tulips need to be separated and stored but, well — you know — those things, like some church services I promised this year, I found hard to *get-at-it*.

Come to think of it, what if — just what if — God's schedule hadn't allowed Him to finish the Creation? He couldn't *get-at-it*. What if Jesus hadn't found time to visit this earth? And what if the inspired writers of our Holy Bible had wanted to record God's Word but just never could *get-at-it*?

Well, I know now what I must do — pick up my share of *get-at-its*. Where is my sewing box? Then a visit to a friend in the hospital, a letter to my recently widowed aunt. And I'll call the church and tell them I'm ready to lead a Bible study group....

Lord, I'll get-at-it right now. —JUNE MASTERS BACHER

24

... There is a lad here, which hath five barley loaves, and two small fishes: but what are they among so many?
—JOHN 6:9

Thomas à Kempis spent his life remote in a monastery in the Netherlands. There he wrote a collection of meditations called the *Imitation of Christ*, which he probably thought would never go beyond the monastery walls. Yet three hundred years later the captain of a slave ship found a copy of this little monk's work aboard his vessel.

During a long voyage, Captain John Newton read the small volume. It had a profound effect upon his life and eventually Newton gave his life to Christ and became a minister. He won many men to Christ. One of them, a member of the British parliament, after his conversion put forth a bill outlawing slave traffic in the British Empire.

The *Imitation of Christ* has changed the entire world. And somewhere behind it all there was only a humble monk quietly writing down his thoughts, never dreaming that they might someday circle the earth.

Now I believe that everything we say and do matters. Nothing we give is too small for God to use — a boy's lunch of loaves and fish, a monk's little volume of words, or simply someone's tiny deed of kindness. The next time you are tempted to think that your small deed is of little consequence, remember: In God's hands it is like the proverbial pebble tossed into the pond. Its ripple may travel much farther than you might ever expect.

May I never become discouraged over doing little things for Your glory, God.
—SUE MONK KIDD

25

. . . Freely ye have received, freely give.   —MATTHEW 10:8

Suppose you had a wealthy father who deposited $86,400 into your checking account each morning, his only stipulation being that you must spend it that day. It would be easy to tithe with such a large sum, wouldn't it?

Well, I happen to have a Father Who *is* that generous. Every day He credits my personal account with 86,400 seconds. I wonder if I could tithe my gift of time. Let's see. After eight hours of sleep, I have sixteen waking hours left. One tenth of that would be roughly an hour and a half. That's not really very much to give to the Lord — especially when He has been so generous to me.

By tomorrow, today's 86,400 seconds will be gone, leaving in their place something that I have traded for them. May that trade include: time spent with my God, my services for others offered in His name and my work dedicated to His purposes.

Are you a time-tither? If not, you may want to think about it.

My time is Yours, Lord. Help me to give it joyfully, according to Your will.   —MARILYN MORGAN HELLEBERG

26

For with the heart man believeth unto righteousness; and with the mouth confession is made unto salvation.

—ROMANS 10:10

A proud young fellow walked into the village blacksmith shop just after the smithy had tossed a red-hot horseshoe on the ground to cool. Noticing it lying there, the young man bent down and picked it up...only to drop it in all haste.

"Kind of hot," isn't it, son?" asked the blacksmith.

"No, not hot," said the fellow, hiding his burned fingers. "It just doesn't take me long to look at a horseshoe."

I've done that — made a mistake and then been too proud to admit it. Jesus said that we all sin. We all burn our fingers. The trouble comes when we allow pride to prevent us from confessing the wrongs we do.

How much better it is to simply say, "I was wrong. I admit it." Confession truly is good for the soul. Without it, we can never experience forgiveness...which is, after all, the only cure for "burned fingers."

Wash away my pride, Lord, that prevents me from confessing my wrongdoing. —SUE MONK KIDD

---

27 *There shall no evil befall thee, neither shall any plague come nigh thy dwelling.* —PSALM 91:10

Boll weevils. We've all heard about the obnoxious little insects. In less than one season they can wipe out the cotton crop for miles around.

As my husband and I once drove through Enterprise, Alabama, we were astounded to see a marble statue of a woman holding aloft a huge boll weevil. When we stopped, we asked a town resident why the pesty little creature was obviously held in such esteem.

He told us that early in the century, boll weevils had devastated all the cotton crops in the area. Disaster threatened the whole region. But instead of despairing, Enterprise lived up to its name: Farmers planted crops other than cotton; town officials sought to bring in new industries to increase employment. And when prosperity returned, Enterprise gave credit where it felt credit was due: to the *boll weevil*!

Most of us don't have to deal with boll weevils. But in the coming year all of us are going to have to face "life-changers" — unanticipated situations or events that may completely rearrange our plans or our lives. Some life-changers may be as small as a phone call in the middle of a hectic morning; others as overwhelming as financial disaster or the death of a loved one. How will we meet them? Will we let them ruin our day, the rest of our lives?

Or will we, like the people of Enterprise, take up the challenge of the Apostle Paul to "give thanks in all circumstances"?

Thank You, Father, for the "boll weevils" in my life and for unexpected opportunities to grow. —PATRICIA HOUCK SPRINKLE

---

28   *Ye ask, and receive not, because ye ask amiss.* —JAMES 4:3

A story that dates back to World War II tells about the soldier who gets trapped behind enemy lines in fierce combat. His prayer goes, "Lord, I haven't bothered You for twenty years now, but I really need Your help today. Get me out of this mess alive and I won't bother You for another twenty!"

The soldier's approach makes us laugh. And, of course, it's ridiculous. You and I know we don't "bother" God. On the other hand, it might be a good idea to stop once in a while and consider how truly sincere our prayers really are.

Next time you catch yourself imposing your solutions on God or looking for quick answers, or complaining that things aren't working out right, stop and listen. Is your prayer making you a demanding, impatient *pray-er*? How about sending God a bit more praise, a bit more thanks, a bit more good news? And don't forget, stop and listen now and then!

Just checking in, Lord, to say thanks for everything.
—JAMES McDERMOTT

309

29 *...Except ye...become as little children, ye shall not enter into the kingdom of heaven.* —MATTHEW 18:3

One day shortly before Halloween I was standing in line at the post office when a mother walked in with her costumed four-year-old. The child wore no mask but her face was fearfully painted; a black cape draped her tiny shoulders, and on her blonde curls a pointed hat was perched.

"Oh, my, I'm scared!" I exclaimed. "I had better be careful. I'm sure I see a witch."

I will never forget the sweetness, the absolute innocence and trust, of those big blues eyes gazing up at me. Or the voice that kindly and gravely reassured me, "Don't worry, it's just a little girl in here."

Just a little girl in here. How often I've thought of that when having to give orders to somebody...advising a teenager...criticizing a manuscript...teaching class...approached by someone who is obviously timid and nervous, thinking me far wiser and stronger than I really am.

I remember the simple child who lives within all of us behind the sometimes fearful costumes we seem to wear as adults. How nice if we could somehow reassure others as sweetly as that tiny witch did and say: "I really want to help you. I wouldn't hurt you for the world. And don't worry, it's just a little girl in here."

Lord, don't let me ever outgrow that little child.

—MARJORIE HOLMES

30

O give thanks unto the Lord; for he is good...
—I CHRONICLES 16:34

I once asked a doctor friend for the name of the most effective prescription he knew of.

"Well, I'll tell you," he said. "A colleague of mine once had a woman patient who suffered from depression. Got to the point where she stayed at home all the time, listless, apathetic, indifferent to just about everything. The usual medications didn't seem to help.

"One day this doctor delivered a small package to the woman's home. 'I want you to take what's in this package,' he said, 'and spend ten minutes of every day looking through it at some object in this room.'

"In the package there was a strong magnifying glass. The woman began looking through it at the warp and woof of the fabric on her sofa, the veins in a flower plucked from her garden, the color dots in an old photograph, even the texture of her own skin. That was the turning point of her illness. She began to get well because the doctor and his 'prescription' had aroused the most curative of all emotions."

"Curiosity?" I asked.

My friend shook his head. "Gratitude," he said. "Gratitude to the Creator of this marvelous gift of life. It's the best health insurance of all."

Let my soul magnify Thee, Lord, with praise and thanksgiving.
—ARTHUR GORDON

31 *For ye were sometimes darkness, but now are ye light in the Lord: walk as children of light...* —EPHESIANS 5:8

Last year the children in my neighborhood received a special kind of treat when they rang doorbells on Halloween. My church had prepared small plastic bags for them. In each bag were several treats, including a little card that told the following story:

ONCE UPON A TIME [house] there was a candle named Candy who had no [house] to shine her [candle] in. Candy was so [sad face] . She couldn't find a [pumpkin] who would let her [candle] in. She needed a [pumpkin] to shine her light through!

On Halloween [moon and stars] Candy wandered sadly from place to place looking for a [pumpkin] who would let her in. When the [moon and stars] was at its darkest, and the Trick-or-Treaters came out, Candy noticed a lonely [pumpkin] who had NO light. Candy asked the [pumpkin] , "May I come live inside you so my light can shine through you?" The pumpkin let Candy's [candle] in, and now it's the brightest [glowing pumpkin] in all the land.

Candy's light will shine only on Halloween night, but *yours* can shine forever, if you let Jesus Christ in.

Jesus is the Light of the world, and He will shine through anyone who will let Him in. Please open the door to your heart and let Him in today.

This "treat" was passed out to children on one night only, but you and I have no time limit on sharing our "treat" of the Good News of Jesus. Every day in the year is a golden opportunity for us to tell someone about Him; to let His light shine through us; to treat someone to the Greatest Story Ever Told.

Jesus, I want to shine for You today and every day. —DRUE DUKE

Praise Diary for October

1

2

3

4

5

6

7

8

9

10

11

12

13

14

15

16

17

18

19

20

21

22

23

24

25

26

27

28

29

30

31

November

Let us come before his presence with thanksgiving,
and make a joyful noise unto him with psalms.

—PSALM 95:2

My heart is filled with thanks, Lord,
For the harvest You bestow,
Not only for the grains and fruits
That You have caused to grow,
But for the harvest of the soul,
The good things that I feel,
The closeness of my family,
The friendships that are real....
And thank You, Lord, for planting
These seeds within me too,
A thirst for knowledge, cherished dreams,
A faith that's deep and true.

—ALICE JOYCE DAVIDSON

PATTERN FOR A BLESSED LIFE

Rejoice, and be exceeding glad: for great is your reward in heaven...
—MATTHEW 5:12

1

A couple of people in our adult Sunday school class were in an argument about Heaven. One said that it's an actual place in the sky; the other considered it to be a spiritual dimension. A third settled the argument by saying, "Heaven is where God is and that's all that matters." That *is* the ultimate reward, isn't it?

As I review the Beatitudes, I see that each tells *who* is blessed and *what* the blessing is. All point toward EXPERIENCING THE PRESENCE OF GOD. Jesus teaches that if we practice His pattern of blessedness, we can experience His *presence*, now and forever. What an irresistible cause for rejoicing!

Knowing You are with me at this moment, Lord, my soul sings for joy! Every day this month let me delight in Your presence.
—MARILYN MORGAN HELLEBERG

2

... Speak, Lord; for thy servant heareth. —I SAMUEL 3:9

The phone call on Saturday from the Port Washington, Long Island, train stationmaster came as a surprise. "There's a dog here in a crate," he told my father, "addressed to you." And, sure enough, when we got to the station, there was a beautiful Llewellyn setter, shivering with fear, inside a big wooden crate. It later turned out that my grandfather had trained the dog and sent her to us from Virginia, but had forgotten to notify us.

My father borrowed a crowbar from the stationmaster and began to pry the crate open. He had taken three boards off when the dog bolted out and tore down the railroad tracks. My father frantically looked for a shipping tag with the dog's name on it and, finding it, muttered, "Ah, it's Victoria." Hearing her name, even in that whisper, our new dog stopped dead in her tracks and came back to us, tentatively wagging her tail.

In her eleven years with us, "Vickie" was an adored member of our family. Although we never made the slightest attempt to refresh her on the training she had received, she never lost a bit of her original obedience. In fact, she seemed to thrive on it. She was the happiest, most serene dog I have ever encountered.

Since then I've often thought that her obedience was the key to her serenity. And I believe our Creator had our contentment in mind when He handed down our most important Commandments. The more closely I adhere to them, the happier I am.

I'm most content, Father, when obeying You. —JAMES McDERMOTT

---

3   *And this is the confidence that we have in him, that, if*
     we ask any thing according to his will, he heareth us.
                                                    —I JOHN 5:14

My grandfather Buchholz had a large buckeye tree on his farm and every fall people would come from miles around to pick up buckeyes — those little round nuts with a tan eye.

"They bring you good luck," they would tell Grandfather with great confidence and he would ask, "Who said so?"

He knew that they would carry one of the tiny buckeyes in their pockets for good luck in hunting, planting, fishing, marketing — in just about all their activities.

"You'll only wear holes in your pockets," Grandfather would warn them. "After all, why fool around with a buckeye when you can get all the goodness you want from God?"

Grandfather was right.

When we carry You in our hearts, God, You fill our lives with goodness. —ZONA B. DAVIS

---

4 *But thanks be to God, which giveth us the victory through our Lord Jesus Christ.* —I CORINTHIANS 15:57

The other day I phoned a dear friend who was going through a severe difficulty. I wanted to talk to her about it. When she answered the phone, it was evident that she'd been crying. I blurted out, "How are you doing?"

I shall always remember her answer. She whispered, "I'm walking in *victory!*"

She could have said, "Oh, didn't you know? Let me tell you what has happened to me...." But, no. None of that. No spoken defeat or fear. No self-pity. No opportunity for me to give her advice. Just a simple, powerful statement of faith.

"Good for you," I answered, stunned, and we hung up.

Later she told me that the victory came shortly thereafter. Not only in her heart, but in her circumstances as well.

Thanks for reminding us, dear God, in every day, in every way, that we walk in victory when we walk with You.

—MARION BOND WEST

5   *Herein is our love made perfect, that we may have*
boldness in the day of judgment...   —I JOHN 4:17

My cousin Jim — that's not his real name — had a serious problem with alcohol. He gave us all a pretty rough time, but we never gave up on him. We anguished and prayed and told him how much he was loved and that he was harming himself, and us, by his continued drinking.

Then, one day on a business trip to Cleveland on the New York Central, he was in the club car, drink in hand, passing the time with another passenger. All of a sudden the passenger turned, stared Jim squarely in the eye and said, "Look here, fella, it's time you got hold of yourself."

Jim was understandably startled. "What are you talking about?" he said, drawing back warily.

"You know what I'm talking about," said the passenger. *"You're an alcoholic."*

Jim squirmed. He was nonplused. He was never to see the man again. But amazing as it might seem, that single remark from a total stranger started my cousin Jim on the road to sobriety.

Recently a friend told me that Alcoholics Anonymous claims that 99 percent of the alcoholics who successfully stop drinking are people who have been helped by *strangers* — not by family members or well-meaning friends — too many emotional ties.

In many respects it seems hard to believe, and yet, the more I've thought about it, the more I recognize how potent advice from outsiders can be. Sometimes a family's love can be overly protective and a problem is never confronted head on. It seems that outsiders are often able to exercise a kind of "tough love" that can be a powerful agent for change. Strangers or family members, we all need to learn to love — wisely.

Father, let me speak Your truth in love.   —VAN VARNER

321

6 *He that hath pity upon the poor lendeth unto the Lord...*
—PROVERBS 19:17

My friend Gregory told me that last Sunday in church he was waiting for the collection to be taken. He had in his pocket two bills, one twice the denomination of the other. The smaller one, he decided, would be a perfectly adequate donation.

"But as I sat there," he said, "without any warning, a little episode that I had read about the Vietnam War came to my mind.

"Two American soldiers in a combat zone were eating their field rations. A young Vietnamese boy of about eight or nine years old, homeless and hungry, was watching them intently. When they had finished their meal, one of the soldiers took the piece of chocolate that was part of his K-ration and handed it to the child. The little boy looked at it for a moment. Then, very carefully, he broke it into three pieces, put the smallest in his ragged pocket and solemnly offered the other two pieces to the soldiers.

"The memory of that story came right out of nowhere," Greg said, "just as the collection plate arrived."

"And so?" I prompted.

He smiled. "Do you have to ask?" he said.

Dear Lord, teach us to give from our plenty as readily as some of your less fortunate children give from their scarcity.
—ARTHUR GORDON

7 *Blessed is the man whose strength is in thee...*
—PSALM 84:5

"You have to lose weight," the doctor told Aunt Lucy. "It isn't healthy to be so heavy."

Lucy was sulky.

Food was one of the great pleasures of her life, not only the enjoyment of it but the cooking and serving of it as well. How could she give up one of her finest joys?

That night, Lucy told me later, she couldn't sleep. She sat up in bed reading her Bible. Then she went downstairs to the kitchen for a glass of milk and some cookies. *I simply can't diet*, she muttered to herself.

Lucy was about to take a cookie when a Bible verse she had just read came to her: "I can do all things through Christ which strengtheneth me."

Yes, she firmly believed that — but certainly it was a promise meant for something truly important, not for merely losing a few pounds.

Or was it? *All things*, whispered Lucy.

The cookie was returned to the cookie jar and the milk would wait until breakfast.

Lucy did lose weight — and as she did, she gained in faith. "I had a lot of help," she says, "once I realized that I couldn't do it by myself."

Is there something you feel that you can't do by yourself? Today why not claim the promise of *all things*?

I will remember in all my endeavors, Lord, to turn to You — in all things.   —PHYLLIS HOBE

---

8 *Blessed is the nation whose God is the Lord...*
—PSALM 33:12

I once read that the reason elections across America are held on Tuesdays is because years and years ago, when we were primarily a rural nation, farmers always spent most of Sunday in church. Then they had a lot of chores to catch up with on Monday.

And it was Tuesday before they had time to hitch up a horse and buggy and travel to the nearest voting place.

I like that. God first. Work second. Civic duty third. Each deserving its own day.

Acknowledgment of God has always been part of our nation's heritage. Maybe that's why our country remains strong today.

God...work...country. Let's practice that — in just that order — every day.

Especially today, Lord. — GLENN KITTLER

---

9 *And let the beauty of our Lord our God be upon us: and establish thou the work of our hands upon us...*
—PSALM 90:17

I should have been writing this morning. But when I looked out the window, I saw a pattern of ice crystals on the storm window and paused for a second to take a closer look. The second stretched to minutes while I sat, chin in hand, fascinated.

A mighty battle was etched in frosty precision on the window. Horses and knights reared above a dense forest of leaves while here and there a cross towered above the melee. One cross had fallen but the knights of truth were holding their ground. Beneath three crosses on a slight hill I saw a stern figure directing the fray and his victory seemed assured.

Even as I gazed, the sun reached the window and the scene dissolved. But the glorious picture of truth triumphant etched on my window by Someone was permanently etched in my memory.

Should I have been writing this morning? How often do those things I "should" do cause me to miss some of God's glory — a moment of special intimacy, a glimpse of rare beauty, an instant of true peace provided for me and me alone?

What glory will God design for you today? Will you take time to enjoy it?

Great and lavish God, Who strews our paths with beauties we often overlook, make us aware of them today.
—PATRICIA HOUCK SPRINKLE

---

10 *Take my yoke upon you... and ye shall find rest unto your souls.* —MATTHEW 11:29

I was standing on the highway beside my car with a number of other frustrated drivers. The rain and freezing temperature had glazed the road with ice and made the steep grade ahead impossible to travel. We were still assessing the situation when suddenly one of the men bolted for his car.

"It's so obvious!" he exclaimed. "I know how we can get up this road!"

Slowly he eased his car across the ice-slicked pavement until the two right-side wheels were fixed on the gravel shoulder. For a few seconds his tires spun but soon they began to bite into the rough gravel surface and he began inching up the mountain. I followed his lead; behind us a long caravan of cars followed slowly. Gradually we were making it up the mountain that had seemed impossible. But something bothered me: Why had the solution been so obvious to that man?

"Easy," he replied when I saw him later. "My wife had been praying and finally she said, 'This one's on Christ's shoulders.' It's kind of a habit of ours — when a problem seems too big for us, we say that it's better on Christ's shoulders. He can handle it. Then, standing there on the road, I thought of that. And I realized that in this situation the road's shoulder could help."

Whenever I face a big problem now, I think of that man running across the slippery Pennsylvania highway exclaiming, "It's so obvious!" Truly it is. Put it on Christ's shoulders — He'll help you from the lowest valley to the very top of the hill every time.

Father, I'll lean on You today if there's trouble up ahead.

—JEFF JAPINGA

---

11 *He that is not with me is against me...* —LUKE 11:23

Somewhere in Germany during the first spring of World War II, an old rabbi was being badgered by his Nazi captors. France had fallen to Hitler's panzer divisions and it looked as though Britain would soon be overwhelmed.

"Well, old man," the Nazi guards scoffed, "now just whose side do you think God is on?"

The rabbi replied quietly and firmly. "That question is not one that concerns me," he said. "What matters most to me is that *I* am on God's side."

Knowing where we stand is something to keep in mind in war, in peace, in any situation, at any time.

Lord, my allegiance to You comes before all else. —VAN VARNER

---

12 *Pleasant words are as an honeycomb, sweet to the soul, and health to the bones.* —PROVERBS 16:24

I have a friend who is a desk clerk in a large motel. Part of her job is answering the incoming calls on the switchboard. For weeks, the same elderly woman's voice was heard every morning asking for the correct time.

Exasperated, my friend finally suggested to the caller that perhaps she should get a good timepiece.

"Oh, I have a watch and two clocks," the caller said. "But I don't have anyone to say 'Good morning' to me, and you always do."

How hungry a lonely heart becomes! How sweet the sound, how soothing to the spirit, to have someone to contact when we are alone and lonely.

Is there someone who has been trying to get a "Good morning" from you and, knowingly or unknowingly, you're sending back a busy signal? Why not pick up the phone right now and dial their number. A "Good morning" from you could change their day. Who knows — yours, too.

Father, a small act of kindness on my part goes a long way.
—DRUE DUKE

---

13 *Let the word of Christ dwell in you richly in all wisdom...* —COLOSSIANS 3:16

Geoffrey Bull, a missionary to the Orient, was imprisoned in a dungeon for three years. There were only two hours a day when enough light came through his small window for him to read by. Every day he spent those two hours reading his Bible and memorizing it. Later his Bible was taken from him, but he continued systematically to go over the Scriptures in his mind. Starting with Genesis and recalling every person and incident he could, he worked his way through the whole Bible — and then started over again.

The threat of execution was constant, and his captors tried to brainwash him, but they didn't succeed, and he was eventually rescued.

How blessed I am to have a Bible and light all day by which to read it! But I don't always have my Bible with me. So I'm going to start pausing after each day's Scripture reading to recall the events and people about whom I've read and the special words I want to remember. Then no matter where I am, no matter what the situation, I'll be carrying God's Word with me.

May Your Word become imprinted on my mind, Lord.

—MARILYN MORGAN HELLEBERG

---

14   *Wherewithal shall a young man cleanse his way? by taking heed thereto according to thy word.*   —PSALM 119:9

"Disciplining *is* a hard chore," my neighbor agreed as we sat over a morning cup of coffee and discussed the raising of children.

"When Randy was just past sixteen, we really worried," she explained, "until his father hit upon a great idea. Taking three-by-five index cards, he began to print on each one a Bible verse that applied specifically to a current problem. Then when the time seemed right, he would leave one of the cards on the dashboard of Randy's car.

"When there were too many girlfriends, the message was from I Peter 2:11. When Randy began going around with a questionable high-school crowd, Proverbs 1:15-16 filled the bill.

"Randy never mentioned the cards but his behavior really changed. He had outgrown *our* words, you see, but not God's."

I liked the idea so much that I began to use the method. I would slip a Bible verse such as "Lie not to one another...." (Colossians 3:9) into a shirt pocket or "Children, obey your parents in the Lord: for this is right" (Ephesians 6:1) into a lunch pail. One day when I saw Neil and Gary comparing cards, I knew that the plan was working.

It's a funny thing. I, too, was learning from my Bible research. Unexpectedly, God was speaking not only to *them* but to *me* too!

Speak to us, Father God. We all need Your guidance.

—DORIS HAASE

JOURNEY OF FAITH

15 Your traveling companion is *CALEB*
. . . who scouted the route. —NUMBERS 13, 14 - JOSHUA 14, 15

As the children of Israel neared the Promised Land, Moses sent twelve men ahead to report on the land to which they were headed. They were to bring back answers to six questions. Was the land good or bad? Was the land rich or poor? Was there wood in it or not? Were the people strong or weak? Were there few or many? Were their cities camps or strongholds?

These are questions those of us embarked on a spiritual journey must answer too. The land *we* are now reconnoitering is the Bible. Settle for yourself this month: Does it proclaim good news or bad news for your life? Will your life in this land be richer or poorer than before? Will the land supply all you need, or must you import building materials from elsewhere?

And what about the resistance you will encounter? Will the opposition be: Strong and traumatic, or easily overcome? Centered on only a few issues, or contesting every step of the way? Temporary, or deeply entrenched?

So the scouts set out. One was Caleb, another Joshua. After forty days spying on the green hills of Canaan, they returned to the wilderness camp and reported. All agreed on what they had seen: *the land flows with milk and honey!* And about the inhabitants the spies were also unanimous: *the people are strong, the cities are fortified and very large, and all the people we saw are men of great stature!*

That was the intelligence report — tantalizing and terrifying. All twelve concurred on the *facts.* But two — Caleb and Joshua — saw those facts with eyes of faith: "Let's go at once and occupy it!" The other ten reacted with fear: "We're not able to go up against those people; they are stronger than we."

The fear-filled words of the ten had the entire people weeping in terror. "Take us back to slavery in Egypt!" they begged Moses. Mob fear turned to mob violence. Only the intervention of God saved Caleb and Joshua from being stoned by the panicky mob, and the children of Israel were condemned to forty years of homeless wandering; a year for every day of the reconnaisance mission that had ended so faithlessly.

Faith versus fear! We know we should have one and renounce the other — but how? What made ten spies see giants; two, opportunity?

The key is not *what* the scouts saw, but *where* they stood while they looked. The viewpoint, not the view, made the difference.

"We seemed like grasshoppers," said the ten. That's the view from the human perspective, obstacles seen from the standpoint of weakness — an insect's-eye view of the situation.

But Caleb envisioned the scene through God's eyes. "If the Lord delights in us, he will bring us into this land and give it to us," Caleb says, and he's willing to stake his life on that possibility.

When we next meet Caleb, he is an old man, survivor — with Joshua — of the forty-year wilderness wandering. The rest have perished. The Promised Land has still to be wrested from the powerful people living there.

"It may be that the Lord will be with me, and I shall drive them out," announces Caleb.

And the Bible records that Caleb did — indeed.

> *Dear Father, give me the ability to put my trust in Your protection as I scout the land You have promised me.*
> — ELIZABETH SHERRILL

---

16 *Let your light so shine before men, that they may see your good works, and glorify your Father which is in heaven.* —MATTHEW 5:16

A wise person once wrote that no act of kindness, no matter how small, goes unnoticed by God. I was reminded of that statement when I heard this apocryphal story recently.

At the pearly gates, so the story goes, a prominent Bible scholar appeared, seeking admission. "I don't see your name on the list," said St. Peter.

"Oh, it must be there," the man replied. "I'm the one who wrote all those religious books."

"Sorry, but I'm afraid I don't recall them."

"And I'm the one who delivered those university lectures on spiritual growth," the man continued. But St. Peter just shook his head. He wasn't persuaded.

Head down and shoulders drooping, the scholar turned and began to walk away. Suddenly St. Peter's face brightened. "Wait a minute," he called after him. "You aren't the fellow who built all those birdhouses and put out seed for the birds every winter, are you?"

"Why, yes, that's me," the man answered.

"Oh, then forgive me," said St. Peter. "Of course we have a place for you."

Lord, when I speak Your Word, let me act on it. —FRED BAUER

---

17 *Cast thy burden upon the Lord, and he shall sustain thee...* —PSALM 55:22

I had found little relief from the burden I was carrying around. Someone I loved was very ill and I could actually feel a heaviness within myself from the weight of it. I had prayed and prayed — but without very much peace.

Late one night, unable to sleep, I slipped into my little girl's room to make sure that she was covered. The night light glowed through the organdy ruffle of her canopied bed, where she lay fast asleep. And just as I suspected, her blanket had been kicked to the foot of the bed. As I drew the cover over her, I noticed that she clutched a half-eaten grape lollipop in her hand. A birthday present from her grandmother that she had carried around all day. Now the candy made a sticky purple splotch on the pillowcase, and a few strands of my daughter's hair were stuck to it.

Why didn't she get rid of this before going to bed? I thought. Of course I knew why. She was reluctant to trust anything so precious out of her sight. Her little fingers were still wound tightly around the stick and I had to pry them away one by one. And as I freed them, I began to see a small lesson in all of this. A fragile lesson that tugged at me. A lesson in learning how to let go.

No wonder I had found so little peace in my concern over my burden. I had been praying with my fingers wrapped tightly around it, afraid to trust anything so precious to anyone else. So there by the bed I bowed my head and, uncurling my fingers one by one, I let go of my burden, transferring it from my hands to God's.

Still holding the big purple lollipop, I bent down and kissed my daughter's face. Her gift...my burden...they were in good hands.

Lord, help me leave my burdens with You when I pray. For there is no better place for them. —SUE MONK KIDD

---

18 *...A little leaven leaveneth the whole lump.*
—I CORINTHIANS 5:6

I tried baking bread one day, but my yeast turned out to be too old. My dough lay, like a gray blob, in the bottom of the bowl. Finally I pushed the bowl to the back of the counter. I was depressed by my failure, just as I had been depressed by a recent problem. My spirit felt as dead as the lifeless dough in that bowl.

Later that night I walked into the kitchen to find the dough, like a huge white creature, puffing high out of the bowl and oozing across the countertop.

Somewhere in that inert lump there had been one vital spore! It had taken hold in the warm kitchen and had multiplied, filling the entire loaf, changing death into life....

I looked inside myself. Was there a tiny bit of God's love hidden somewhere? Just one tiny, yeasty piece that might expand and change my soul from a lifeless lump into a living spirit?

"Touch me, Lord," I whispered. "Fill me with Your love."

A rush of warmth spread through me. And with that warmth, something began to stir.

Today, Lord, help me find the leaven of Your love.

—MADGE HARRAH

---

19 *But grow in grace, and in the knowledge of our Lord and Saviour, Jesus Christ.* —II PETER 3:18

When asked about his success, popular playwright Bill Davis replied that he likes to think of himself as *succeeding*, rather than as being a success. The latter, he says, makes him think of someone who has arrived at the top, has no more to learn, nothing else to accomplish. He does not want that; he hopes to be succeeding, to continue growing.

This has to be my goal too, as a Christian. I must never consider myself a successful Christian. No, there is ever so much to learn and accomplish.

Each day, Father, help me be a succeeding Christian.

—DRUE DUKE

20

And they continued stedfastly in the apostles' doctrine and fellowship, and in breaking of bread, and in prayers.
—ACTS 2:42

An icy gale was blowing off nearby Lake Michigan and big, wind-swept snowflakes fell from a slate-gray sky. I sat huddled in my college dormitory, wrapped in two woolen blankets, sniffling and sneezing from a serious head cold and trying to study for an upcoming exam. And since it was Sunday and the dormitory cafeteria was closed, my lunch was a peanut-butter sandwich I had hastily slapped together.

Sneezing again, I put aside my psychology text and picked up the bulletin a friend had dropped off after the church service I usually attended. *Darn, I missed communion today*, I thought sadly, glancing at the order of worship.

I broke off a corner of the sandwich and took a sip of orange soda. *Do this*, I murmured, *in remembrance of me.* I closed my eyes.

Then — there alone in that drafty dormitory — a peace came over me, a calm assurance that God was with me and cared for me, even though I was sick and harried.

When I opened my eyes, I saw that the sun had broken through the clouds, its light reflecting off the snow like a million glittering diamonds. I know that it was God's way of showing me that in remembering the sacrifice of His Son and by drawing close to Him, He would remember me and be close to me. Anywhere — and any time.

For the love and care You always extend at all times, Father, we praise You.
—JEFF JAPINGA

21   *As we have therefore opportunity, let us do good unto all men, especially unto them who are of the household of faith.*
— GALATIANS 6:10

Here is one of my favorite stories about my boss, Norman Vincent Peale. He can tell very amusing stories on himself and as a matter of fact, he told me this one. It concerns a problem that we all face from time to time — even, it seems, a distinguished minister of God.

It happened back in the days when "rock 'n roll" was first blasting its way into our eardrums. Dr. Peale had just boarded a California-bound plane and was in the process of fastening his seat belt when down the aisle came an extraordinay sight — a young man with a guitar in one hand and a flight bag in the other. Dressed in a lavender-colored velvet suit, he wore gold chains and his hair flowed over his shoulders.

Dr. Peale watched with fascination as the young man took the seat next to him.

"Howdy," the man said.

"Howdy," Dr. Peale responded — but not quite with his customary enthusiasm. Dr. Peale had talked with many individualists in his long life but surely he would have a hard time in finding common ground with this one.

They began by trading casual information. Dr. Peale was going to give "a talk" in Los Angeles. His seatmate was heading for "a gig" on what he called "The Strip." Then, after a few more routine remarks, the young man reached into his flight bag and took out a book. It was the Bible.

"Well, sir," the musician said to the astonished man beside him, "do you know Jesus Christ?"

Dr. Peale beamed, somewhat sheepishly.

Now what's the problem I mentioned earlier, the one we all face from time to time? It's the folly of prejudging, which is a form of prejudice. And it always can be avoided.

Father, help me to meet others through Your eyes of love.
— VAN VARNER

---

22 *For my people have committed two evils; they have forsaken me the fountain of living waters, and hewed them out cisterns, broken cisterns, that can hold no water.* —JEREMIAH 2:13

In a letter from Jacques Cousteau imploring his many friends to help save the world's oceans, he speaks of the seas as "living waters." He points out that when scientists had tried to keep salt-water fish alive in man-made sea water, the fish had died.

When I read of this, I was reminded of a body of "dead water" in Israel. A thick, odorous body called the *Dead* Sea. Why is it dead? Because there is no outflow. It receives living waters from the Sea of Galilee and the Jordan River but it does not pass them on. Like raindrops held fast in a cistern, the waters stagnate, then evaporate. In a word, die.

Christ calls us to life. When He says, "Freely ye have received, freely give," He is leading us to the fountain of living waters. With no outflow, we die.

Lord, I would hoard nothing. Let all I receive flow freely that others too may be blessed. —ELAINE ST. JOHNS

23 *...In the morning will I direct my prayer unto thee...*
—PSALM 5:3

When I was a child, we had a fire in the fireplace most of the winter. Every night my father would pile extra logs on the fire "so in the morning there'll be a live ember to start with." And in the morning I felt safe and warm and loved, and that feeling followed me throughout the day.

Our bedrooms are warm now, but I still like to have a warm ember to start my day with. So at bedtime I read from my Bible to stoke up my faith, choosing a phrase to hold in my heart as I fall asleep. Then, when the alarm rings, I awaken to the live ember of those words, still in my heart. Warmed by the flow of His Word, I begin my day feeling secure, protected, loved.

Thank You, Lord, for the warming glow of Your Holy Word all through the night and day. —MARILYN MORGAN HELLEBERG

24 And God said, Let us make man in our image, after our likeness...
—GENESIS 1:26

The neighborhood where I live in New York City has in recent years acquired a large Puerto Rican population. One November afternoon I heard the sounds of a basketball game in the school yard adjacent to my home and I went to the window to watch it for a few minutes.

I heard one boy say, "Today our teacher told us what Americans eat for Thanksgiving dinner." His voice took on a rather bitter singsong ring as he chanted "turkey and dressing and gravy and sweet potatoes and pumpkin pie and—" his litany went on and on.

The tone of the boy's voice made me wonder. Wouldn't some

Americans prefer to have rice and beans and stewed chicken for *their* Thanksgiving dinner? Wouldn't some be eating their Thanksgiving dinner with chopsticks? Wouldn't some prefer veal Parmigiana, a tangy salad and pasta, or boiled pork shoulder and sauerkraut?

America is known as the world's "melting pot." For that reason let us never forget the real meaning of our Thanksgiving holiday — gratitude to God for His guidance and protection equally bestowed on all pilgrims to this new land. The pilgrims are still arriving. Let us be thankful for every one of them.

Father, thank You for our differences and for our common bond — our fellowship with You. —GLENN KITTLER

---

25 *But they that wait upon the Lord shall renew their strength; they shall mount up with wings as eagles...*
—ISAIAH 40:31

My husband told me that he was very moved when he first visited Kitty Hawk, North Carolina, the site of the Wright brothers' first flight in 1903.

"It was a bleak November day, gray and overcast. I had climbed the tower that had been erected to their memory and, looking down, I could see the plaque that marked the spot from which their little plane took off. It cleared the ground and actually flew for about a hundred feet. But it did leave the earth, it *flew*, and a dream that man has had since the beginning of time, the dream of being able to fly, became a reality.

"Then as I stood there on the tower, imagining the scene — the Wright brothers with their cheerful determination and their belief in their machine, and the twenty or thirty people who had come to watch, most of them to scoff — I heard a sound overhead. Looking up, I saw a plane that resembled a silver needle. As it cut smoothly through the clouds, a burst of sunlight — like a benediction — glinted on its wings. And I thought, *Here I am, barely fifty years later, on the very spot where it all began, witnessing the fulfillment of a dream.*

"I was so overwhelmed by awe that mere man should possess such a creative imagination that I fell to my knees. I thanked God for the miracle of His creation — and for all the people who have dared to use their dreams to make this world a better place."

Dear God, it is You who give us our dreams. Give me the faith and determination to make the most of mine. —MARJORIE HOLMES

---

26 But godliness with contentment is great gain.
—I TIMOTHY 6:6

"It's not much of a day for skiing," I remarked to the new friend I had made at the ski lodge. The sunshine had disappeared and the day had deteriorated into wet snow and a wind that seemed to blow right through me.

"Oh, it's going to be a great day!" Dolph enthused. I followed along halfheartedly, disappointed by the bad turn in the weather.

"Ah, what lovely fresh air!" Dolph exclaimed. He took a deep breath and then tore off down the mountainside. I careened breathlessly after him.

When he pulled up for a breather, he caught my wondering look and said: "It's a little trick I play on myself but the more I play it, the more I wonder whether it's a trick or not. I know the weather's lousy but look at all this good snow. There are no icy patches and we have the mountain to ourselves. We can ski the whole mountain!"

I caught the spirit. "Well, with the no-visibility condition, we won't have to cope with any distracting views!" I shouted.

"Right on!" Dolph said. "Let's have a look at your technique."

And indeed it was a wonderful, exhilarating, great, great day.

Thank You, Lord, for the weather of this great day. Let me rejoice and be glad in it. —JAMES McDERMOTT

MARY'S MEDITATIONS

During the four Sundays of Advent...and on Christmas Eve and Christmas Day...experience the wondrous events surrounding the birth of the Christ Child as seen through the eyes of Mary, His mother.

We hope that these six Meditations, sensitively written by one of Guideposts' favorite writers, Sue Monk Kidd, will prepare your hearts to celebrate this Holy Season. —THE EDITORS

27 THE FIRST SUNDAY OF ADVENT
Mary's Wonder

The sky of Nazareth burns with a low orange light. I step along under the sunset, following the little shining path, careful not to stumble. After all, I am expecting a child soon. But I could not resist coming once more to the place where the mystery began. I settle on a rock by the spring and watch the sun's low rays sparkle in the water. I remember as though it were yesterday....

I had come with my water skins that day, hurrying ahead of the sinking sun. I, a peasant girl moving in the predictable regularities of life. The same spring. The same chore. The same routine. But somehow that day found me full of heightened awareness, alive to God and the world and the

340

possibilities hidden all around me. I was like a child, full of wonder and expectation.

The spring was deserted. I stood there alone for a moment, alert to the presence of God in the rushing water. I dipped my water skin into the stream.

"Mary." The voice broke into the silence. I looked up. No one was about. Only a slanting shaft of sunlight.

"Mary!" The voice poured forth from the streaming light. I froze, my hands steeped in the waters of the cold spring. Slowly I lifted my eyes.

He stood only a few feet away, surrounded by the light. "Do not be afraid, Mary," he said. "I am sent from God. You will conceive in your womb and bear a son. You shall call him Jesus."

"How can that be?" I whispered. "I have no husband."

"The Holy Spirit will come upon you, and the power of the Most High will overshadow you. Therefore the child to be born will be called holy."

Silence hung like a white mist around us. Slowly the words arose from my heart. "Let it be," I said. And the stranger was gone.

The memory fades. Yet even now as I sit by the spring, I feel the wonder of that time. And think of how strange it is that God breaks through to us in the midst of small, common moments...how strange it is that every ordinary moment of existence is poised on the brink of a miracle.

And I wonder. If on that day my eyes and ears had been closed...if my sense of awe and expectancy had been asleep...if my sensitivity to God's coming had been dim...would I have heard the angel's voice? And even too, long ago, would my forefather Moses have seen the bush burning in the wind had he not been alert to God's Presence? The spring gurgles and the question looms large in the gentle, falling light.

No, I think. God comes. The extraordinary occurs. And common bushes burn. And there are those who are aware.

28 *I will sing of the mercies of the Lord for ever…*

—PSALM 89:1

What's a *mercy?*

We hear a lot more about miracles than mercies these days. But the Bible speaks of the *mercies* of God nearly eight times as often as it mentions the miracles of God. Webster's dictionary defines a mercy as a blessing, an act of divine favor or compassion. I like to call mercies "God gifts." And you know, I receive mercies every day:

—The joy of making applesauce with the family from apples we picked together.

—Good roads for a midwinter journey.

—A beautiful ice fern etched on a window.

—A parking space right outside the post office when it's zero degrees outdoors.

—Dropping a full jar of mayonnaise from the top shelf of the refrigerator — and it doesn't break.

All these are daily little messages from God that say: "I'm here! I care!"

But often mercies are taken for granted because they seem to occur so naturally. That's the reason we hung a banner in the stairwell of our house. It shows a figure with outstretched arms greeting the rising sun with the joyful cry: "Morning by morning new mercies I see!" Each day as we come downstairs to breakfast, the banner reminds us to look for the mercies God is *planning* for us that day.

Are you watching for your "God gifts"?

Dear Lord, I think I see one coming…

—PATRICIA HOUCK SPRINKLE

29 *Come now therefore, and let us take counsel together.*
—NEHEMIAH 6:7

Recently a neighbor knocked on my door and asked, "What have I done to offend you? When I last visited you, why did you tell me that I wasn't welcome?"

How very odd! Then and there we tried to reconstruct her visit and what had been said. She had thought she heard me say, "Go on home," when what I had actually said was, "Make yourself at home."

Humorous? She didn't think it was funny at all — until we had cleared the air.

I'm glad that she went right to the point. The next time I sense a coolness between myself and a friend — or my spouse or my child — I'll go to that person right away and try to set the matter straight. It may be only a simple misunderstanding, just as it was between my friend and myself.

But whatever the problem is, nothing could be worse than ignoring it. If you or someone you know feels hurt, try sharing the healing balm of kind words between you.

Show me the sin of pride, Father, if I resist resolving a difference between myself and another because of it! —ISABEL CHAMP

30 *But without faith it is impossible to please him: for he that cometh to God must believe that he is, and that he is a rewarder of them that diligently seek him.*
—HEBREWS 11:6

I once asked my seminar professor if Jesus was aware of His identity on the night He was born in the Bethlehem stable.

"Yes," my teacher answered, "Jesus knew."

343

"Who else knew?" I asked.

He replied, "Mary knew. Joseph knew. Mary's cousin Elizabeth knew. Elizabeth's husband knew."

Then I asked, "Why didn't other people know — and why do so many people not know even now?"

He answered, "Knowing is not a matter of fact. It is a matter of faith. And faith is given to anyone who seeks it."

Father, I believe. I don't need facts.   —GLENN KITTLER

Praise Diary for November

1

2

3

4

5

6

7

8

9

10

11

12

13

14

15

16

17

18

19

20

21

22

23

24

25

26

27

28

29

30

December

*Light is sown for the righteous, and gladness for the
upright in heart.* —PSALM 97:11

Praise to You, O Holy One,
Source of our salvation,
For out of darkness You brought light
That first day of creation....

And when the world went dark again
And evil walked this earth,
You sent a Guiding Light to us,
O praise His Holy Birth....

He leads us out of darkness
He gives new hope to men—
O praise His Name, His Holy Name
As Christmas comes again!

—ALICE JOYCE DAVIDSON

PATTERN FOR A BLESSED LIFE
Building on the Beatitudes Blueprint

1   When I accompany my architect husband as he inspects buildings under construction, I notice that the workmen constantly refer back to the working drawings and specifications. As the building begins to take form, the carefully designed pattern becomes a reality.

In the Beatitudes, Jesus gave us His blueprint for living a blessed life. Month by month we have been trying to understand His blessedness. Now it's time to build. This is a life-long task but if we can keep referring back to the plan of the Master Architect, our lives can be shaped by His blueprint. Here's a pattern for you to tack up on your walls — in both your house and your heart.

TODAY I WILL TRY TO:
Lean on God, knowing that without Him I am nothing;
Bring my sorrows to the Father;
Do my work quietly and humbly;
Let prayer fill my emptiness;
Perform an act of mercy;
Keep my heart centered in Jesus;
Lay my problems in God's hands and share the peace this brings;
Give thanks for my freedom to worship;
Value God's approval above that of men.

Lord, be the Architect of my life, now and forever.

—MARILYN MORGAN HELLEBERG

2   *For if, when we were enemies, we were reconciled to
    God by the death of his Son, much more, being
    reconciled, we shall be saved by his life.*   —ROMANS 5:10

During the bitter winter of 1777, General George Washington was visited in his tent by an elderly civilian named Peter Miller.

Miller told the General, "I have come to ask you to pardon Michael Wittman."

Washington could hardly believe the man's words. Wittman was a spy who had betrayed the Continental army and collaborated with the British. He had been tried and was sentenced to be executed on the following day.

"I cannot do that," Washington said. "Spies must be severely dealt with, even one who is your friend."

"He's no friend of mine!" Miller declared. "He has treated me dreadfully for years. He has even spat on me!"

"And still you ask me to pardon him?"

The old man nodded.

"Why?" the general asked.

"Because Jesus did as much for me."

Without speaking, Washington turned to his desk. He sat down and began to write with a quill pen on white paper. When he arose, he handed the paper to Miller. It was a pardon for Wittman.

Is there an "enemy" who needs *your* pardon?

Forgive us, Lord, our trespasses as we forgive those who trespass against us.   —DRUE DUKE

3   *The Lord upholdeth all that fall, and raiseth up all those that be bowed down.*   —PSALM 145:14

Ten yards and whap! Down I went. Another twenty yards and I tumbled again. I got up. Another thirty yards down the hill and I fell again. This time I stayed down.

"Why didn't you turn, honey?" my wife asked as she skied over to me gracefully, trying unsuccessfully to hide a tiny smile.

"Because you didn't tell me *how* to turn," I growled.

Lynn laughed. "Did you really expect to be ready for the Olympics the first time you skied?"

"Of course not," I retorted. "But I do feel foolish with all these half-pints skiing circles around me, laughing at the big klutz."

"Maybe they should laugh, but not at your skiing. It's your *attitude* that's klutzy. They've probably been skiing for years — and working hard at it. You sound as though you want everything to be magically granted to you." And with that she skied off.

By the end of the day, gaining a new-found patience, I could ski the entire beginner hill without falling. I had picked up a lot of bumps and bruises and no doubt I did look foolish at times, my lanky 6'5" frame sprawled across the slope. But I had done it!

Don't ski? Well, I found out that there's one principle that applies to nearly every activity — and especially walking with God. I can't expect to know it all from the beginning, and I may look foolish. But when I went the distance of an entire hill without falling, the bruises I got on the other hills didn't count.

Father, thank You for a faith that is always a challenge.

—JEFF JAPINGA

4

SECOND SUNDAY OF ADVENT
Mary's Promise

The stigma follows me like a shadow in the Nazareth street. And although I fight them, tears sting my eyes. For even now after all these months, the women whisper when I pass. And the scandal grows thick with gossip. "There goes Mary. She sinned before her wedding and now she blasphemes God by claiming that her child is conceived from the Holy Spirit. Does she think we are mad to believe such a lie?"

I glance back at the whispering women. Their eyes stare at me with raw accusation, piercing my heart. *Dear Joseph, at least you believe me*, I think as I hurry into the courtyard of our house. I drop my market basket with sudden weariness. The long months of rejection and hurt wash over me in great black waves. "Oh, God, what have You asked of me?" I cry.

The air is quiet except for the sound of Joseph's hammer thudding rhythmically in his carpenter's shop behind the house. His voice, too, drifts out in faint song, the cadence weaving through the pounding of the hammer. In those quick, decisive blows I seem to hear my own words as they answered the angel. "Let it be...let it be." I had freely accepted the extraordinary proposal of God. Yet, how can I go through with it? What good will come of it?

I sit down beside the gate. Joseph's hammer pounds and pounds. His song grows louder. He is singing one of the ancient psalms of King David. "Sing praises to the Lord...weeping may endure for the night. But joy comes with the morning."

The words suddenly suffuse me with their promise. The promise that all of God's nights are followed by His mornings. The assurance that He brings light out of dark, hope out of hurt, good out of trials.

Joseph's voice dies away now but the promise remains, warm and deep and certain inside of me. The accusing eyes, the stigma, the tears — they will fade just as the night fades. Joy will arise as God's purpose is fulfilled.

Here by the gate I whisper the words again, "Oh, yes, my Lord. Let it be."

---

5   *When I said, My foot slippeth; thy mercy, O lord, held me up.*   —PSALM 94:18

It was a colorful sight in the otherwise dismal winter scene. A little girl of about two — dressed in a pink snowsuit and white rubber boots — toddled along confidently upon the frozen snow, clinging to one of her father's fingers with her little mittened hand.

Suddenly her foot slipped on the ice and down she went. Sobs followed.

As I continued down the street, careful to watch out for treacherous patches of ice myself, my thoughts dwelt on the little girl.

Living the Christian life sometimes resembles that incident, I thought. Like the child in the snow... if I hold only God's finger, I can slip. But with my whole hand firmly clasped in His, I may slip but He will never allow me to fall.

This day, Father, I entrust myself to Your loving hands.
— ISABEL CHAMP

---

6   *Give to him that asketh thee, and from him that would borrow of thee turn not thou away.*   — MATTHEW 5:42

Standing on my doorstep was the neighborhood "borrower," a fierce old lady who constantly wandered our block demanding, with no thought of repayment, eggs, onions, sugar and so forth — quite as though they were her due. That day, a day of heavy summer heat when I was rushed and irritable, it was of all things, cup hooks!

About to deny her, I suddenly recalled the voice of my seven-year-old grandson who had come in earlier to take forty cents from his allowance box to buy lemonade at an improvised sidewalk stand.

"One for me," Bogart had said, "and one for my friend Tom."

"Why not let him buy his own?" I had asked, thinking of Tom's lucrative paper route and Bo's dwindling savings.

"Grammy," Bo had replied, "I like to be nice." Then, earnestly, "It's *nice* to be nice!"

Looking now at the "borrower," I saw for the first time a lonely lady who may not have needed eggs and onions, but who went around ringing doorbells in search of a cup of kindness.

"Come in while I look to see if I have any," I urged. There were no cup hooks but I could give her a cup of coffee. When she left, gravely smiling her thanks, I felt calm and refreshed. In return for that cup of kindness, my cup overflowed.

Bogart was right. "It's *nice* to be nice!"

Lord, help me to recognize my neighbor's true need and to fill it, and mine, for Thy sake. — ELAINE ST. JOHNS

7 *...Brethren, give diligence to make your calling and election sure: for if ye do these things, ye shall never fall...* —II PETER 1:10

The end of the term was near and we were terrified of the final examinations. We sweated over our books and visited the chapel with pleading prayers every day. One evening the dean said, "I see that many students are spending a lot more time than usual in chapel lately. They are wasting their time. The Holy Spirit can't do anything for them unless they have already given Him something to work with."

That remark has always stayed with me. So often I went for stretches of time without giving a thought to God. Then when I found myself in trouble, I cried out to Him. What did I expect? Had I given the Holy Spirit something to work with?

Now I find that regular periods of daily prayer are an investment in my spiritual future. When I steadfastly communicate with God, it's easier to find Him when I need Him quickly. Maybe prayer is like a snowplow on a blocked country road: It clears the path to our destination.

Father, we have been told to pray ceaselessly, not only in the storms of life. —GLENN KITTLER

---

8 *Serve the Lord with gladness…* —PSALM 100:2

Our family stood in church to sing a hymn with the rest of the congregation. A little girl in the row in front of us turned around and began to study us. She stared. I kept on singing, looking down at her from time to time. A cute child. But she looked so…unhappy. *Why in the world doesn't that child smile?* I thought.

Just as we were finishing the hymn, I glanced down once again and noticed that a bright smile was now on her face. But she wasn't looking at us any more. She was quite obviously looking at someone behind us. I turned my head slightly to see who had won a smile from this unhappy-appearing little girl.

I saw an ordinary-looking woman, singing with joy. She had the most wonderful smile I'd ever seen. Looking at my family I noticed that none of us smiled as we sang — not even me. The solemn child who had stared at us so intently was merely reflecting our family.

Father, let my face reflect Your joy and may it be contagious to those around me. —MARION BOND WEST

9

For where your treasure is, there will your heart be also.
—MATTHEW 6:21

About ten years ago a scientist at an Inca "dig" was probing an ancient burial ground in South America when he uncovered a small pile of perfectly formed, gleaming pearls. His mind raced. Here was an unprecedented discovery! He might very well make headlines as the discoverer. On the other hand, no one else was near and the pearls could easily be pocketed....

He leaned closer and noticed a film of dust on the little trove. Impulsively he blew on them, and instantly they crumbled to dust. Thousands of passing years had rotted their cores so that their luster was barely more than a hint of a shell.

This little story told me something about worldly treasures. Does it do the same for you?

Lord, deliver me from being tricked by glitter into loving false things.
—JAMES McDERMOTT

10

Jesus Christ the same yesterday, and today, and for ever.
—HEBREWS 13:8

When my husband and I left the annual Christmas party, we felt something amiss. It had been a beautiful party: children stringing cranberries, their mothers ladling out spiced punch, the ceiling-high tree decorated with herb-laden fruits. The theme was "Christmas As It Was Then."

On the way home, my husband rolled down the car window. Suddenly the air came alive with Christmas chimes from one of the local church towers. "Silent Night, Holy Night.... "

"Tonight's party didn't go back far enough," he said softly.

That was it, I realized, squeezing his hand in appreciation.

It's fun to remember the ways of our ancestors, but the real joy comes from digging down to the roots of Christmas, feeling the loving arms reach out from a manger, holding us close to the heart of God. That's Christmas — as it was Then. As it is Now. And as it will be Forevermore.

Father, as the Christmas season approaches, remind me of Your unchanging Gift, the same yesterday, today and tomorrow.

—JUNE MASTERS BACHER

---

11 THIRD SUNDAY OF ADVENT
Mary's Calling

The night is well-aged, yet I am sleepless. The tiny unborn one inside moves and thrashes about. What *are* you doing, little one? Don't you know the hour? I stroke my abdomen as though my touch may somehow serve as soothing lullaby. Yet he stirs again, anxious, it seems, to be free of his safe and silent cocoon, eager to take his place in the stream of life.

Oh, it will not be long, little one. Soon you will nestle in my arms. Soon you will romp on the hillsides, chase the fat lambs and toss pebbles into the spring. And too soon you will skin your knees, and later you will taste the pain and heartbreak that await in this world. When that time arrives, I cannot protect you as I do now. I pray that I am ready for the fearful responsibility of being your mother. It seems beyond me now, and I am humbled at the thought.

The night grows older. I lie still now, not daring to shift upon my bed. For at last he is quiet...he sleeps. I alone am awake, listening to the distant night sounds, pondering the stillness within me and the life that grows as it was bidden.

Why have I been chosen? How mysterious it is! God could simply speak this child into existence should He wish. Yet we are collaborators, God and I. I smile to myself in the darkness. For to share with God is, I know, the deepest joy of human life. And I know, too, that the joy is given not to me alone. It is a gift to all who would participate as God's partner in the world, transforming His creation into His kingdom.

Outside, the moon glides across the sky too quickly, drawing the night away from us. "Sleep on, little one," I whisper. "Very soon you too will enter upon your high and holy alliance with the Lord."

12

This is the day which the Lord hath made; we will rejoice and be glad in it.
—PSALM 118:24

Both my dog Clay and I are getting old and arthritic. In dog years, Clay's a lot older than I and maybe he's more arthritic too (at least I can still climb up on the bed without being boosted). No, my arthritis is the mild kind that moves around from my left hip to my fingers to the heel of my right foot with just enough pain to make me complain about it. And that's exactly what I was doing — complaining — to a friend of mine recently when she said, "Why can't you be more like your dog?"

I couldn't tell whether she was being serious or sarcastic — or both. "Meaning what?" I asked.

"Well, does Clay complain about *his* arthritis?"

I've been watching Clay lately and there's something to my friend's comment. On our long walks in the morning, Clay will trot ahead of me, his ears at half-alert, the soles of his paws flicking back like the hoofs of a race horse, his tail swinging pleasurably from side to side, when suddenly, without any warning, those old legs of his will give way and he'll go crashing down into the dirt, a startled look of noncomprehension in his eyes. I'll rush to help him but before I can get there, he'll be up again and back on the trail, the tail swinging pleasurably as though nothing had happened. No complaining. No feeling sorry for himself.

Come on, Van, take a tip from your old dog Clay: Stop complaining, get up, get on with the joyous business of living!

Today, Lord, yet will I rejoice! —VAN VARNER

---

13 *If ye know these things, happy are ye if ye do them.*
—JOHN 13:17

Her name is Ethel and everybody who knows her loves her. She always remembers your birthday. If you're not feeling well, she calls you. If she makes an apple pie, she makes one for you too.

"How do you do it, Ethel?" I asked her.

"I guess I don't *think* about it. I just do *it*," she said. "If I think about something I intend to do, it takes too long."

Well maybe that was the reason I couldn't fit all those wonderful, caring gestures into my life....

Being thoughtful doesn't take much time at all — it's *intending* to that does!

Dear Lord, help me to be more of a doer than an intender.
—PHYLLIS HOBE

---

14 *... Establish thou the work of our hands upon us; yea, the work of our hands establish thou it.* —PSALM 90:17

Sometimes I become discouraged when faced by a complicated task. I don't know where to start, how to proceed. Then I like to remember the scene from Dickens' *David Copperfield*. Young, starving David shows up at the door of his Aunt Betsy. Horrified at the responsibility of bringing up her scruffy little nephew, she appeals to her cousin, Mr. Dick, for advice.

Mr. Dick screws up his face, scratches his head and finally says, "If I was you, I should wash him."

"The very thing!" the aunt exclaims in delight. "Mr. Dick, whatever would I do without your help!"

So it goes, step by step, with Mr. Dick advising the aunt on every little detail. She follows his advice and succeeds in her task.

When I think of that story, my discouragement changes to hope. After all, isn't a big task really just a series of little tasks linked together and leading toward a final goal?

Today, Lord, with Your help, I will choose one small task and do that well. —MADGE HARRAH

JOURNEY OF FAITH

15 Your traveling companion is *JOSHUA*
... *who entered the Promised Land.* —THE BOOK OF JOSHUA

We began our pilgrimage this year with God's word to Abraham: "Go from!" We end our journey with His command to Joshua: "Go in!"

How to *receive* what belongs to us — that is our question for December. The Biblical territory we have surveyed this year is ours. "Every place that the sole of your foot tread upon I give you."

Are we living as though we believe this? Or do we stand within sight of the Promised Land, and not enter? Let's look at how Joshua went in.

Walking on Two Legs. "YOU are to pass over this Jordan to go in to

TAKE possession of the land which THE LORD your God GIVES you." Does God give it or do we take it? Both, Joshua would say.

The ark, symbol of God's presence, went ahead of the people. Sometimes do you get the order reversed and rush at your Promised Land? Maybe it's a healing that you think should come sooner...or a marriage partner you want changed. Don't get discouraged and conclude that a particular promise isn't meant to be. God may still have some growing in mind for you.

Walking Through Water. Between the children of Israel and the Promised Land lay an impassable barrier — the Jordan River. Now, Joshua did not set about constructing a bridge; instead, Joshua invited God right down into the threatening situation itself.

And when he did, a solution appeared. The water stopped flowing. It didn't happen by magic. The temporary cutting off of the Jordan's flow has been observed in modern times, when spring floods undercut cliffs upstream, toppling tons of earth and rock into the river to create a natural dam. But we learn from Joshua that when we ask God *into* our problems, He gets involved through His natural processes of change.

The Edge of the Sword. We're apt to shrink, nowadays, from the grisly details of Joshua's campaign — to find them primitive and bloodthirsty. What, after all, is a Christian of today to make of God-fearing men who utterly destroyed men and women, the young and old, oxen, sheep and asses, with the edge of the sword? Precisely that they feared and followed God more than they cared for *anything* else.

Reading ourselves into this account means doing battle with any "barriers" to *our* Promised Land. Whatever it is, if it stands between us and God's promises, it must be destroyed!

The Choice. Joshua's last words to his people — *choose THIS DAY whom you will serve* — are a perfect conclusion for your year-long journey.

In some areas of your life you are living now in the Promised Land — where you can relax, right? Not at all, cautions Joshua. When you stop traveling, two kinds of false gods can tempt you: the gods your fathers served — old idolatries, outgrown ways of problem-solving; and the gods of those in whose land you dwell — the current standards of the world around you.

To choose is a daily matter, not a once-and-for-all achievement.

I promise, Lord, to start each morning — now and into the new year — with Joshua's joyful declaration, "As for me and my house, we will serve the Lord!"

—ELIZABETH SHERRILL

---

16   *And while they went to buy, the bridegroom came; and they that were ready went in with him to the marriage: and the door was shut.*   —MATTHEW 25:10

One summer Marge and Johnny gave me a key to their cabin in Big Bear Lake.

"Keep it," Marge told me, "and if you want to come up for a vacation, feel free to do so. If we aren't here, just walk in and make yourself at home. The door is always open to you!"

For a long time I kept the key looped over a spindle on my desk. But somehow something always came up and I kept putting off the visit. Then they sold the cabin and I lost the opportunity.

A personal letter arrived from my pastor this morning. "Christmas Greetings!" it read. "I hope you will attend our special Christmas Sunday service...."

Oh, dear, I thought. *I still have to buy my Christmas tree and there are a few late Christmas letters and last-minute gifts....*

"Dear Pastor," I wrote. "I'm sorry...." Then my eye fell on the key that was still hooked over the spindle.

I began again. "Dear Pastor, I shall be very glad to come...."

Father, since friends and special kindnesses that come my way are precious, let me ever respond with joy.   —DORIS HAASE

17

When they saw the star, they rejoiced with exceeding great joy.　　　　　　　　　　　　　—MATTHEW 2:10

Of all the symbols of Yuletide, surely the Christmas tree is one of the most beloved. Once a pagan symbol, today its branches are decorated with angels, and on high, crowning all, Bethlehem's star shines. So this is the time for all good men to take wife and children in hand and venture forth to buy a Christmas tree!

You ask the man if the tree you have picked out is a good one. "Of course!" he replies (knowing no more about it than you do). You shake the tree a couple of times to make sure the branches are firmly attached (they always are). You grasp the trunk firmly, shoulder the tree (the needles stab you, but never mind) and you stagger blindly to the car (inhaling the heady aroma of balsam and crashing into anyone in your path). You brush needles out of your ears and a few stray twigs from your hair. You contemplate your hands, sticky with sap (just think of all that gummy residue on the steering wheel).

Then you return and pay the man cheerfully (suppressing the thought that he's trimming you, not the tree). You drive home (if you can see your way past all those branches). And on the way everyone sings carols....

Why sing? Because you are happy. Why are you happy? Because it really isn't a tree that you're bringing home....

It's the spirit of Christmas.

Lord, don't let the tasks of Christmas take away my Christmas cheer.　　　　　　　　　　　　　　　—ARTHUR GORDON

18 FOURTH SUNDAY OF ADVENT
Mary's Journey

The black and silver sky bends over us like the dome of a shining temple. Far in the East a lone star gleams with a peculiar intensity. I watch it as Joseph adjusts the pack on the donkey.

"We must hurry if we are to be off before day breaks," he says.

It will be a long journey to Bethlehem, where Joseph must pay his tax. Five...even six days. We must cross the Jordan and climb the treacherous Judean hills. What I fear most is that my child may be born on the cold, lonely road. My time is so very near.

As Joseph lifts me upon the donkey's back, I cannot ignore the sudden rush of fears. The donkey's hoofs ring hollow on the cobbled street. *Oh, stop!* I want to cry out. *Let me remain here in my safe bed. Here, when I can deliver this child while surrounded by my mother and my aunts.* But Joseph and I plod on, silent shadows in the fading night, moving as though in a dream.

At the edge of Nazareth where the stone street gives way to dirt, I turn and look back. Somehow I know that nothing will ever be the same again...the journey has begun.

I watch Joseph's sure hand tug the little donkey forward into the darkness. I am struck by a simple thought: *Are we not led by God as surely as Joseph leads the donkey?* High up in the clear purple night sky the strangely bright star once more draws my attention. It gleams before us like a map in God's window. Would God send us on a journey without lighting the way with His guidance?

Now the sound of the donkey's hoofs on the road does not seem as lonely, nor does the dark distance seem as ready to swallow us up. *This is not a journey of uncertainty, it is a journey of faith*, I tell myself. How can I fear the unknown when I travel through life with the One Who is always there to place a lamp in the window and gently draw me in the right direction?

19 *For unto you is born this day...a Saviour, which is Christ the Lord.* —LUKE 2:11

At the office Christmas dinner we were seated around a long, festive table. An identical package, wrapped in red foil, lay beside each plate.

Some people shook their package, a few checked their neighbor's — and some opened their gift with excitement, taking it out of its wrapping for others to see and touch and admire.

How like another Christmas night, I thought. God gave an identical Gift to all men two thousand years ago. Some merely observed it with faint curiosity, some only commented on it — but some received it with rejoicing and hurried to share it with others.

This Gift is still offered to each of us. We can save it for later or we can simply observe our neighbor's gift — or we can receive it with delight and thereafter thank God for the magnificence of His generosity.

Lord, I will rejoice in Your Gift! —ZONA B. DAVIS

20 *And ye shall seek me, and find me, when ye shall search for me with all your heart.* —JEREMIAH 29:13

It had been raining all day. Christmas was just a week away and I was still taking exams at college. Where I come from, Christmas means snow, not a soggy, gray wetness.

"This is sure a rotten Christmas season," I said to my friend. "I have three more exams, there's no snow, no family, and I've heard this Christmas album four million times already! I'm going out to take a walk before I tackle any more sociology."

Outside, the trees were dripping wet. I turned up my coat collar

— a deceptively cold north wind had sprung up. *What a Christmas*, I thought. *Even the carols are stale.*

And then I heard it in the distance: "*O little town of Bethlehem, how still we see thee lie; Above thy deep and dreamless sleep, the silent stars go by.*" Automatically I looked up at the sky — and was shocked to see a multitude of stars where only gray clouds could be seen minutes earlier. And I sensed the feeling the shepherds must have had when they first heard the singing and looked up.

Where was the singing coming from? I went searching. Around the corner I found a group of students, huddled around a makeshift manger and singing.

"*Yet in thy dark streets shineth,*" I joined in, "*the everlasting Light. . . .*" The light of Christmas had reappeared, shining brighter than ever! Just as the shepherds of old, I had to come to worship the Babe of Bethlehem. What is the Christmas season? I know now that it is the love that lies in the hearts of those who seek Him.

Truly, Father, Christ is the Good News, which has been given to all people. —JEFF JAPINGA

21 *Thanks be unto God for his unspeakable gift.*
—II CORINTHIANS 9:15

It is almost Christmas. This year I have decided to give my eight-year-old niece a tea set I received when I myself was only eight — a "real china" set with pink rosebuds and gold rims.

But now as I unwrap the tiny cups and saucers from the box where they have lain for many years, I wonder. Will she really appreciate the meaning of this gift? Will she see it as a gift of love? Or will she wish that I had given her something new? A sadness comes over me for I realize that no matter what she decides to do with the tea set, I will have no say in the matter once it is hers. She may cherish it, ignore it or even smash it — never knowing that she has smashed a part of me in the process. For just an instant I hesitate, a tiny cup cradled in my hand...maybe I'll buy her something else after all.

Then my eyes fall on the crèche and the infant lying in the straw. A gift of love. Freely given. Never retracted, no matter what those who receive the gift do with it.

Tenderly I rewrap the tea set and tie it up for my niece. A part of myself, offered in the pain — and the joy — of love. Isn't that what Christmas is all about?

Dear God, thank You for letting us too share in the pain and the joy of giving, in memory of the gift You gave to us. Amen.
—PATRICIA HOUCK SPRINKLE

---

22 *The Spirit of God hath made me, and the breath of the Almighty hath given me life.* —JOB 33:4

Once Joni Eareckson told me about her first Christmas following a diving accident that left her a seventeen-year-old quadriplegic. "One of the most depressing things was that I couldn't go out and shop for that extra-special gift for people on my list," she recalled. "The thought that I had nothing to give left me feeling blue."

Then she remembered reading her Bible one day and coming to the realization that Christ's best gift to the world was Himself. Suddenly she had the answer to her dilemma; she would give herself.

The next day she went to her physical therapy class, a chore she had previously entered into halfheartedly. This day she really tried to paint candy dishes with brushes placed in her mouth. And although she didn't know it then, it was the beginning of an artistic endeavor that would lead to her career.

Joni's real Christmas gift that year was her affirmation of life — and giving herself back to her loved ones. It's something for all of us to think about this Christmas.

Father, thank You for the best gift of all — life itself. —FRED BAUER

---

23 *I am Alpha and Omega, the beginning and the end.*
—REVELATION 21:6

The young couple down the street was celebrating the first Christmas in their new home. And since it was their little boy's first Christmas as well, I expected to see a large, lavishly decorated tree. Instead, a tiny potted evergreen, not more than a foot high, stood decorated on a table by the window.

"It's a very special tree," the wife explained to me. "For years I've watched people discard used Christmas trees. Christmas day was over, and that was the end of it. But Christmas is not an end. It's a *beginning*. It's Christ's birth, a beginning.

"And this little plant," she said, touching a slim branch lovingly, "is the *beginning* of a tree. We'll plant it in our yard, our first planting. Then as the years go by, it will stand as a symbol of beginnings — the beginning of our new home, the beginning of our little boy's life, the beginning of our Saviour's life and salvation for all the world."

Make this Christmas a new beginning for me, one that will go on and on with You, my Saviour and Lord. —DRUE DUKE

24 CHRISTMAS EVE
Mary's Miracle

"It is finished," I whisper, touching my lips to his tiny ear. "You are born, little Jesus."

In one dark and obscure moment it is done. I lie back in the straw, breathless from pain but also from the strange aura of wonder that has settled so thickly upon our tiny stable.

A clean, black night wind stirs the air. The lantern flickers yellow. Dust dances up like swirling gold. I draw the baby closer, watching Joseph arrange tufts of hay in a cow trough. The silence grows deeper.

I kiss the small face nestled against my cheek. And I count his fingers. One...two...three. One by one they uncurl as the memory of the angel's voice whispers in my ear, "The child to be born will be called holy." *Holy.* The word echoes. Suddenly my heart is beating hard, the eternal question arising within me as I regard the ten tiny, pearl-like fingers. "Oh, human child, whose fingerprints do you bear? With whose fingerprints do you enter into the human world? *Who are you?*"

Joseph turns as though the question had tapped him on his shoulder. Now all is still in the little stable. The moment seems to hang on the end of a thread, held in suspension by God Himself. And ever so slowly the answer comes, until it bursts into full-blown awareness. This baby — my baby — who stares at me from the depths of his eyes is of us, and yet...and yet he is not. He is *Emmanuel. God-With-Us.*

I gaze up at Joseph, my heart and soul too full to speak. And somehow Joseph knows as well. It was there all along — in the prophet's foretelling, hidden in the words of the angel's announcement, quietly in the virgin birth, in the awed wonder that has clasped the stable. And now the answer is alive in the light that pierces my heart.

I hold little Jesus close against the night, knowing even now that his birth belongs not to me alone. For this baby, so newly born, will be reborn to all generations of people as they too ask the eternal question: *Who are you?* And they will hear the same answer ring out from their hearts.

And so now, here in the shadowed stable where the miracle has arisen like dawn upon the still-sleeping world, I touch my lips to my child's ear once more. "No, my little son," I whisper. "It is not finished. It has only just begun."

---

25 CHRISTMAS DAY
Mary's Offering

I awaken suddenly, forgetting for a moment where I am. Brilliant sunlight pours through the doorway, forcing my eyes to close again. Then I remember: I am a mother! I sit up to face the shimmering light. *Jesus? Jesus — my baby — where is he?*

Across the stable Joseph cuddles a small bundle in his arms. "Now, now," he says with a smile. "Didn't I tell you your mother would soon be awake?" He tucks Jesus into the straw beside me. Such a tender little miracle is this child! I kiss the top of his tiny nose, my thoughts floating back to the events of the night just past...the silent band of men dressed in shepherds' garb who appeared so soon after his birth, kneeling beside my child. When they departed, they were curiously different men, their voices raised in song and praise to God. Do they know who my baby is?

Now, here in the daylight, the knowledge of his identity arises within me like a fresh new wind, a wind that will gather strength and sweep across all humanity, forever changing its destiny. Beyond the stable walls I hear the sounds of the world as it plods by — Roman horses, wagon wheels, Jewish sandals — moving to the jingle of Caesar's coins, churning the ancient dust through the streets. How strange that the throng should file by in this manner, so close to God's own revelation and yet so unaware.

In the stable a lamb bleats softly and a gentle breeze moves chill shadows through the air. Joseph draws a blanket about us. I trace my finger across the sleeping baby's face. *My precious one, I do not know why you have come. Perhaps the reason has to do with all these people outside who wander past so casually.*

"Oh, Joseph, if only they knew.... How could they hurry on by?"

Joseph smiles down at me. His face reflects a yearning that has already begun to kindle within my soul — a hope that one day all will discover this stable and leave it in awe and wonderment as did the shepherds.

I reach for Joseph's hand. The truth shines radiant in the air, brighter even than the sunlight: *God is alive in the world!*

Yet I wonder. How will people respond? What will be their thoughts as they depart this stable? In what manner will this child affect the rest of their days?

Deep in the straw Jesus cries. I bend down and lift him up. And suddenly I know that in this very act my question is answered. I will leave this stable forever lifting Him up....

This Child is mine, and He belongs to all.

---

26 *To every thing there is... a time to love...*
—ECCLESIASTES 3:1, 8

One special lesson that I learned as a youngster stands out in my memory. It concerns the day *after* Christmas.

My mother had a friend whose husband had died on Thanksgiving day. Mrs. Warner had no children or relatives close by and as Christmas neared, Mother made certain that we did everything we could to include her in our own family activities.

We took her with us to candlelight service at church. My brothers and I made presents for her. She came to our house for Christmas dinner. And when we saw her safely home that night, we were happy with the knowledge that we had helped someone over a period of loneliness.

Late the next day a delivery man went to Mrs. Warner's door. Through the living-room window he saw that she was slumped over awkwardly in a chair; he sensed that something was the matter. Something was. If he hadn't quickly summoned help and broken in, the gas escaping from a fireplace jet would have been fatal to Mrs. Warner.

I am happy to say that she recovered and later remarried and enjoyed a long, productive life. But what I remember most about Mrs. Warner is that she told my mother, "I braced myself for the sadness that I knew I would feel on Christmas. But I wasn't ready for the day *after*. It was so quiet in the house. I was simply overwhelmed by loneliness."

Do you know someone who is unprepared for the holiday letdown? Pick up the phone, now.

O Lord, I truly want to help others. Guide me with Your wisdom. —VAN VARNER

---

27 *O give thanks unto the Lord, for he is good: for his mercy endureth for ever.* —PSALM 107:1

This year when I find myself caught up in the bounty of Christmas, grateful for all that has been bestowed upon me, I'm going to try to remember the following story, told to me by a friend.

A small boy was carefully pulling his shiny new wagon down the street on Christmas day. Carefully, because in the wagon was the statue of the Christ Child that he had taken from the crib of the outdoor nativity scene. He had tenderly wrapped it in an old sweater.

Seeing what her son had done, the mother asked him why he had removed the Christ Child from the manger.

"Baby Jesus gave me the wagon for Christmas," the little boy explained. "Shouldn't He have the first ride in it?"

Will I first give to God my appreciation for all the blessings I receive? Maybe *that's* what tithing is all about. It can start with Christmas. Better yet, it can start with me.

Father, I want to return to You with all my love that which You have bestowed upon me. —ZONA B. DAVIS

---

28 *In my Father's house are many mansions...I go to prepare a place for you.* —JOHN 14:2

We were taking a winter walk, my daughter and I. She was four years old, prancing between the trees, busy discovering life. All at once she came upon a little dead chipmunk lying beside a pile of firewood. She bent over him, her eyes shadowed with the mysteries of death. Then she asked the timeless question, "Mama, what happens when you die?"

I drew a long breath and sat down on a log, trying to find words a child could understand. Words that even I, myself, might. Across the street there stood a grand old house, beginning to crumble on its foundation like an old man leaning on a cane. It seemed deserted.

"Do you see that old house?" I asked, pointing to it. "Our bodies are sort of like houses. At first houses are very new. But over the years the paint peels and the roof leaks a bit and finally the foundation gives way. And then it's time for the person who lives in the house to move out."

She was staring at the house, frowning in the winter sun.

"Do you understand?" I asked, frustrated by my rather poor and simple effort at explaining such a complex question. "You see, when you die, it's kind of like moving out of your old house and into a better one."

Then she smiled. "You mean God's house?"

I nodded. She cast me a satisfied look and ambled off to other mysteries. And I stood there for a moment studying the old house, feeling that strange mixture of excitement and regret that characterizes moving days.

I know one day the tenant in my house will move out. All of us must, eventually. But Christians will never be homeless. Jesus said He was going to prepare a place for us — God's house. A home with a warm welcome mat.

Thank You for the promise of heaven, Jesus. —SUE MONK KIDD

---

29 *Therefore if any man be in Christ, he is a new creature: old things are passed away; behold, all things are become new.* — II CORINTHIANS 5:17

Every so often I like to pore over the few pictures we still have that were taken when I was a boy growing up in a small town in Ohio. There I am, a winsome little lad, tucked away in a back row or off by myself in a corner. And all by choice, for I was painfully shy as a child. Why, the little fellow staring back at me from those old pictures hardly seems to be me at all.

The fact is that little boy hardly *is* me. If you can believe the doctors — and I do! — he's undergone ten complete cell changes since that time. He's no longer shy; he's developed into the sort of person who loves people and wants to be with them. And he's no longer afraid of his own shadow for the simple reason that he has come to know Jesus Christ as his all-powerful Redeemer and Saviour Whose followers need fear no evil.

I am a great deal older now but I still firmly believe in the possibilities of change. Not long ago the Lord and I licked a weight problem that had crept up on me. My point is, if you don't like the way you are now, you can change. Your chemistry is changing every day and you can change right along with it, for the better.

Right now, Lord, I'm going to select an aspect of my life that both You and I would like changed, and with Your help, I am going to change it. — NORMAN VINCENT PEALE

---

30 *In every thing give thanks: for this is the will of God in Christ Jesus concerning you.* —I THESSALONIANS 5:18

As December nears its end, it's traditional to depict the "dying" year as the hoary and decrepit victim of Father Time, tottering off stage to make way for the bright-eyed, infant New Year bursting with health and vitality.

But does this really make sense? Isn't the old year an old friend? In the past twelve months hasn't it offered countless moments of joy and excitement, new faces, new places, new opportunities? Yes, some bleak moments too. But didn't we grow because of them?

So before we sit down to write all those fresh resolutions for the next year, let's look back and thank God for all the blessings of the year just past. List the best things it brought, and as you do, remember what a good companion this sturdy old year really was. Then you'll see it not as a senile, worn-out adversary, but rather as a strong, steady, wise ally. And you can say, "Thank you, old year, old friend, three hundred and sixty-five times."

Thank You, Jesus, for the gifts of the past as well as the gifts that lie ahead. —ARTHUR GORDON

31   *...Though your sins be as scarlet, they shall be as white*
as snow...   —ISAIAH 1:18

High in the mountains of North Carolina snow was falling on the roof of the little cabin. Inside, a fire burned on the grate. My husband Sandy and I were spending New Year's Eve by the warm bricks of the fireplace. Sometimes the flames leaped high with an illusive beauty, reminding me of bright dreams for the year ahead. And then they'd turn low and brooding like sad regrets of the year past. How tenaciously our mistakes and regrets hang on...tiny stumbling blocks to the future.

Midnight drew near. "It would be nice to burn all the failures of the past year and start clean," Sandy said.

So we each got a pencil and paper and began to search within ourselves for all the unwelcome baggage we didn't want to carry into the new year. Old mistakes, bad habits, guilt feelings, burdens. My list grew long, seeming dark and heavy by the blue firelight. How, I wondered, had I managed to drag all that around for so long.

At the stroke of midnight we let our lists float down into the fire. The papers curled with brown edges, then ignited suddenly. Watching them burn, I whispered a prayer, "God, I want to start anew. Cleanse me now."

The next day, taking the shovel from the hearth, I raked the gray ashes from the fireplace and dumped them behind the cabin. Away in the clean, white morning they blew, swirling toward heaven. Gone. It was a new beginning.

Wash me and I will be whiter than snow, Lord. —SUE MONK KIDD

Praise Diary for December

1

2

3

4

5

6

7

8

9

10

11

12

13

14

15

16

17

18

19

20

21

22

23

24

25

26

27

28

29

30

31

COME...*and meet the authors:*

JUNE MASTERS BACHER is a columnist-poet-teacher turned full-time inspirational writer. She writes from two to eight hours a day on a book-length manuscript and sends at least one short piece a day to one of her many publishers. She still finds time to take a daily five-to-eight-mile walk in and around Escondido, California where she lives with her husband, George.

FRED BAUER. A former editor with *Guideposts,* Fred now heads Little-brook Publishers, Inc. He began his career as a radio and newspaper reporter in his native Ohio and is the author of many inspirational books. When not exploring the byways of America in their handsome *Winnebago,* Fred and his wife Shirley and three sons live in Princeton, New Jersey. Daughter Laraine lives with her husband in Pennsylvania.

ISABEL CHAMP. "It's easy to sit hour upon hour at my typewriter," says Isabel. Her view from her writing room looks out upon a trout-stocked pond in the deeply wooded acres of her Oregon home. A busy photo-journalist, Isabel has two grown sons and three grandchildren.

ALICE JOYCE DAVIDSON. A long-time friend of the late Helen Steiner Rice with whom she worked for many years, Alice has created more than 3,000 greeting cards and several books. "God gave me two very special gifts, imagination and faith," she says. "I cannot imagine what my life would be without them." Alice is a resident of Cincinnati, Ohio and the mother of two grown children.

ZONA B. DAVIS "wrote the news," as she describes it, for forty-five years for the Effingham (Illinois) *Record* and continues to be a correspondent for the leading international news syndicates, radio and television. The Davises have one son and three grandchildren and, at one time or another, some twenty "teenagers with problems" have called the Davis house their home.

DRUE DUKE, who is employed by the United Way in Sheffield, Alabama, treasures a letter from President Franklin D. Roosevelt about a congratulatory poem she wrote to him as a child. She has not stopped writing since the age of eight. Her stories have appeared in national and regional magazines and newspapers. The Dukes, who have one daughter and two grandchildren, enjoy traveling, cooking and square dancing.

ARTHUR GORDON, who retired in December, 1981 from *Guideposts* after seven years as Editorial Director, is the author of many short stories and a number of well-received books, two of which were made into motion pictures. He continues his distinguished writing career as a contributor to *Guideposts* and other magazines. With his wife, Pam, he now travels between his ancestral home in Savannah, Georgia, and New York City. He has five grown children.

DORIS HAASE. California born and raised, Doris has two grown sons, one of whom is studying for the ministry. Since 1961, she has been employed as an educational secretary by the Los Angeles Unified School District. Her interest in teenagers' problems has led to volunteer work with the Help Line and other local volunteer groups.

MADGE HARRAH is one of a handful of triple talents in the National League of American Penwomen to qualify in writing, composing and illustration. She married the boy she met in the eighth grade who went on to become a physical chemist. The Harrahs have lived in Albuquerque, New Mexico since 1966, where they raised a boy and girl. Madge says her goal now is to keep doing what she's doing, "keep busy."

MARILYN MORGAN HELLEBERG has been a contributor to *Guideposts* since 1967. "I love writing devotionals because it forces me to search out the deeper meanings in everyday life events," she says. She has taught at Kearney State College in Nebraska where she lives with her husband, an architect, and three children.

PHYLLIS LAURA HOBE. "My parents were always reading and I guess it rubbed off on me," says the prolific writer of books and stories. Phyllis is also the editor of some of *Guideposts'* most popular collections. "Although I have written many kinds of books, the ones I love most are my collections of stories, poems and memories from many writers all over the world."

MARJORIE HOLMES. Few women writing today have touched the lives of as many people as has Marjorie Holmes. Novelist, syndicated columnist and inspirational writer, she was born in Iowa and now lives in Pittsburgh. She says, "Talent imposes two responsibilities: To use it. And to use it for good."

JEFF JAPINGA. At 25, Jeff is one of the youngest contributors to *Daily Guideposts*, and is an assistant editor of *Guideposts*. "I was born and raised in Holland, Michigan, known for tulip festivals and pretty Dutch girls (one of whom I married last year)." Jeff commutes from Princeton, New Jersey where his wife, Lynn, is a student at Princeton Theological Seminary.

SUE MONK KIDD is a former nurse whose work has appeared in many magazines since she began writing in 1977. She lives with her husband, a minister, and two children in South Carolina. "I am an exercise enthusiast and swimmer and share the sport of white water canoeing with my husband," says Sue.

GLENN KITTLER is the author of some forty books and many magazine articles. He lives in New York City and has been a contributor to *Guideposts* for thirty years. Says Glenn, "I am looking forward to the next thirty."

JAMES McDERMOTT is a Senior Editor of *Guideposts*. Apart from writing and editing, Jim says he spends his time "Fishing, traveling to odd destinations, planting trees and fixing up old houses," the latter two in Brooklyn where he lives with his wife and young son.

NORMAN VINCENT PEALE. Founder, Co-publisher and Co-Editor-in-chief of *Guideposts* with his wife, Ruth, Dr. Peale celebrates his fiftieth anniversary as minister of Marble Collegiate Church in New York City. He is the author of 21 inspirational books.

RUTH STAFFORD PEALE. Being General Secretary and Editor-in-chief of the Foundation for Christian Living is a priority activity for Ruth Peale. The author of several books, she is a nationally syndicated columnist and lecturer who travels widely with her husband. The Peales have three grown children and seven grandchildren. They live in Pawling, New York.

ELAINE ST. JOHNS is the daughter of author, Adela Rogers St. Johns, and granddaughter of one of the West's most exciting criminal lawyers, Earl Rogers. A free-lance writer, known for her work on national magazines, Elaine has been a *Guideposts* contributor for some twenty-five years. She lives in her native California. The mother of two children, she says unequivocally, "my hobby is my six grandchildren."

ELIZABETH SHERRILL does most of her writing with her husband, John. The Sherrills met aboard ship on their way to Europe and married in Switzerland. Elizabeth joined *Guideposts* in 1963, twelve years after John had been on staff. In 1970 the Sherrills founded Chosen Books.

PATRICIA HOUCK SPRINKLE is a pastor's wife and the mother of two young boys, both under five. She has written children's stories, plays, short stories and several church curricula, in addition to many inspirational articles. "I enjoy anything to do with Scotland, reading almost anything, and telling stores — most of which are true," she says.

VAN VARNER has been Editor of *Guideposts* since January, 1982, but he has been on the staff since 1954. He began his career at Doubleday & Co., after receiving a master's degree in history from the University of California at Berkeley. He also attended Princeton University. Van comes from Louisville, Kentucky, but now he's a *real* New Yorker who loves theatre and horses and whose idea of country is Central Park (he and his venerable bird dog, Clay, live across the street from it).

MARION BOND WEST reveals that she had "twenty-two years of rejection slips before ever having an article accepted." Her persistence was rewarded with four published books to date and a growing demand for her work from many inspirational magazines. She is married and has four children, three of whom live at home. The Wests live in Lilburn, Georgia, where her husband is Health Services Manager for the Georgia Power Company.

A NOTE FROM THE EDITORS

This devotional book was prepared by the same editorial staff that creates *Guideposts*, a monthly magazine filled with true stories of people's adventures in faith.

If you have found enjoyment in *Daily Guideposts*, we think you'll find monthly enjoyment — and inspiration — in the exciting and faith-filled stories that appear in our magazine.

Guideposts is not sold on the newsstand. It's available by subscription only. And subscribing is easy. All you have to do is write Guideposts Associates, Inc.; Carmel, New York 10512. A year's subscription costs only $5.95 in the United States, $7.95 in Canada and overseas.

When you subscribe, each month you can count on receiving exciting new evidence of God's presence, His guidance and His limitless love for all of us.